THE NEW EDUCATION PHILANTHROPY

THE EDUCATIONAL INNOVATIONS SERIES

The Educational Innovations series explores a wide range of current school reform efforts. Individual volumes examine entrepreneurial efforts and unorthodox approaches, highlighting reforms that have met with success and strategies that have attracted widespread attention. The series aims to disrupt the status quo and inject new ideas into contemporary education debates.

Series edited by Frederick M. Hess

Other books in this series:

The Strategic Management of Charter Schools
by Peter Frumkin, Bruno V. Manno, and Nell Edgington

Customized Schooling
Edited by Frederick M. Hess and Bruno V. Manno

Bringing School Reform to Scale
by Heather Zavadsky

What Next?
Edited by Mary Cullinane and Frederick M. Hess

Between Public and Private
Edited by Katrina E. Bulkley, Jeffrey R. Henig, and Henry M. Levin

Stretching the School Dollar
Edited by Frederick M. Hess and Eric Osberg

School Turnarounds: The Essential Role of Districts
by Heather Zavadsky

Stretching the Higher Education Dollar
Edited by Andrew P. Kelly and Kevin Carey

Cage-Busting Leadership
by Frederick M. Hess

Teacher Quality 2.0: Toward a New Era in Education Reform
Edited by Frederick M. Hess and Michael Q. McShane

Reinventing Financial Aid: Charting a New Course to College Affordability
Edited by Andrew P. Kelly and Sara Goldrick-Rab

The Cage-Busting Teacher
by Frederick M. Hess

Failing Our Brightest Kids: The Global Challenge of Educating High-Ability Students
by Chester E. Finn, Jr. and Brandon L. Wright

THE NEW EDUCATION PHILANTHROPY

Politics, Policy, and Reform

FREDERICK M. HESS
JEFFREY R. HENIG

Editors

Harvard Education Press
Cambridge, Massachusetts

Library of Congress Control Number 2015938382

Paperback ISBN 978-1-61250-871-9
Library Edition ISBN 978-1-61250-872-6

Published by Harvard Education Press,
an imprint of the Harvard Education Publishing Group

Harvard Education Press
8 Story Street
Cambridge, MA 02138

Cover Design: Saizon Design
Cover Photo: Robert Morrissey/EyeEm/Getty Images
The typefaces used in this book are Minion Pro and Myriad Pro

Contents

Introduction

The New Education Philanthropy

Frederick M. Hess and Jeffrey R. Henig

Contemporary philanthropy plays an outsized role in schooling and school reform. Leading donors have influenced policy and practice around the Common Core, teacher evaluation systems, extended learning time, and charter schooling. Major foundations have worked closely with the Obama administration on visible programs like Race to the Top and Investing in Innovation (i3) and provided crucial support for teacher voice groups, advocacy groups, think tanks, and university research.

This involvement has earned kudos from some and backlash from others. For all the commotion, though, it's striking how rarely the strategies, scope, and import of "edu-philanthropy" are subjected to extended scrutiny and analysis. Even basic descriptive questions of what foundations do and how they do it have drawn far less attention than one might expect. For all the ink devoted to foundations like the Bill & Melinda Gates Foundation, the Lumina Foundation, The Walton Family Foundation, The Eli and Edythe Broad Foundation, the Michael & Susan Dell Foundation, the Ford Foundation, the Carnegie Corporation of New York and the like, we know remarkably little about patterns of giving and the purposes funders seek to achieve, much less about how these patterns and purposes have changed over time.

This book is framed by our sense that what foundations do has changed in notable ways and that these changes matter. Our experience suggests that funders have become more intentional in their strategy, more attentive to politics, more focused on metrics of success, and more aggressive about changing policy. In the pages that follow, we and the contributors seek to illuminate what foundations are doing; to inform our understanding of what they're doing and why they're doing it; and to provide an opportunity for

1

educators, policy makers, advocates, scholars, and funders to reflect on the nature of today's education philanthropy.

This volume is not about all of the different kinds of philanthropy in education today. After all, there are thousands upon thousands of education donors, of all shapes and sizes. Some support local scholarship programs, some give schools technology and textbooks, some pay for a new building on a beloved college campus. That kind of localized activity is not the focus of this book. Here, we focus on those funders engaged in the "new" education philanthropy—those who seek to promote significant change in how America's schools and school systems go about their work.

Now we'll put our cards on the table. We believe that what we call *muscular philanthropy* can play an enormously healthy role. Amid the fragmentation, bureaucracy, and deep-set routines of American education, this kind of giving can prove a valuable catalyst. Muscular philanthropy provides a vehicle for identifying and supporting promising individuals and ideas that may be an uncomfortable fit for education bureaucracies and routines. Such giving can light the way forward, especially as long as other donors provide a balancing wheel that can counter fads and the groupthink of the moment. At the same time, muscular philanthropy also poses important questions about who gets to influence public decisions and how they should do so.

Approached this way, it seems to us that the relative virtue of the "new" philanthropy doesn't exist in a vacuum—it depends on what donors do and the context in which they do it. What matters is not just what individual foundations may choose to do, but also whether on the whole foundations provide that balancing wheel and whether philanthropy enriches or short-circuits the messy process of democratic decision making. In all of this, there is an especially acute need for a mix of funders that support a diversity of strategies and improvement agendas—nurturing the clash of ideas that is such a distinctive and healthy feature of the American system. Philanthropy can play a similarly valuable role in providing a balancing wheel that can help ensure that competing visions and voices are not stifled by the current shape of government policy. Clearly, determining whether donors are sufficiently diverse or independent of government are judgment calls—but they're crucial ones. A primary goal of this volume is to help clarify what foundations are doing and how they're going about it, precisely so that readers will be better equipped to make these determinations for themselves.

A TUMULTUOUS DECADE FOR PHILANTHROPY

As recently as ten or fifteen years ago, there were concerns that the nation's philanthropic community was retreating from the K–12 public school arena, frustrated with what it regarded as school districts' stubborn resistance to change. In March 2002, the $500 million Annenberg Challenge, which had been unveiled eight years earlier at a joyous White House ceremony, petered out on a disappointing note. The Challenge's own final accounting comprised a pro forma recitation of accomplishments followed by the acknowledgment that "repeated setbacks, rapid turnover in leadership and sudden changes in direction . . . took everyone by surprise."[1] Less generous reviewers declared the effort an outright failure.

On the heels of Annenberg, in the early 2000s, several major traditional funders redirected their efforts away from K–12 to preK or to other sectors. In one noteworthy development, in July 2002, three major Pittsburgh-based foundations—Heinz, Pittsburgh, and Grable—announced they would stop funding the Pittsburgh Public Schools. More generally, the major new education philanthropies started to evince a heightened interest in structural change by giving to nontraditional providers rather than school systems, supporting a coherent and coordinated reform agenda, and more precisely measuring the impact of their funds.

In an attempt to make sense of these shifts, back in 2005, one of the editors of this volume published perhaps the first book to take a hard look at contemporary education philanthropy. That book, *With the Best of Intentions: How Philanthropy Is Reshaping K–12 Education*, examined the new, muscular brand of philanthropy while raising questions about some of the challenges it posed.[2]

Since those early years of the twenty-first century, the nature of foundations has changed dramatically. A Council of Foundations survey conducted in 2010 found that program staff had held their positions for an average of only three years.[3] Just as the death and replacement of individual cells means that the human body is almost wholly remade every few years, so it is true that most foundations are almost wholly remade within a period of a half-decade or so. While the mission and key leadership may remain, lots of grant officers—the "street-level bureaucrats" who make many of the decisions that matter—turn over, sometimes taking institutional memory and existing relationships with them.[4] Today's foundations have recruited more Teach for America and business school graduates than in previous generations, and unsurprisingly, the decision calculus of foundations is becoming more focused on accountability and the tenets of contemporary reform.

The last decade has seen such notable education developments as ED in '08, *Waiting for Superman*, Race to the Top, i3, the Common Core, the Gates Foundation's Measures of Effective Teaching project, the Relay Graduate School of Education, the Khan Academy, the *Vergara* lawsuit, statewide voucher programs, Democrats for Education Reform, Students for Education Reform, StudentsFirst, the "parent trigger," and much else that comprises today's education landscape. Just about all of these were driven in important ways by philanthropy.

While many welcome this resurgent education philanthropy as a source of badly needed resources, energy, and ideas, it has also generated serious concerns. Opponents charge the newer foundations with backing the wrong reforms, undermining democratic control, and even pursuing malign agendas. Even those who generally support the means and ends of the philanthropic resurgence see things that give them pause.

Indeed, the visibility of philanthropy and the controversy over its role has taken on a shape that once would have been astonishing. While it was once rare to hear attacks on education philanthropy, today, many education funders are subject to furious backlash from teachers and union leaders over proposed reforms—from left-leaning progressives opposed to testing and what they perceive as a creeping privatization of schooling and from Tea Party critics of the Common Core and new data collection initiatives. This volume is an attempt to make sense of these developments: to understand the new education philanthropy, its nature, its promise, and the issues it poses.

HAVE WE WITNESSED A REVOLUTION IN EDUCATION PHILANTHROPY?

The most vehement critics of contemporary philanthropy have asserted that the new emphasis on policy has transformed the nature of giving—turning it into something threatening and undemocratic. Historian Diane Ravitch, perhaps the most influential of these voices, charged in 2014, "[Those in] the philanthropic sector . . . are using their vast fortunes to undercut public education and impose a free market competition among competing schools. As they go merrily about the task of disrupting an important democratic institution, they work in tandem with the U.S. Department of Education . . .

Big money—accountable to no one—and big government have embarked on an experiment in mass privatization."[5]

Ravitch is right that the new philanthropy reflects a growing emphasis on advocacy, structural reform, and public-private partnership. But it's not clear that these practices are as dramatic a departure as she and others suggest. While most foundation giving has historically focused on less controversial efforts to support programs and practices, there have been plenty of efforts to promote a more muscular approach to giving.

The phenomenon of muscular educational philanthropy is not wholly unprecedented. Critics seem to forget that the Ford Foundation was aggressive and unapologetic about its push to radically restructure New York City's schools in the 1960s. In the 1970s and 1980s, Ford and other donors spent heavily to bankroll litigation and policy advocacy that sought to boost and revamp education spending. The Bradley and Olin Foundations played critical roles in supporting the research, advocacy, and policy experimentation that helped bring school choice to the national stage. If one is inclined to go back further, to the first half of the twentieth century, foundations like Rockefeller and Carnegie are responsible for helping to create much that eventually came to be seen as unobjectionable and even inevitable—from the SAT to the "Carnegie unit." Active engagement by individuals, associations, communities, businesses, and nonprofits has long been part of America's pluralist tale. We've always been a Tocquevillian nation, where progress springs not from the genius of central planners but from the pushing and shoving of a hearty scrum of self-interested actors.

That said, it's clear that some things about today's education philanthropy are distinctive—and some of those things are potentially worrisome. Ravitch rightly points out the extraordinarily close working relationship between major funders and the federal government. Especially in an era of unprecedented federal involvement in schooling, this threatens the philanthropic sector's ability to support competing visions and strategies—and even threatens to make some independent observers hesitant to criticize federally supported efforts for fear of crossing influential funders. While some foundations have always taken an active interest in policy and reform, the shared priorities, prescriptive metrics, emphasis on advocacy, and coordination of several of today's most prominent and deep-pocketed education donors are noteworthy developments.

A decade ago, philanthropists were frequently frustrated that they would invest heavily in exciting programs or practices, only to see them fail to deliver lasting improvements. A piloted reading or mentoring program would offer promising results, then disappoint when scaled. Or a foundation would underwrite professional development for several years, only to see it die on the vine when external funding dried up.

Whereas an earlier generation of donors chalked such failures up to problems of implementation or program design, the new philanthropists were apt to blame policy, system inertia, and a lack of political willpower. Donors who had made their fortunes in the new economy increasingly staffed their foundations with Teach For America alums and MBAs and embraced a focus on leadership, policy, and advocacy. The new approach was fueled by three insights.

First, as University of Arkansas professor Jay P. Greene observed in 2005 in his pioneering contribution to *With the Best of Intentions*, the dollar amount of education philanthropy is so small that it's tough to imagine that investments in programs or practice will have a significant impact. Greene estimated that all private giving to K–12, combined, amounted to, at the very most, one penny out of each dollar spent. Consequently, he argued, philanthropy mattered only when it funded "high-leverage investments" (e.g., changes in policies governing the use of public funds).[6]

Second, although these private funds typically account for small dollars in the grand scheme of things, they can have an outsized influence because they are relatively agile and can be used to fuel promising but relatively untested initiatives. In contrast, it's politically and bureaucratically difficult to redeploy more than a sliver of public funds.

Third, leverage can be enhanced by strategic investment in research and advocacy to shape policy. Foundation-backed research can overcome skepticism by providing proof points that innovative approaches are possible and effective. Foundation-backed advocacy can shape policy proposals and add pressure and legitimacy to the call to alter priorities in order to create the conditions for long-term, systemic change.

IT'S NOT JUST PHILANTHROPY THAT'S CHANGED

It's not just foundations that have changed; the landscape of education policy, politics, and reform today is dramatically different from that which prevailed up through the early 2000s. In the world of education, shifting political dynamics have fueled an array of aggressive policies addressing teacher evaluation, school choice, school turnarounds, state standards, and more.

The changes have played out in Washington, DC, and across the land. Great power has been concentrated in the US Department of Education, and the role of states has increased as well, creating opportunities for a new class of aggressive state-level education officials. Both of these trends have greatly reduced the autonomy of district-level leaders.

School choice has increased dramatically; today, charter schools enroll about 5 percent of the nation's students. By 2015, at least twenty cities had 25 percent or more of their students enrolled in charter schools.[7] Statewide voucher programs (in Louisiana and Indiana), the rapid growth of tuition tax credit programs, and the sharp increase in online options have helped unlock a world of new opportunities, choices, and tensions.

Teacher policy has also undergone dramatic change. Tenure has come under intense pressure through California's *Vergara* lawsuit and ensuing imitators. The US Department of Education pushed states to incorporate value-added metrics into teacher evaluation, and states complied. Meanwhile, teacher preparation programs have faced new competitors and heightened calls for accountability.

Foundations have helped support many of these shifts: fueling the growth of charter schooling and online education, supporting efforts to overhaul teacher tenure and evaluation, and funding scrutiny of teacher preparation and the emergence of new options. They have done so even as they have found themselves reacting to the new circumstances that these changes have created. And much of the animus directed at foundations is due to unease about the direction of this activity. This is all accentuated because we have entered an era in which education policy has lost some of the bipartisan framing and support it long enjoyed. As partisan and ideological forces infuse debates over the Common Core, teacher evaluation, and the federal role, foundations cannot easily avoid getting caught up in the currents.

The Danger of the Echo Chamber

We're immensely dubious about the charge that Bill Gates or other wealthy donors are out to buy America's schools as a way to further line their pockets; if these billionaires were really focused on accumulating additional millions, giving away huge sums might not be the most obvious strategy. That said, there are real causes for concern about the new philanthropy. And, as exasperating as it might seem to foundations, especially in the face of ad hominem attacks, it seems to us that foundations that wade into policy have a responsibility to embrace criticism more proactively. After all, choosing to give funds in a way that changes policies for millions of children and communities is different from underwriting a mentoring program. High-leverage giving can be appropriate and may be enormously healthy for students and schools, but it brings with it a new level of civic responsibility.

Most of the leading donors make a pretty sincere effort at self-appraisal. They evaluate grants, engage in self-criticism, and convene groups to offer feedback on their giving—and they deserve kudos on this front. However, the groups and individuals tapped by foundations for their insight and feedback tend to include, naturally enough, friends, allies, and grantees. These aren't the people most likely to challenge comfortable assumptions—especially given the sensible disinclination of grantees to offend benefactors. Robust public discussion, not private conversations, is the most effective forum for surfacing overlooked challenges, forcing difficult issues to the fore, or understanding how others may see an issue through an entirely different lens.

In the absence of robust public discussion, a vacuum emerges that gets filled by incendiary voices and marginal figures with ideological agendas and nothing to lose. Our hope is that the analysis and insights that follow suggest some opportunities for foundations, analysts, and critics to find more constructive ways both to listen and to speak up.

THIS BOOK FROM HERE

The United States has a rich and vital ecosystem of local donors and unobtrusive philanthropy, and we place enormous value on their activity. However, for better or worse, this is not a volume that tries to address the tens of thousands of smaller donors that enrich K–12 and higher education. Instead, as noted above, it's an examination of the few dozen foundations that have given millions in a conscious effort to help reform American education. Foundations that will merit repeated mention in this book include influential and recognizable names like Gates, Ford, Broad, Wallace, Walton, Dell, and Carnegie.

In the chapters ahead, a terrific lineup of contributors explore the giving of major foundations (new and old), the shift to advocacy, the backlash phenomenon, the impact of giving on research and policy, lessons learned in recent years, and the extension of "reform" philanthropy to higher education. The aim is to understand both what has changed and why it matters. How significant is the shift into advocacy or the heightened cooperation between the federal government and major donors? What are donors really doing differently, and what does that mean for students, teachers, schools, policy, and democratic decision making?

In chapter 1, Jay P. Greene shows that major foundations are more focused on changing public policy than they used to be, but he argues that these efforts are generally undermined by the failure of foundation staff to understand how their ability to mobilize advocates is limited. Greene suggests that foundations do not have natural constituents and that all they can do is hire mercenaries. Advocating for policy change without self-sustaining constituents, he says, is a recipe for failure.

A critical question is how more traditional foundations have responded to the emergence of the "new" education philanthropists. Have older foundations changed their patterns of giving, magnifying the shift represented by the new philanthropy? In chapter 2, Jeffrey W. Snyder takes a look at traditional donors like Ford and Carnegie and finds that they have embraced an emphasis on advocacy and policy that looks increasingly similar to that of newer foundations.

Chapter 3 takes a closer look at two of the most prominent new foundations. Sarah Reckhow and Megan Tompkins-Stange analyze the giving and thinking of the Bill & Melinda Gates Foundation and The Eli and Edythe Broad Foundation. Both have sought to influence federal education policy and politics in areas such as the Common Core, teacher evaluation, and charter schooling. Drawing on an analysis of giving and dozens of in-depth interviews, Reckhow and Tompkins-Stange examine how these foundations developed their advocacy strategies, how their strategies have unfolded, and how they think about their impact.

While "venture philanthropy" has grown familiar in K–12 education, it is still a relatively new phenomenon in higher education. Philanthropy in higher education has drawn important lessons about high-leverage investing from K–12, due in part to the Gates Foundation's influential role in both arenas. In chapter 4, Andrew P. Kelly and Kevin J. James take a look at how the new philanthropy has played out in higher education. How have funders turned to or modified the strategies of K–12 reform? How have they tried to change the fragmented, market-driven world of higher education?

One place where the new philanthropy has consciously sought to exert leverage is in the realm of research. From value-added measures of teacher effectiveness to charter schooling, philanthropy has played a catalytic role in spurring research that has had a substantial impact on policy and practice. In chapter 5, Dana Goldstein takes a careful look at the Gates Foundation's expensive, enormously influential Measures of Effective Teaching research. She examines the project itself, how its findings were communicated, and its impact on national policy.

In chapter 6, Michael Q. McShane and Jenn Hatfield examine the backlash against the new philanthropy. Although education philanthropy has sometimes been met with skepticism or localized pushback in the past, today's philanthropic ventures face what may be unprecedented hostility. McShane and Hatfield first quantify the amount of criticism—finding that it has grown, but less than casual observation might suggest—and then interview some of the critics to explore the nature of their discontent.

In chapter 7, Larry Cuban asks whether the new philanthropy—or any philanthropy—changes what teachers do behind the closed doors of their classrooms. He suggests the answer is no and explains why, unless things change, the impact of today's educational philanthropy is likely to be only skin deep. Cuban discusses the tendency to focus on state and federal policy, or on system leadership, while overlooking the crucial role of teachers as "gatekeepers" to what actually happens in classrooms. He argues that this inattention to how reform affects teachers means that the new philanthropy generally fails to change classroom practice or the teaching profession.

What lessons have foundations taken from all the goings-on of the past decade? In chapter 8, Alexander Russo tries to answer that question by interviewing a number of current and former foundation officials. He offers their frank assessments of shifts in strategy and tactics and their lessons learned. He notes their mixed feelings about what has happened when foundations have worked closely with government, the emphasis on more intrusive accountability, and the challenges of advocacy.

In the concluding chapter, we will do our best to summarize key findings and takeaways. We will try to make sense of what the contributors have to share and to understand how much that matters. After all, the intriguing thing about the new philanthropy, love it or loathe it, is that it has the ability to illuminate much that's distinctive and important about the shape of education policy in the first decades of the twenty-first century.

1

Buckets into Another Sea

Jay P. Greene

Most large foundations working on education policy have broader objectives than simply helping the direct recipients of their giving.[1] They aspire to make significant changes to the entire system of K–12 education so that their efforts help many more students than they can directly touch and continue to do so for a long time after their funds stop flowing. Unfortunately, very few foundations are engaged in a strategy of philanthropy that is likely to lead to broad and enduring changes in the education system.

In this chapter, I will describe cultural, institutional, and political characteristics of our education system that commonly prevent foundations from producing broad change in the K–12 system. I describe what types of strategies foundations would have to adopt to overcome these obstacles. I then document, based on an analysis of their grant making, how foundations rarely pursue these strategies. Lastly, I will consider why foundations frequently fail to adopt more effective strategies.

OBSTACLES

Foundations would be better positioned to have broader and enduring effects on the K–12 system if they were to grasp a few key features of education politics. The following review of the political context prevailing in K–12 education forms the basis of my subsequent analysis.

First, foundations do not possess sufficient resources to purchase change in a system that spends over $600 billion annually.[2] Foundations have billions in endowment but annually spend no more than $2 billion on K–12 education in aggregate.[3] That is about 0.33 percent, or almost rounding error, of the total resources available to public schools. It is certainly less than the average increases in spending that public schools have enjoyed in the past or can reasonably expect in the future. Between 2000 and 2011, total spending on public K–12 education increased from $522 billion to $632 billion (adjusted for inflation), an average increase of over $10 billion each year.[4] So there is nothing foundations can buy that the public school system as a whole could not afford if it wished.

Second, public schools are no more in need of foundation ideas than they are of foundation dollars. The K–12 system is awash in theories about effective practices. As I will argue, foundations cannot hope to produce broad change by modeling an effective practice in a limited location. Other schools are unlikely to learn about, let alone adopt, something that is claimed to be effective somewhere else. They have good reason to be skeptical about such claims and have their own ideas of effective practices to pursue. They doubt the sincerity and competence of outsiders. Once foundation funding is withdrawn, even effective practices may be discontinued in the limited locations where they are piloted. Any theory of change based on the idea that schools are sitting around waiting for foundations to tell them what works is horribly naive.

Third, the public education system is dominated by a large, well-financed, and very well-organized set of political interest groups. This means that foundations face active and strong opposition that they would not face if they were trying to cure a disease or put up an art exhibition. Education policy is characterized by interest-group politics. I am primarily talking about the two national teachers' unions here, but this description could also include other professional associations of educators, administrators, and school boards. These groups are all very resistant to efforts by others to control any meaningful aspect of the education system. And the main feature of interest group politics is that concentrated and organized interests tend to prevail over dispersed and unorganized interests. If there is a conflict, unions and their allies are very likely to prevail over foundations. And even if they lose, the established education interests can bide their time to repeal, dilute, or co-opt an unfavorable measure at some later point.

Fourth, education is a highly decentralized system, with most policies controlled by state or local officials. To be sure, there has been a shift toward greater centralization over the last few decades, but the bulk of education funding, policymaking, and operational control remains highly decentralized and is likely to remain that way far into the future. This means that foundations pursuing top-down policy reforms have two highly unattractive options. They can attempt to reform schools one state or district at a time, then try to replicate policy victories in each state and local jurisdiction, spreading their already thin political and financial resources across many policy battles. Or, instead of fighting district by district, they can try to increase centralized control so that they only have to win once. But the long-standing traditions and entrenched interests associated with decentralized control make efforts at imposing a centralized solution extremely difficult and costly. And even in the unlikely event that foundations can impose centralized solutions, the chance that they will be able to retain control over those centralized solutions for any length of time is near zero.

Fifth, monitoring and enforcement costs in education are very high. That is, it is extremely difficult to know what teachers are actually doing in their classrooms or to change what they are doing. Observations of teacher classrooms typically have to be arranged in advance, are limited in number, and follow a strict protocol. If you cannot observe what teachers are doing, it is nearly impossible to impose any instructional practice or content. Other methods of monitoring classrooms and altering teacher behavior, such as using the results of standardized tests, can be effective only if those measures are used to impose real consequences on teachers for noncompliance. Again, this is something that teachers and their unions fiercely oppose. It is hard enough to use test results to grade whole schools or districts, and remarkably rare that those scores affect teacher pay, job security, or anything else. Some school systems have attempted to base compensation and termination decisions on test performance, but those policies are often blocked, diluted, or co-opted.[5]

If these five things are true about education politics, how are foundations supposed to produce broad change in the K-12 system? The one thing they can't do is compel change. They can't buy it because even billionaires don't have enough money. They can't use the power of effective practices or good ideas because schools are rightly skeptical and have their own vision of effective practices and good ideas. Any effort to impose a top-down solution faces opposition from well-organized and extremely powerful interests, has to navigate a remarkably decentralized system, and has virtually no mechanism for getting teachers to implement it.

OVERCOMING OBSTACLES

Change can occur only when it is in enough people's interests and when people are organized to accomplish it. Change needs a constituency that can advocate for its own interests independent of foundation support. The main role of an effective foundation seeking to make broad and enduring change should be to fund and advocate for programs that can attract their own constituencies. Foundations could also help pay the fixed costs associated with organizing a constituency so that it can then advocate for its own interests without continued foundation support.

The essence of an effective foundation strategy is to recognize scarcity of both financial and political capital. Foundations do not have enough money to buy the broader change they want. Instead, they have to redirect how public funds are used by changing public policy and practice. This was the point of my chapter, "Buckets into the Sea," in the 2005 volume on philanthropy and education edited by Frederick M. Hess.[6] And it is a lesson that foundations are increasingly incorporating into their thinking. According to Sarah Reckhow and Jeffrey W. Snyder's analysis, total foundation grants for advocacy and research jumped from $69.9 million to $110.6 million between 2005 and 2010.[7] Even with the increase in total giving during this period, the share devoted to advocacy and research expanded from 9.5 percent to 13.1 percent. Around the same time I was urging foundations to recognize the limits of their financial resources and focus on changing public policy, foundations were making greater efforts to do precisely that.

The problem is that foundations have not been sensitive to the constraints on their political resources. They are increasingly focused on changing policy, but often attempt to do so without generating and organizing constituencies that benefit from these changed policies. Foundations need these self-sustaining constituents so they can independently advocate and multiply foundation efforts. Giving to typical DC-based groups that stream endless talking points in Tweets, blog posts, and at conferences does not create a self-sustaining constituency for programs or practices. These groups are largely paid mercenaries and will drop their advocacy efforts if funds for advocating a particular cause disappear. In addition, even when these groups are being paid, their advocacy is of limited usefulness, given that they are mostly talking to each other.

In "Buckets into the Sea," I emphasized the need for leveraging limited foundation dollars by redirecting public funds. The heart of my argument in this chapter is that foundations seeking broad change in the education system need self-sustaining strategies that both redirect public resources in support of their policy objectives *and* create and organize new constituents who can fight to expand and protect changes independent of foundation support.

THE UBER ANALOGY

Rather than reiterating my argument as an abstract set of principles, it might be best to illustrate it with an analogous real-world example. The technology/transportation company Uber is currently attempting (and largely succeeding) at doing in transportation policy what foundations are seeking to do in education policy. Uber wants to introduce broad changes in how local taxi service is provided, just as foundations want to change how local education is provided. The policies and regulations governing taxi services, like those governing education, are highly decentralized and dominated by well-organized political interests.

But Uber is not doing any of the things that foundations have traditionally done with respect to education. Uber did not attempt to purchase the change it sought in the transportation model, whereas foundations have tried to pay for the programs they prefer. Uber understands that it does not have enough capital to purchase enough taxi medallions to influence how the local transportation system operates. Nor has Uber tried to persuade taxi companies to change by demonstrating their alternative model with successful pilot programs. Taxi companies have reasons for preferring to operate in the way they currently do.

Uber also clearly recognizes that taxi companies dominate the local authorities that set policies and the regulations that govern third-party transportation. So Uber's first move was not to go to each local government in an attempt to persuade it to change its regulations to allow Uber's model to operate. In a head-to-head political contest with taxi companies, Uber would lose, just as foundations are likely to lose in a head-to-head battle with teachers' unions. Uber understands that, at least initially, it cannot achieve change by imposing its political preferences over the well-organized interests of local taxi companies.

Instead, Uber is mostly accomplishing its goals for changing transportation policy by creating a constituency that will advocate on its own for those changes. Uber operates in many cities where its services are not fully compliant with local policies and regulations. Uber's hope is that by nevertheless starting operations in those places, it will create constituents who benefit from its services and will then help lobby for changes. Once drivers start to work for Uber and riders start to use their services, both groups start to recognize how they would benefit from changes in policies and regulations that would allow Uber to operate more freely. Uber may help subsidize organizing drivers and riders into effective interest groups, but those constituents are motivated by their own interests to fight for the change in transportation policy and regulation.

The *Washington Post* recently recounted exactly how Uber uses this constituency-generating political strategy.[8] In June 2014, public officials in Virginia warned Uber that its service was illegal and that it needed to immediately stop operating in the state. The paper then described how Uber reacted:

> Far from being intimidated, Uber was ready to fight back. The company immediately called on one of its most potent weapons: its ever-growing list of smartphone-wielding customers. A notice sent to Uber users in Virginia included the e-mail address and phone number of the ordinarily low-profile official in charge of the decision. The notice instructed the company's supporters to demand that the DMV "stand up for you."
>
> Hundreds of them did and, by Sunday, Commissioner Richard Holcomb's inbox was flooded. Holcomb did his best to respond—working through the weekend, even crafting e-mails to irate Uber customers as he lay in bed at home . . .
>
> While Uber pushed its riders to lobby Holcomb, the company also moved quickly to mobilize its newly hired team of high-powered lobbyists in the state capital. After the lobbyists agreed to meet in the ensuing days with aides to Gov. Terry McAuliffe (D), the state's transportation secretary instructed the DMV not to interfere with Uber drivers, according to documents obtained through a public records request. Within 48 hours of the order, Uber had, in effect, won a reprieve.
>
> Then, seeking a longer-term fix, Uber lobbyists submitted a draft of a proposed temporary operating permit. State officials granted a revised version several weeks later, permitting Uber as well as Lyft, a smaller company, to continue normal operations for the time being.
>
> In an era of government dysfunction, the Virginia example shows how San Francisco–based Uber has pioneered not just a new sort of taxi service but also a new way to change long-standing local ordinances.
>
> Uber's approach is brash and, so far, highly effective: It launches in local markets regardless of existing laws or regulations. It aims to build a large customer base as quickly as possible. When challenged, Uber rallies its users to pressure government officials, while unleashing its well-connected lobbyists to influence lawmakers.

Teachers' unions and their allies are too strong to be defeated by the foundations and the advocacy organizations they pay. Like Uber, foundations need to leverage their scarce financial and political resources to get others to work toward their goals. They need to redirect public funds to pay for the programs and practices they prefer. Foundations also need to get others to realize how they would benefit from policy changes and work independently to fight for those changes.

REFORM EXAMPLES

Foundation support of school choice is an excellent example of how this strategy works in the field of education. Some foundations have worked to expand school choice, either by paying directly for those programs or advocating for their creation. Once students start attending schools of choice and educators start working in them, they may come to recognize how they benefit from the existence of school choice. They can then be mobilized to defend those programs or fight for their expansion. In this way, school choice helps create its own constituency to protect it.

In fact, we witnessed how beneficiaries of choice could be mobilized to defend and expand the program when New York City Mayor Bill de Blasio tried to crack down on charter schools located in district buildings. Thousands of choice students, families, and educators took to the streets of Albany to rally for charter schools.[9] Governor Andrew Cuomo and other state officials took note of this organized interest, recognized the political benefits of helping that interest, and adopted measures to protect charter schools in New York City.[10]

If foundations had not initially subsidized the development of charter schools in New York and elsewhere, there would not have been a thriving charter sector with thousands of enrolled students. And if foundations had not supported the organizations that helped mobilize those beneficiaries of charters into an organized interest, constituents may not have turned out in such large numbers and parlayed that strength into victory in Albany. With school choice, foundations leveraged their limited resources for political influence by creating advocates who fought for the programs on their own. Before the foundations took action, these constituents did not know they could benefit from this change and could not be organized to fight for it.

It is important to keep in mind that for this leverage strategy to work, the beneficiaries need to be able to organize and exercise political influence. It is an oft-said but still true aphorism that programs for the poor tend to be poor programs. Because charter schools in New York and most other places benefit middle- and upper-middle-class families as well as the poor, those more advantaged beneficiaries are better able to engage in political activity and prevail. Programs that target only the most disadvantaged have a hard time mobilizing constituents to come to their defense.

Many other education reform strategies do not create a set of beneficiaries and are therefore unlikely to survive organized political opposition. Take, for example, efforts in Chicago to change the method by which teachers are evaluated and to attach real consequences to those evaluations.[11] Linking student test scores to teacher evaluations and then linking merit pay or dismissal to those evaluations does not generate a sizable set of beneficiaries who will fight for those reforms. It is true that the teachers who would receive bonuses would benefit, but they mostly do not know who they are and are necessarily a minority subset of all teachers. In fact, attempting to implement a merit pay system generates a group of well-organized people who believe that they will be harmed. Teacher outrage in Chicago over the controversial teacher evaluation and compensation system fueled a historic strike, after which the union largely prevailed in neutering the reform—a good illustration of how teachers' unions can so easily block, repeal, dilute, or co-opt test-based evaluations and merit compensation efforts.[12] Who will come to the streets to rally for those reforms? If there are any beneficiaries, they are dispersed students and parents who are largely unaware that they may be beneficiaries and incapable of being organized politically.

In addition to expanding school choice, reform strategies based on building new institutions also stand a better chance of being self-sustaining. Examples of philanthropy creating new institutions that are self-sustaining can more easily be found historically than in recent times. Julius Rosenwald, the founder of Sears, helped build almost five thousand schools to educate black children across the South in the early part of the twentieth century.[13] Those schools required matching public and community funds, so they also leveraged public dollars. The Rosenwald schools educated a large portion of the black middle class in the South, who were then able to organize and fight for full equality in education as part of the civil rights struggle decades later.

Other institution builders included Andrew Carnegie, whose philanthropy helped build thousands of libraries across the United States in the late nineteenth and early twentieth centuries. Once built, those libraries received public funding, thus leveraging public dollars. They also helped develop and organize constituents to advocate for improving literacy and education in communities all across the country. In the area of higher education, John D. Rockefeller Sr. helped build the University of Chicago, Rockefeller University, and Spelman College. Leland Stanford helped build Stanford University. Cornelius Vanderbilt founded Vanderbilt University. Carnegie helped start Carnegie Mellon.

The super-rich of the Gilded Age knew something that the super-rich of today seem to have forgotten. They knew that paying people to lobby for changes in existing institutions was unlikely to yield broad and enduring change. You are better off building institutions, leveraging public dollars, and creating constituents to advocate for more. If you want to improve literacy, getting state boards of education to adopt new standards that declare that all children should learn how to read will not actually result in widespread literacy. Instead, you should do as Carnegie did and build libraries that generate local, public funding and support for community-based efforts to promote literacy. Gilded Age philanthropists who wanted to transform American universities like Harvard, Yale, and Princeton from divinity schools into modern, scientific institutions did not attempt to do so by nagging them to meet "best practices." They built new universities that competed with the old and forced them to change or fade into oblivion.

In more recent years, we have seen philanthropists back school choice, charter schools, and the development of new small schools, but, as I will show, the bulk of philanthropic effort does not embrace these self-sustaining strategies. While I clearly see how efforts to expand school choice and build new institutions help generate their own constituencies, I do not see how many top-down reforms, including those focused on standards and assessments, accomplish this. It may be that these top-down reforms possess an inherent political weakness in that they fail to generate independent constituents. If so, then foundations are very unlikely to succeed in supporting these efforts, regardless of the substantive merits of those reforms. It is also possible that my political vision is limited and I do not understand how policies like Common Core, merit pay, and mandated instructional approaches will generate groups of organized supporters who can defeat the already established organized interests that are likely to fight against these reforms. If that is the case, supporters of those policies should be able to articulate exactly who the beneficiaries would be and how they could be mobilized into organized interests.

DATA ANALYSIS

In my observation, most large foundations working on K–12 education policy are not pursuing the strategies I mentioned for leveraging their limited
resources, even though they need to do so to be successful in achieving broad
and enduring policy change. To test this suspicion, I collected information
on recent grants from fifteen of the largest foundations working on K–12
education. To identify these foundations, I started with the Reckhow and
Snyder *Educational Researcher* analysis of foundation giving, which lists the
fifteen largest donors to K–12 education in 2010.[14] I searched for the most
recent detailed description of grantmaking for these foundations and found
information on all but these three: GE Foundation, Communities Foundation of Texas, and Daniels Fund. I then added three replacement foundations, which I selected largely because they appear to be active funders of
education reform according to education media: the Laura and John Arnold
Foundation, the William T. Grant Foundation, and the Joyce Foundation.
There are some indications that the Arnold Foundation has subsequently
reduced its effort on K–12 education, but their previous active role is still
worthy of examination.

I then had two research assistants independently review and classify grants
from these foundations. For most foundations, they were able to use lists
and descriptions of grants provided on foundation websites, although sometimes they had to rely on 990 tax filings. The grants examined were generally
from 2013. However, the grants available for analysis were from 2010 for the
Robertson Foundation; 2011 for the Doris and Donald Fisher Fund; 2010–
2011 for The Broad Foundation; and 2011–2016 for the Arnold Foundation.

In total, the 1,596 grants were coded into eight categories:

1. Not education
2. Self-sustaining advocacy
3. Non-self-sustaining advocacy
4. Indeterminate advocacy
5. Research
6. Self-sustaining program
7. Non-self-sustaining program
8. Indeterminate program

Education grants could be classified as supporting advocacy, research, or
programs. *Advocacy* included grants that supported organizations whose

primary purpose appeared to be to persuade others to adopt or support particular education policies or practices. *Research* included efforts to analyze the effects of education policies or practices. *Programs* included grants to organizations that directly provided services to students.

Within advocacy and programs, grants could be subdivided into being self-sustaining, non-self-sustaining, or, if the research assistants coding them were unable to tell, indeterminate. *Self-sustaining* advocacy or programs support efforts that are likely to develop beneficiaries who could then be mobilized to provide political support for them. *Non-self-sustaining* advocacy or programs support efforts unlikely to generate constituents who could provide the necessary political backing.

To illustrate the distinctions between these categories, I will describe a number of grants, all made by the Gates Foundation. I chose Gates because it is by far the largest foundation and because it has grants in all categories.

In 2013, the Gates Foundation gave $4.2 million to Green Dot "to support the expansion of Green Dot Public Schools into the state of Washington and the launch of at least one school in 2015–2016."[15] This is an example of a self-sustaining program because it involves the creation of a new institution that will be supported in the future with redirected public funds. The Gates grant pays to get it started and its support becomes self-sustaining, as the institution will receive public funds.

An example of a non-self-sustaining program can be found in the $75,000 grant from Gates "to support School District of Philadelphia teachers to share their teacher effectiveness work with each other and key community members by engaging in workshops and other learning opportunities that will elevate and celebrate effective teaching in Philadelphia."[16] Although this community sharing may be a beneficial practice, the district could have funded such a program before the grant, so there is little reason to believe that it "needed" the money to engage in it. The fact that the district did this only when paid to do so suggests that there is little reason to believe that it will continue the program after Gates stops funding it. In addition, it is unlikely that this program will generate its own constituency that will advocate for redirecting public funds to continue it in the future.

An example of self-sustaining advocacy can be found in the $250,000 grant that Gates provided to the Center for Education Reform "to advance high quality charter policies."[17] Finally, an example of non-self-sustaining advocacy can be seen in the $240,000 grant to Pennsylvania Partnerships for Children "to enhance understanding and support to implement the new teacher evaluation system and the Common Core."[18] As described above, I see charter school advocacy as creating its own independent, organized group of supporters, whereas advocating for top-down reforms like teacher evaluation systems and Common Core standards does not.

Grants were classified as *indeterminate* within programs or advocacy when it was unclear whether they would create their own constituents. Research grants were largely self-evident, although it was sometimes difficult to distinguish true research from disguised advocacy. If something was described as research, we accepted that at face value and classified it as such.

Obviously, making these distinctions involves difficult judgments with incomplete information. Despite this messiness, the two research assistants were remarkably consistent in how they independently classified grants. As can be seen in table 1.1, they agreed on how grants should be classified 72.6

TABLE 1.1   Inter-coder reliability of fifteen top funders

Foundation	Cohen's Kappa	Agreement quality	Number of total gifts	Percent agreement
Arnold	0.53***	Moderate	74	63.5
Broad	0.51***	Moderate	66	63.6
Carnegie	0.30**	Fair	43	55.8
Dell	0.61***	Substantial	43	81.4
Fisher	0.76***	Substantial	33	81.8
Ford	0.29***	Fair	105	53.3
Gates	0.66***	Substantial	677	77.3
Grant	0.49**	Moderate	25	72.0
Hewlett	0.24***	Fair	95	56.8
Irvine	0.48**	Moderate	16	75.0
Joyce	0.43***	Moderate	32	56.3
Kellogg	0.12	Slight	21	42.9
Robertson	0.69***	Substantial	34	79.4
Silicon Valley	0.36***	Fair	41	85.4
Walton	0.71***	Substantial	291	79.4
Overall	**0.63***	**Substantial**	**1,596**	**72.6**

***$p < .001$, **$p < .01$

percent of the time. Using Cohen's Kappa as a test of inter-coder reliability yields a Kappa of .63, which indicates "substantial" agreement between coders. The categories are vague, descriptions of the grants were difficult to find, and reasonable people might disagree on how things ought to be classified. But, perhaps like pornography, the independent coders appeared to be able to know it when they saw it.

In the instances where the two coders disagreed, they met to explain their reasoning and see if they could resolve the difference in classification. In almost all cases, they were able to do that successfully. In the handful of cases where they could not agree on how to classify a grant, I reviewed the information and served as the tie-breaker.

After eliminating grants that were not related to US K–12 education, there were 1,390 grants, representing $889.6 million. Given that almost all of these grants were from 2013, this represents approximately the amount that the largest fifteen foundations devoted to K–12 education in a single year. Table 1.2 provides a summary of the results. The largest group of grants, representing nearly half (47.5 percent) of the total dollars, goes to non-self-sustaining programs. As I documented in "Buckets into the Sea," the bulk of foundation giving goes to these programs.

The next largest category of giving is to self-sustaining programs, with 17.1 percent of the total dollars. These programs largely consist of subsidies to charter schools. Close behind is giving to non-self-sustaining advocacy, with 16.5 percent of total dollars. This includes organizations advocating for changes in teacher evaluation, merit pay, instructional techniques, or other measures that teachers tend to oppose and for which parents are unlikely to hold rallies. Self-sustaining advocacy, accounting for 8.5 percent of total dollars, includes groups advocating for choice, changing the structure of schools, and small schools.

Toward the bottom of the categories is research, which receives only 5.9 percent of total dollars. For the most part, foundations work on and advocate for programs with little or no research basis for their activity. They appear confident that they know what is good and just want to do it. Little effort is devoted to determining whether reforms actually are effective or how they can best be implemented. And little thought is given to the potential for research to have long-term advocacy benefits. Instead, foundation-supported organizations tend to have a lot of guns but no bullets.

In total, nearly two-thirds (65.3 percent) of giving goes to programs and barely one-third (34.7 percent) goes to advocacy or research, as shown in

TABLE 1.2   Funding from the largest fifteen foundations to K–12 education, 2013

Category	Total dollars	Number of gifts	Percent of giving
By category of giving			
Self-sustaining advocacy	75,821,298	80	8.5
Non-self-sustaining advocacy	146,341,857	259	16.5
Indeterminate advocacy	33,965,024	61	3.8
Research	52,259,572	115	5.9
Self-sustaining program	151,872,039	241	17.1
Non-self-sustaining program	422,598,143	620	47.5
Indeterminate program	6,713,169	14	0.8
By advocacy/research or program			
Advocacy/research	308,387,751	515	34.7
Program	581,183,351	875	65.3
By advocacy or research or program			
Advocacy	256,128,179	400	28.8
Program	581,183,351	875	65.3
Research	52,259,572	115	5.9
By sustainability			
Non-self-sustaining	609,618,193	954	68.5
Self-sustaining	279,952,909	436	31.5
Total	**889,571,102**	**1,390**	**100**

figure 1.1. In addition, more than two-thirds of total giving goes to non-self-sustaining programs or advocacy.

After reviewing the "indeterminate" subcategories of advocacy and programs, I determined that they most likely belonged in the non-self-sustaining groups. For this reason and for the sake of simplicity, I combined indeterminate with non-self-sustaining to generate this overall split between self-sustaining and non-self-sustaining grants.

In table 1.3, I report the results broken out by foundation. Some of the foundations have distinctive patterns of giving. For example, the Grant Foundation is unusual in that it devotes the bulk of its giving (71.6 percent) to research. Some organizations give almost entirely to programs, including

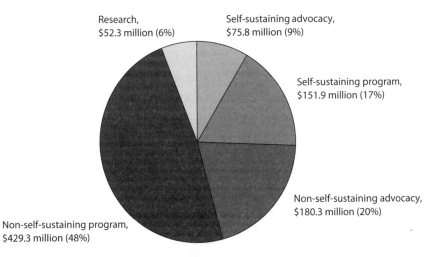

Research,
$52.3 million (6%)

Self-sustaining advocacy,
$75.8 million (9%)

Self-sustaining program,
$151.9 million (17%)

Non-self-sustaining advocacy,
$180.3 million (20%)

Non-self-sustaining program,
$429.3 million (48%)

FIGURE 1.1   Percentage of giving, by category

TABLE 1.3   Percentage of giving in each category by foundation

Foundation	Self-sustaining advocacy	Non-self-sustaining advocacy	Research	Self-sustaining program	Non-self-sustaining program	Total
Arnold	31.7	27.2	0.0	5.1	35.9	100
Broad	4.4	24.0	1.0	17.6	53.0	100
Carnegie	0.6	44.5	0.6	0.0	54.3	100
Dell	0.0	0.6	0.9	24.1	74.4	100
Fisher	39.0	7.5	0.0	40.5	12.9	100
Ford	0.0	29.7	9.9	0.0	60.4	100
Gates	1.8	13.0	12.3	9.3	63.6	100
Grant	0.0	7.2	71.6	0.0	21.1	100
Hewlett	0.0	42.6	6.6	5.7	45.0	100
Irvine	0.0	4.9	1.1	0.0	94.0	100
Joyce	9.7	42.9	11.6	1.4	34.3	100
Kellogg	2.5	19.3	1.4	2.1	74.6	100
Robertson	19.6	4.4	0.0	29.7	46.3	100
Silicon Valley	0.0	0.0	0.0	2.2	97.8	100
Walton	13.7	23.6	0.7	48.3	13.8	100
Overall	**8.5**	**20.3**	**5.9**	**17.1**	**48.3**	**100**

the Michael & Susan Dell Foundation, the James Irvine Foundation, and the Silicon Valley Community Foundation. Some tilt heavily toward advocacy, including the Arnold, Carnegie, Fisher, Hewlett, and Joyce Foundations, each of which devotes more than 40 percent of its giving to advocacy. The Arnold, Fisher, and Robertson Foundations focus significantly on self-sustaining advocacy, while Carnegie, the William and Flora Hewlett Foundation, and Joyce Foundation focus significantly on non-self-sustaining programs. The organizations that seem to best grasp the need for supporting self-sustaining efforts are the Fisher, Grant, Robertson, and Walton Foundations, each of which devotes roughly half or more of its giving to research or self-sustaining advocacy or programs.

WHY DON'T FOUNDATIONS FOCUS MORE ON SELF-SUSTAINING EFFORTS?

If my argument is correct that self-sustaining grants are most likely to produce broad changes in education policy, why don't foundations devote more of their resources to that strategy? First, I think some foundations have only recently begun to realize that just funding attractive programs is insufficient to accomplish this goal. In this analysis, grants supporting advocacy and research constitute more than one-third (34.7 percent) of total giving, with nearly two-thirds still going to programs, most of which are not self-sustaining.

Several forces may be hindering foundation adoption of self-sustaining strategies. First, foundations may be increasingly aware of their financial limitations, but they may not understand how weak they are politically. Foundations may not appreciate how hard it is to achieve and sustain political victories in the face of well-organized, well-funded, and persistent opposition in the form of teachers' unions and their allies.

Second, many foundations have acquired much larger staffs with more bureaucratic governance of their operations. This shift away from small, mission-based foundation staffs operating largely on personal trust has increased what economists call *agency costs*. That is, it may increasingly be the case that program officers and senior staff are protecting their own jobs and power at the expense of the organization's mission. The performance of staff and their grantees are judged by metrics that often invite manipulation and deviation from the mission of the organization. For example, even if a foundation decided that it needed to improve its political influence, the metrics that are typically used to assess influence do not correspond to actual political effectiveness. In particular, influence is often judged by measures such as Klout scores, web hits, article placements, and other metrics that are easily manipulated. All grantees have to do is Tweet, blog, and speak continuously, regardless of whether anyone with any power is actually listening. Constant communication is not the same as influence. In addition, these metrics can be goosed by easy tricks, like picking fights to generate more online traffic or colluding with other similar organizations to promote each other's work. The behavior of teenagers in an echo chamber does not constitute influence in the grown-up political world. To assess actual influence requires human judgment about what actually constitutes influence. The less foundations rely on human judgment, the more they rely on metrics that do not accurately capture what they are trying to accomplish.

Third, resistance to focusing on funding self-sustaining efforts may come from the top. The founders of many of these organizations earned their wealth at a young age and remain actively involved in the strategy and operations of their foundations. Their business competence may not translate well into the political world of education policy. In business, the boss is generally able to produce a desired change simply by imposing his or her will on subordinates. But this kind of control does not apply in a democratic system dominated by organized interest groups. You have to recruit people to your way of thinking by making it in their interest to do so.

Interestingly, John D. Rockefeller Sr., who was a real pioneer in modern philanthropy, learned the importance of cultivating support because of the complicated and decentralized structure of trusts controlling Standard Oil.[19] Because he presided over a committee of the heads of related but separate companies, Rockefeller could prevail only by mobilizing the interests of these separate power bases for a common effort. This is also the way Rockefeller ran his philanthropy, with a clear eye on creating self-sustaining institutions and policies that would not be dependent on his support. All foundation boards and their staff should study the example Rockefeller set.

The problem is that many founding donors did not have a path to great wealth similar to Rockefeller's. They were often solely responsible for their companies and could impose their solutions from the top down. In addition, their wealth was often accumulated at a younger age than Rockefeller or inherited, so they may never have lost the overconfidence of youth, especially if it was reinforced by the inordinate praise and deference that wealthy and powerful people tend to receive.

Adopting self-sustaining strategies in philanthropy is all about humility. It requires the realistic expectation that change is likely to be gradual and limited. It also requires understanding that even large fortunes and enormous power are not enough to produce even that gradual and limited change in highly decentralized, democratic systems dominated by well-organized interests. Of course, failure in philanthropy is a humbling experience. Some foundations headed by wealthy entrepreneurs may become frustrated with non-self-sustaining strategies and walk away from education reform, convinced that change is too hard. But some will acquire wisdom from those frustrating experiences and adapt their strategies. This chapter is intended to provide some guidance on how they might adapt to improve their chances of producing broad and enduring change in K–12 education.

2

How Old Foundations Differ from New Foundations

Jeffrey W. Snyder

I n early 2008, the *New York Times Magazine* featured a conversation between individuals with different viewpoints on education philanthropy that discussed the sector's changes. Steve Barr, founder and then-CEO of a well-known Los Angeles–based charter school operator, Green Dot Public Schools, explained why his organization received large amounts of grant money from philanthropist Eli Broad: "Because I'm a disruptive force. And he's betting on that force gaining enough momentum that it will ultimately change the system, not just in L.A. but elsewhere, too, in a way that really realigns the education debate."[1] This type of grantmaking is commonly referred to as *venture philanthropy*. Like venture capital, venture philanthropy seeks to maximize "returns" on foundation investment. Unlike venture capital, where returns are often measured in profit, philanthropic returns come through social change. Although this concept is not new, even to education philanthropy, its scope as undertaken by newly emergent education foundations like the Gates, Broad, and Walton Foundations is a relatively recent phenomenon.[2]

The largest new national foundations are characterized by living benefactors who built their business fortunes in the late-twentieth-century economy. Among the philanthropists included in this chapter's analyses, Bill Gates and Michael Dell built their fortunes through computer technology, Eli Broad and Julian Robertson through investment, and the Walton family through multinational retail. These magnates typically established their eponymous foundations in the 1990s, and their K–12 education philanthropy became most prodigious after 2000. Older foundations were typically established between 1900 and 1950 and based on industrial-era manufacturing and print publishing fortunes.[3]

Another key difference between old and new foundations lies in the types of organizations they fund.[4] The Annenberg Challenge exemplifies traditional foundation approaches. Announced in late 1993 by former ambassador Walter Annenberg, the Annenberg Challenge remains the largest single gift to American public education—$500 million to help reform struggling schools. The largest portions of this money went to ten sites across the United States and generated over $600 million in matching funds. Challenge grants supported collaborative reforms developed at each site, requiring that programs include both traditional school systems and local nonprofits. The Annenberg Challenge sought to change entire systems by mobilizing communities and school districts in tandem to make concerted reforms, unlike other efforts that might seek to improve individual schools (for example, charter schools or vouchers). After Challenge grants expired in the late 1990s and early 2000s, many described the initiative as a failure. Said one evaluation, "The Annenberg Challenge was not set up to challenge the status quo; rather, it relied upon much the same set of relationships and processes that had yielded the status quo in large public school systems."[5]

Although those involved with the Challenge dispute this characterization, the contrast between this approach and new foundation initiatives is stark.[6] New foundations seek to generate the greatest change and frequently support actors outside traditional education systems pursuing reform (like Green Dot and Steve Barr). Traditional foundations, as shown by initiatives like the Annenberg Challenge, typically target their funds to grantees aligned with traditional school systems. In the Carnegie Corporation's 2000 Annual Report, President Vartan Gregorian further distinguished traditional organizations like his from newer groups by explaining, "Unlike traditional philanthropies, which make grants to a great many capable organizations with promising proposals, the new philanthropists work intensely with relatively few nonprofit organizations."[7] Thus, older foundations grant to a broad set of groups to influence traditional public school systems, but new foundations often maximize social change by funding a smaller set outside traditional education organizations.

Many accounts of philanthropy in education after 2000 often, in one way or another, focus their attention on roles played by new foundations. In *Reign of Error*, her newest book on education reform, Diane Ravitch mentions the Gates Foundation on twenty-two pages, The Broad Foundation on ten, and the Walton Family Foundation on eight, with nary a mention of the more traditional Annenberg Foundation, Carnegie Corporation, or Ford Foundation.[8] Other scholarly work also emphasizes newer groups like the Gates and Broad Foundations.[9] This focus often makes sense—the new foundations, their scale, and their investment styles are important developments in education philanthropy. A second set of analyses groups together the largest education givers in terms of dollars granted.[10] This method also inherently focuses on the outsized role played by new foundations and their disproportionately large coffers, especially in more recent years. For example, in 2010, one of the most recent years for which data is available, the Gates Foundation accounted for 17 percent of total K–12 philanthropy and the Walton Foundation represented approximately 10 percent.[11] Thus, when considering the largest funders, analyses may overlook old foundations' uniqueness because they do not grant as many dollars as new foundations.

Like Barr and Green Dot, new foundations have been a disruptive force. The philanthropic landscape has shifted in no small part due to new foundation funding. What remains unclear is whether and to what degree other actors within the philanthropic system have changed to follow new foundation leads. Traditional foundations still give substantial amounts around education and have long been trying to improve K–12 schooling in the United States. As new foundations became dominant, did older foundations alter their grantmaking to align more closely with new foundation approaches, just as Eli Broad hopes Green Dot affects older organizations in its sector? Or, as shown by the Annenberg Challenge's focus and Gregorian's suggestion in 2000, have new and old foundations remained distinct in what they fund and how they target their resources?

It may be that older foundation grantmaking has become more similar to that of new foundations. Some social theorists contend that isomorphism occurs among organizations within a sector, meaning that they behave in ways that maintain their credibility.[12] One way to do this is by operating in ways that have established legitimacy within the field. As new foundations grew, their giving to nontraditional education organizations in a more focused way gained credibility. Simultaneously, vocal critics delegitimized the goals emphasized in the Annenberg Challenge by claiming it was ineffective. Thus, older foundations may have changed granting behavior because new funding approaches and issues gained credibility just as efforts like the Annenberg Challenge faced criticism.

Conversely, sociologists argue that institutional entrenchment confronts organizations in well-developed fields, so old organizations might have continued to operate in their usual manner.[13] Although new foundations expanded K–12 grantmaking, traditional philanthropies have a far more established history. Rather than become more like new foundations, traditional foundations may have continued giving broadly to organizations working with traditional school systems. Thus, two possible expectations make sense. First, old foundations could have granted in more focused ways and to more nontraditional organizations, following the lead of new foundations. Second, old foundations could have remained entrenched in their funding and methods, choosing to eschew new models and broadly fund those working with traditional school systems.

In two ways, this chapter empirically investigates whether and how old foundation grantmaking changed. First, it shows which types of grantees new and old foundations funded over time. Second, it examines a trend found in other research called *convergent grantmaking*. Several studies have shown that, when examining the largest education philanthropies, grantees more frequently shared funders as time progressed.[14] These results suggested that the largest education funders increasingly shared funding priorities and targeted funds into a small subset of grantees. This chapter explicitly investigates whether old foundations' convergent grantmaking differed from that of newer philanthropies.

This study uses data from the years 2000, 2005, and 2010. Although these data are not as up-to-date as I would prefer, 2012 is the most recent year for which granting data is available. The delay between when foundations make grants and when they are reported through publicly available Internal Revenue Service documents means that this chapter is not an explanation of how new and old foundations currently operate. Instead, it looks at how old foundations operated in the first decade of the twenty-first century, as Annenberg Challenge–era grantmaking faded and new foundations emerged as the largest grantors.

This investigation yields two sets of findings. First, old and new foundations maintained mostly distinct funding priorities. Old foundations tended to give to support traditional education organizations as well as groups and programs working closely with traditional establishments. Old foundations supported their priorities by giving a substantially higher proportion of their grants to universities and state- or national-level policy research and advocacy than did new foundations. Meanwhile, new foundation grants more frequently flowed to public, private, and charter schools, as well as to venture philanthropy organizations providing seed money to nontraditional education organizations. Unlike old foundation grantees, organizations funded by new foundations tended to work on education reform outside traditional systems.

Second, old and new foundations differed in the degree to which they converged their grantmaking. In 2000, few new foundation grantees shared multiple funders. By 2005, new foundation grant recipients more frequently had and shared multiple funders, suggesting that new philanthropies had overlapping priorities and funded the same organizations based on these goals. This trend became more pronounced in 2010, when the grantee network showed a greater number of preferred organizations connected by shared funders. Old foundations did not converge their grants to preferred grantees in the same way. Examples existed in 2000 and 2005, such as organizations affiliated with the Annenberg Challenge, but there were relatively few organizations with shared grantors. By 2010, old foundation beneficiaries were still not nearly as interconnected as new foundation grantees, even though the old foundation network did expand.

These findings cumulatively suggest, as Gregorian stated in 2000, that old and new foundations differed in their priorities and in the degree to which they converged grantmaking while pursuing their goals. Old foundations, perhaps due to institutional entrenchment, supported a wide variety of grantees only loosely connected by their common tendency to work closely with traditional education organizations. Such continuity would likely lead Annenberg Challenge critics to assess old foundation grantmaking similarly from 2000 to 2010.

DATA AND METHODS

To examine whether and to what degree differences existed between new and old foundation granting, analyses compare funding by ten philanthropies, five old and five new. Although more foundations in each group would be preferable and allow for more complete comparisons, finding and culling grant data requires substantial time. Therefore, this chapter focuses on a smaller set that includes some of the most prominent old and new foundations. The Foundation Center's Foundation Stats dashboard provided summary data for the most recent eleven fiscal reports (2002–2012), allowing analyses to target new and old foundations that rank in the top fifty largest education grantors (by dollars) in at least six of eleven possible years. This ensures that analyses are focused on those philanthropies consistently giving to K–12 education on a large scale. Each foundation ranked as at least the twenty-fifth-largest education philanthropy in the years it made the rankings.[15] Using these criteria, The Eli and Edythe Broad Foundation, Michael & Susan Dell Foundation, Bill & Melinda Gates Foundation, Robertson Foundation, and Walton Family Foundation form the new foundation group. The Annenberg Foundation, Carnegie Corporation of New York, Ford Foundation, W. K. Kellogg Foundation, and Wallace Foundation (formerly Wallace-Reader's Digest Funds) comprise the old philanthropy group.[16]

Data came from each foundation's 2000, 2005, and 2010 Internal Revenue Service Form 990-PF, where foundations reported external grants made in that tax cycle.[17] In most cases, tax documents included grantee names, addresses, and funding amounts. Some philanthropies also included a statement with each grant, indicating its purpose. These data provided a granting snapshot in each year and, when assessed over time, substantiated conclusions drawn throughout this chapter. Once recorded, each grant was then coded into one of forty-seven different categories based on the grant's purpose statement and/or Internet searches about a recipient organization's activities. Some examples of applied codes include: public school district, charter school, charter management organization, policy research or advocacy, teacher or administrator training/recruitment, university, association of elected officials, and arts education.[18] Analyses throughout this chapter group similar codes. For example, totals for "charter schools" discussed below include grants to individual charter schools as well as to charter management organizations. Unless otherwise noted, figures are reported in 2010 inflation-adjusted US dollars.

When assessing convergent grantmaking, analyses focused on organizations with multiple old or new foundation funders. The convergence section first highlights the ratio of grantees receiving funds from multiple old or new foundations, as well as the proportion of grant dollars these recipients collected. Then, using UCINET software version 6.537, analyses visually present links between organizations that received at least $1 million in old or new foundation dollars.[19] In these graphics, a link between organizations means they share at least two funders. Should organizations that receive large amounts from philanthropies share multiple funders, they may also share missions and expectations from their funders. As these affiliation networks grow larger and more intertwined, they often highlight priorities

resonating among foundations and suggest increas¡
grantees. Before delving into these networks, the
trends in foundation giving from 2000 to 2010.

GENERAL TRENDS IN NEW AND OLD FOUNDATION GRA

In 2009, Associated Press journalists wryly opened a report on Bill Gates's
influence in education by saying, "The real secretary of education, the joke
goes, is Bill Gates."[20] Quips like this stem from the Gates Foundation's K–12
education philanthropy, which provides far more funding than the next
largest funders. For example, Gates gave 75 percent more than the second-
place Walton Foundation in 2010. Jokes about Bill Gates's education policy
influence would have been less accurate in 2000, when Gates Foundation
grants did not total far more than other foundation funding.

To be sure, Gates was the largest K–12 philanthropy in 2000. When
compared with second-place Annenberg, however, Gates's $93.8 million
in spending did not vastly outpace Annenberg's $89.1 million. Similarly,
the Walton Foundation's third-place sum, $38.9 million, did not dwarf the
Ford Foundation's fifth-place $32.5 million. In fact, the five old founda-
tions granted $42 million more than the five new foundations in 2000 (see
figure 2.1). These figures show that, although narratives often focus on the
amounts given by new philanthropies, old foundations combined to grant
more at the decade's beginning than new philanthropies.

By 2005, new foundations gave far more to K–12 than did old philanthropies. Relative to their 2000 funding totals, Walton nearly doubled and Gates
more than tripled their funding. Broad, Dell, and Robertson all increased
their grant totals more than tenfold. New foundations especially grew their
charter school, state and national policy, and venture philanthropy grantmaking. Although old foundations also increased their aggregate giving,
growth was comparatively modest because only three old foundations grew
their K–12 grantmaking. Carnegie, Kellogg, and Wallace each roughly doubled their funding. Growth for these three was driven by grants for new
university-based teacher preparation, aligning community and school
resources, and leadership development programs, respectively. Ford's total
grants fell by 45 percent, largely because it made a few large grants in 2000
that it did not also make in 2005. These expiring grants included one to
help sustain Annenberg Challenge sites following the program's completion and a series of grants for university-based teacher and administrator

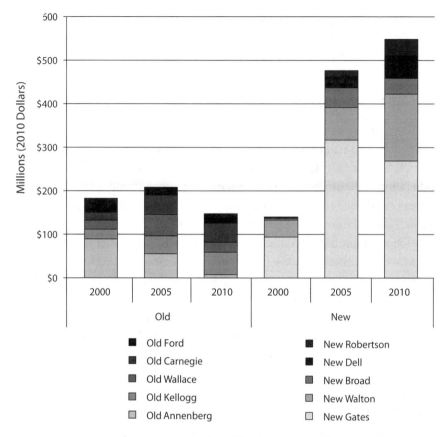

FIGURE 2.1   K–12 Education Giving by Old and New Foundations 2000, 2005, 2010

development programs. Annenberg's total also fell by $34 million as grants associated with the Annenberg Challenge expired.

The disparity between old and new foundations grew in 2010. Old foundation K–12 grantmaking shrank by 29 percent from 2005 to 2010, largely due to decreases by the Annenberg and Wallace Foundations. Annenberg's funding declined from $55.3 million in 2005 to $7.6 million in 2010 as granting to former Annenberg Challenge sites ceased. As Wallace's school leadership grants expired after 2005, the foundation's funding returned to near-2000 levels. New foundations, meanwhile, increased their aggregate giving by 15 percent, with grants to charter schools, alternative teacher training organizations (for example, Teach for America [TFA]), and national-level policy research and advocacy being the largest growth areas.

Overall, these general trends show the emergence of new foundations and suggest some distinct priorities. New foundations grew rapidly, largely based on steady increases in giving to charter schools and other reformers outside traditional education systems. As Annenberg Challenge grants ceased, old foundation granting declined overall. Further, old foundations continued prioritizing a wide array of issues while still maintaining primary support for traditional education institutions. The next section further examines differences between new and old foundation granting priorities.

WHERE THE DOLLARS GO: NEW AND OLD FOUNDATION PRIORITIES

Aggregated grants show what types of initiatives old and new foundations prioritized with their grantmaking. Although these findings do not encompass every grant, the categories described cumulatively represent at least two-thirds of each group's funding in a given year. Three sets of priorities emerge from this type of examination.

The first set highlights granting areas emphasized more by old foundations. Figure 2.2 shows grantmaking for old and new foundations in 2000, 2005, and 2010. Darker bars represent old foundations, moving from dark to light as time progresses. Lighter bars represent new foundations, moving from darkest in 2000 to lightest in 2010. The leftmost cluster, grants to university-based K–12 projects, shows that old foundations gave a substantially larger proportion of their funds to this area—18 and 19 percent of all grants in 2000 and 2010, respectively—than did new foundations. In 2000, the largest grants frequently funded university-based leadership and professional development. Although old foundations' grants to universities continued to fund human capital projects in 2010, more of the largest grants also sought to drive student improvement in other ways. For example, Carnegie granted $1.6 million to the University of Texas at Austin to help develop math and literacy networks, and Kellogg gave $1 million to Utah State University to study extended school year programs. University grants consistently comprised less than 5 percent of new foundation dollars throughout the decade, showing that such grants were not a priority. When new foundations did give to universities, it was often to support human capital development programs, small school redesign initiatives (in 2000 and 2005 only), and improve education data systems (primarily in 2010). Although similar issues arose in both old and new foundation grants to universities,

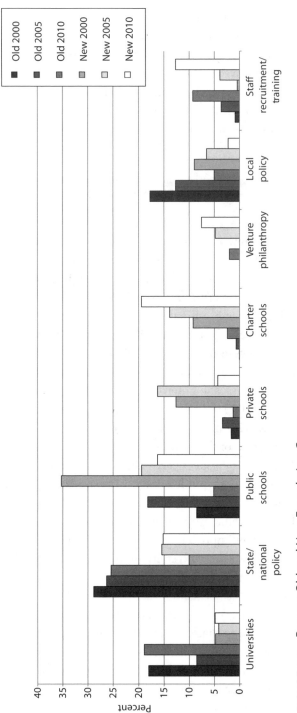

FIGURE 2.2   Percent Old and New Foundation Grants

especially leadership development, old foundations emphasized university-based projects far more than new foundations did.

Figure 2.2 also shows emphasis on state and national policy granting. These figures are the sum of three different grantee types: state-level policy research and advocacy nonprofits, national-level policy research and advocacy nonprofits, and associations of elected officials. These grantee types are grouped together because they predominantly seek to influence policy development or implementation. Old foundations devoted a larger proportion of their granting—over 25 percent each year—to state and national policy organizations. Grants also went to organizations with diverse purposes, promoting policy work around issues like early childhood initiatives, improving university-based teacher education programs and teacher preparation policies, and developing capacity in support of local school districts. In 2000, although new foundations directed 10 percent of their giving to state and national policy work, almost half came from a single Walton Foundation grant to a group advocating for school choice (Children's Educational Opportunity Foundation). Considering this single large grant, new foundations as a whole prioritized state and national policy work far less than old foundations did in 2000. In 2005 and 2010, new foundations devoted roughly 15 percent of their funds to state and national policy work. Grants also flowed to a greater number of priorities in 2005 and 2010, including school choice advocacy, measuring and raising teacher effectiveness, small high school redesign, and improved education data systems. Takeaways from this category are thus twofold: old foundations gave more to state and national policy work, and they mostly gave in support of traditional education organizations, whereas new foundations gave more to groups outside traditional systems.

A second set of grants shows areas that were more heavily prioritized by new foundations. As seen in figure 2.2, one such area was funding for public school systems. Two short-term spikes disturb what would otherwise be consistent patterns for both foundation types. In 2005, the Wallace Foundation awarded eleven districts each $1 million (in 2005 dollars) to support "strategies aimed at improving the training of leaders and at creating working conditions that allow them to succeed."[21] Together, these grants represented more than three quarters of all public school giving that year. Similarly, three large Gates Foundation grants spiked new foundation public school granting in 2000. Two grants totaling a combined $11.7 million supported technology use in schools, and one grant for more than $19 million went to a teacher leadership project in one Washington State Educational Service District. If omitting these one-time spikes from each respective year, the percentages supporting public schools show a more consistent pattern for both new and old foundations. Considering the data in this way, new foundations prioritized giving to public schools 5–10 percent more than old foundations did in a given year. Qualitatively, the largest old foundation grants to public schools focused on school-community engagement and school leader development, whereas new foundations funded efforts to improve teacher effectiveness and enhance school performance management systems.

New foundations also supported private and charter schools more than old foundations did. Old foundations did not prioritize these areas—funding never rose above 3.4 percent for private schools or 2.4 percent for charters. New foundations, meanwhile, gave 12.6 percent to private schools in 2000 and 4.3 percent in 2010. What seemed like a precipitous drop in 2010 was misleading, because 2005's total included a $40 million Gates grant to Lakeside School in Seattle (Bill Gates's high school alma mater). If this very large grant is omitted, new foundations' proportion of funding going to private schools shows a pattern of steady decline as the decade progresses. Most private school grant recipients were individual schools, but Children's Scholarship Fund also consistently received large amounts—$11.7 million in 2000, $15.1 million in 2005, and $13.7 million in 2010. Children's Scholarship Fund, cofounded by John Walton, provides scholarships for low-income students attending private schools. New foundation granting to private schools is thus characterized by two consistencies, funding for Children's Scholarship Fund and gradual decline.

The decline in new foundation private school grants corresponded with an increase in charter school funding from 9.2 percent of new foundation dollars in 2000 to 19.5 percent in 2010. These concurrent trends suggest that new foundations shifted their attention away from private schools and toward charters as their preferred nontraditional education priority. Another trend also emerges in the charter school grants: new foundations placed increasing emphasis on charter management organizations (CMOs). CMOs like Aspire Public Schools, KIPP, and Green Dot Public Schools operate multiple schools and launch new schools, often in different cities or states. In 2000, individual charter schools received 71.5 percent of all charter school dollars, with CMOs receiving the remainder. The inverse was true in 2005; CMOs received 73.8 percent of all charter school money. By 2010, the forty-six largest charter school beneficiaries were CMOs, and these organizations represented 81.1 percent of all new foundation charter school grants. Thus, new foundations shifted their granting emphases in two ways: from private to charter and from individual schools to organizations managing multiple schools. By increasing support to CMOs, new foundations funneled money into those organizations most likely to expand the charter school sector, which may help maximize return on investment.

Figure 2.2's venture philanthropy cluster shows an emerging new foundation priority. Two organizations typify this type of grantee: NewSchools Venture Fund (NSVF) and Charter School Growth Fund (CSGF). Each grantee applies venture capital principles to education reform in efforts to maximize return on investment. To this end, CSGF contributes to charter management organizations to fuel their expansion. NSVF similarly invests in nontraditional education organizations, including charter schools, alternative teaching programs like TFA, and alternative leadership development organizations like New Leaders for New Schools. Over all years, these two organizations received 87.9 percent of all venture philanthropy grants from both new and old foundations. NSVF, established in 1998, is also the only consistent venture philanthropy grantee that existed prior to 2000 (CSGF was founded in 2005). Thus, given venture philanthropy's recent development as an education field, it is predictable that neither old nor new foundations made any such grants in 2000. Venture groups again received no old foundation funds in 2005, but did receive 2 percent of their grants in 2010, mostly via three grants from Carnegie to NSVF for over $2.6 million. New foundations awarded nearly 5 percent of their grants to venture philanthropies in 2005 and 7.6 percent in 2010, with the vast majority going to NSVF and CSGF. Although the share of new foundation grants going to venture philanthropy may seem small, relatively large growth suggests that it became an important new foundation focus as time progressed. Indeed, venture philanthropy had the third-largest growth of any new foundation granting priority, behind only charter schools and grants to teacher or administrator recruitment and training organizations (see below).

A third and final set of priorities are those where old and new foundation trends closely resembled each other. Figure 2.2 shows these two grant areas: local policy research and advocacy, and organizations providing alternative teacher or administrator recruitment and training. Although old foundations' grants to local policy research and advocacy were roughly double the amount that new foundations gave, the very similar trends signal comparably declining emphasis on these grantees. Compared with the share that local policy work received in 2000, new foundations decreased funding by 74.8 percent and old foundations by 71.7 percent to these organizations by 2010. In 2000, the largest old foundation grants went to groups affiliated with the Annenberg Challenge, while more than three quarters of new foundation funding went from Gates to organizations supporting Seattle schools. In 2005, over half of old foundation local policy dollars went to groups formerly affiliated with the Annenberg Challenge, and over half of new foundation grants were made by Gates to small school redesign in Boston, New York, Oakland, and San Francisco. A single organization, New Visions for Public Schools, received 58.7 percent of old foundation grants and 35.5 percent of new foundation grants in 2010. New Visions works on education reforms in New York City and was affiliated with the Annenberg Challenge, Gates's small school initiatives, and efforts to create a diverse school provider network. Cumulatively, these data show that local policy research and advocacy grants primarily supported single new or old foundation issues, and both foundation types simultaneously gave fewer of their resources to such grantees throughout the decade.

The starkest example of shared priorities between old and new foundations was their granting to teacher and administrator recruitment and training organizations. In 2000 and 2005, both foundation types gave virtually the same percentage of their funds to these groups. Qualitatively, however, old and new foundations did differ at times. In 2000, only two new foundations gave in these areas—one grant each from Walton and Broad to TFA to provide alternative routes into teaching. Meanwhile, three of four old foundation grants went to the National Council for Accreditation of Teacher Education, which works to strengthen university-based teacher preparation. Nontraditional organizations received more attention in 2005. TFA and the New York City Leadership Academy, an alternative principal training program initially launched by former New York City chancellor Joel Klein, received roughly 82 percent of old foundation 2005 training grants. Similarly, new foundations devoted over 90 percent of these funds to TFA, The New Teacher Project, New Leaders for New Schools, and the Broad Center (founded by Eli Broad). Each of these organizations provides alternative pathways into teaching and school leadership. This trend continued in 2010 for new foundations; all grants went to alternative preparation programs. Old foundation grants split in 2010 between alternative programs and those that work with universities. One large grant by Kellogg went to the Woodrow Wilson National Fellowship Foundation, which recruits people with science backgrounds into teaching and puts them through university-based training. This single grant represented 63 percent of 2010's old foundation total in this category. Of the remaining dollars, nearly two-thirds went to alternative programs like TFA. Overall, when giving to organizations that were not universities but focused on teacher or administrator preparation, new foundations gave almost exclusively to nontraditional groups like New Leaders for New Schools. Old foundations split their grants fairly evenly between these alternative grantees and organizations focusing on university-based programs. Thus, although this remained an area where the traditional versus nontraditional difference existed, it was not as pronounced as in other granting areas.

Cumulatively, the patterns discussed above suggest that old and new foundations maintained mostly distinct funding priorities. Old foundations primarily supported traditional education organizations or organizations working closely with the traditional system, while new foundations focused their efforts on nontraditional organizations like charter schools and education entrepreneurs. Although these differences exist, it remains to be seen whether and to what degree old and new foundations employ different tactics in their grantmaking. Put another way, did new or old foundations fund the same organizations to pursue their different priorities, or did they spread their funds across a wide variety of organizations? The next section examines the grantees receiving funds from multiple new or old foundations.

CONVERGENT FUNDING AMONG OLD AND NEW FOUNDATIONS

Research over the past five years finds that, rather than funding many different organizations, the largest philanthropies started to direct more money to the same organizations, a strategy known as *convergent grantmaking*.[22] Grantees that share funders may also share goals, and identifying those receiving grants from the same foundations provides a better indicator of aligned funder priorities. Furthermore, by drawing connections between those grantees with multiple overlapping funders, clustering can help identify the most salient shared issues to funder groups. To observe funding overlaps, this section focuses only on those organizations receiving grants from at least two old or at least two new foundations.

Table 2.1 identifies the percentage of grantees that received funds from multiple new or old foundations and the proportion of new or old foundation dollars granted to these organizations. Among old foundation grantees, the percentage of grantees with at least two old foundation benefactors remained relatively stable over the decade—9 percent had multiple old foundation funders in 2000 and 8.6 percent did in 2010. These grantees also received similar percentages of total old foundation funds, 24.3 percent in 2000 and 25.5 percent in 2010. The Public Education Network and Schools of the 21st Century each received over $10 million from old foundations in 2000, far more than others with multiple old foundation grantors. Grants to each also had similar goals. Schools of the 21st Century was Detroit's Annenberg Challenge lead agency. The Public Education Network, similar to the Annenberg Challenge's mission, worked to develop civic capacity and support public education in cities throughout the United States. By 2010, the organizations receiving large amounts of funding from multiple old foundations had more diverse objectives. For example, Public Interest Projects, a philanthropic association, received $4.5 million to build grassroots school reform collaborations. New Visions for Public Schools received $4.4 million, almost all of which was for small-school redesign initiatives. Old foundations granted Big Thought $3.5 million to improve arts education in Dallas and Harvard University $2.2 million for various research projects, the largest grants being for studies of a summer reading program in North Carolina and the Harlem Children's Zone.

Unlike old foundations, larger proportions of new foundation grantees had more than one new foundation funder as time progressed, and these organizations represented increasingly large shares of new foundation funds. The percentage of new foundation grantees that had multiple new foundation funders grew from 1.8 percent in 2000 to 10.1 percent in 2010. The ratio of new foundation grants collected by these recipients rapidly grew as well, from 10.4 percent in 2000 to 46.8 percent in 2010. The issues represented

TABLE 2.1   Grantees with more than one funder

	Old foundations			New foundations		
	2000	**2005**	**2010**	**2000**	**2005**	**2010**
Percentage with >1 funder	9	6.8	8.6	1.8	5.6	10.1
Percentage of $ to organizations with >1 funder	24.3	19.1	25.5	10.4	25.5	46.8

by grantees with multiple new foundation funders stayed somewhat consistent over the decade, primarily funding private school scholarships, charter schools, and other nontraditional education initiatives. In 2000, Children's Scholarship Fund received $11.7 million, the vast majority of new foundation money that went to organizations with multiple new foundation grantors. By 2010, the grantee with most incoming new foundation money was Teach for America, which received $37.5 million. $22 million in new foundation grants went to the DC Public Education Fund, almost all of which was to support DC Public Schools' teacher merit-pay system. Charter School Growth Fund attracted $21.1 million to help expand charter networks nationwide, and KIPP's national office received $14.9 million to support and expand its charter school network. NewSchools Venture Fund received $16.2 million to help seed a variety of projects like charter school expansion and evaluation, data system planning and implementation in Newark, and teacher recruitment/development projects.

Examining grantees with multiple new or old foundation funders further clarifies distinctions between the foundation types. When old foundations funded the same groups, these organizations worked with traditional education systems in a variety of ways. The proportion of old foundation grantees with multiple old foundation grantors also stayed consistent over time, as did the share of old foundation grant dollars these groups received. New foundation grants went increasingly to those with multiple new foundation funders, and these grantees overwhelmingly worked to expand nontraditional education options. This suggests that the biggest change over the decade was a narrowing new foundation focus on organizations supporting nontraditional education organizations.

Old and New Foundation Grantee Networks

An additional way to observe convergent grantmaking is by identifying a more specific subset: those organizations that shared funders and received the most grant dollars. Thus, the following analyses consider groups attracting at least $1 million in old or new foundation grants in a given year that also share at least two funders with another recipient. Using social network analysis, the diagrams below link grantees according to funder relationships. Lines between grantees indicate two shared funders, bolder lines signify a greater number of overlapping funders, and larger circles or squares (nodes) represent organizations that received relatively more funds. Grantees sharing funders may have similar missions and grants to the same organizations may clearly signal more concerted efforts among foundations to pursue their shared priorities.

Figure 2.3 shows the old foundation network for the year 2000. Although links can be drawn between old foundation grantees, no such network can be made for new foundation recipients because only one organization (Children's Scholarship Fund) had multiple funders and received over $1 million. Within the old foundation network, two distinct clusters emerge. The left side includes organizations whose grants were related to teacher or leader development. Even the research institutions in the year 2000's network, Harvard and RAND Corporation, received most of their grant dollars to work on improving school leadership. The left side's primary funders were Carnegie and Ford. The right side, which includes Brown University, the Boston Plan for Excellence in the Public Schools, and New Visions for Public Schools, were organizations associated with the Annenberg Challenge. The other grantee on the network's right side, Public Education Network, received money to build local capacities in efforts to assist traditional public schools (issues very similar to the Annenberg Challenge's mission). Primary funders for the network's right side were Annenberg, Carnegie, and Ford. Overall, the network shows old foundation priorities most overlapped in efforts to bolster staff development and support school-community linkages.

In 2005, networks emerge for both new and old foundations. Of the old foundations, two Annenberg Challenge organizations, Boston Plan for Excellence and New Visions for Public Schools, remain on the right side of the 2005 network and share Annenberg and Carnegie as funders (see figure 2.4). Three of the other four organizations—Jobs for the Future, the University of Michigan, and the Academy for Educational Development—received grants to develop university-based programs for school staff preparation or university capacities to support traditional schools. Annenberg, Carnegie, and Kellogg primarily supported these groups. The Fund for Public Schools worked broadly to support New York City's public schools and received grants from Annenberg, Carnegie, and Wallace. Most of 2005's old foundation money to this group, however, came from a single Annenberg grant in support of the New York City Leadership Academy alternative principal training program. Despite this one grant, 2005's old foundation network maintained focus on traditional education institutions and, absent clearly defined clusters, suggests these actors and issues were common throughout these philanthropies.

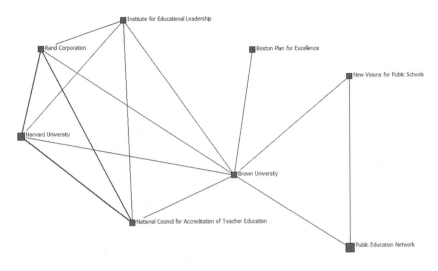

FIGURE 2.3   Old foundation grantee networks, 2000

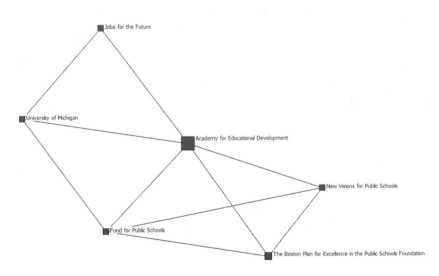

FIGURE 2.4   Old foundation grantee networks, 2005

The 2005 new foundation network in figure 2.5 is far denser than the old foundation network. The lack of any isolated areas suggests shared priorities among new foundations, and the bold lines at the center show many grantees shared three and even four funders. Although most grantees are connected, some similar groups cluster within this network. Charter school organizations occupy the bottom and center right, including operators KIPP, Aspire, and Green Dot as well as the California Charter School Association, which supported charter school operators. Near the top of the network are venture groups NewSchools Venture Fund and Pacific Charter School Development, which seeded charters and developed charter facilities. On the left of the network are groups like the Council of Chief State School Officers, National Governors Association, and National Center for Educational Accountability. These grants were to help exchange best practices about accountability data systems and small high school redesigns. Finally, two alternative staff-training organizations, Teach for America and New Leaders for New Schools, are in the middle and right of the network. The network's high degree of interconnectedness clearly emphasizes shared priorities, especially a preference for groups creating or supporting nontraditional education organizations.

Figure 2.6 shows the old foundation networks in 2010. The 2010 old foundation network has more organizations sharing funders than the 2000 or 2005 networks. Contrasted with 2005, 2010's old foundation network

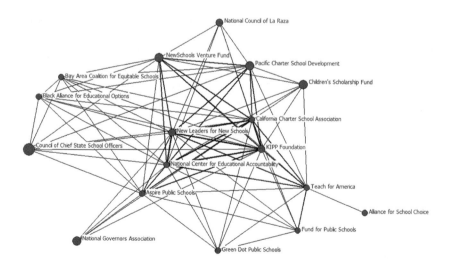

FIGURE 2.5   New foundation grantee networks, 2005

includes fairly clear groups with similar roles. Parts of the network, especially the bottom right, have greater density than in years past and show more interconnectedness between grantees. Recipients in the bottom right tended to have grants purposed for research or dissemination about traditional school reforms in a variety of areas like school redesigns, teacher effectiveness policies, expanded learning days, and arts education. Organizations comprising the network's bottom left arm received funds to provide technical assistance for expanded learning time reforms and improved community engagement in public schools. Grantees in the top left cluster mostly supported early childhood education programs and school data system improvement. As in 2000, although distinct purposes cluster together, each tended to support traditional education institutions and initiatives.

The 2010 new foundation network became much more crowded and dense, showing that new foundations shared more priorities and funded the same groups to these ends in 2010 (see figure 2.7). Although the network's density makes it hard to see, those organizations at the network's center have more connections than in years past.

Teach for America and NewSchools Venture Fund, for example, each received funds from all five new foundations. Beyond TFA and NSVF, other organizations providing alternatives to traditional education institutions are well represented in the network's core, especially charter school organizations and alternative teacher or leader training groups. Compared with the

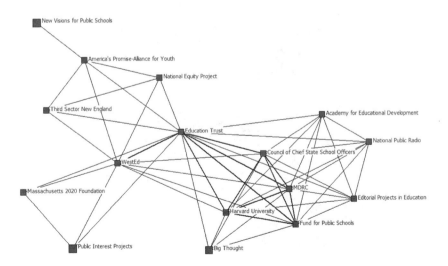

FIGURE 2.6   Old foundation grantee networks, 2010

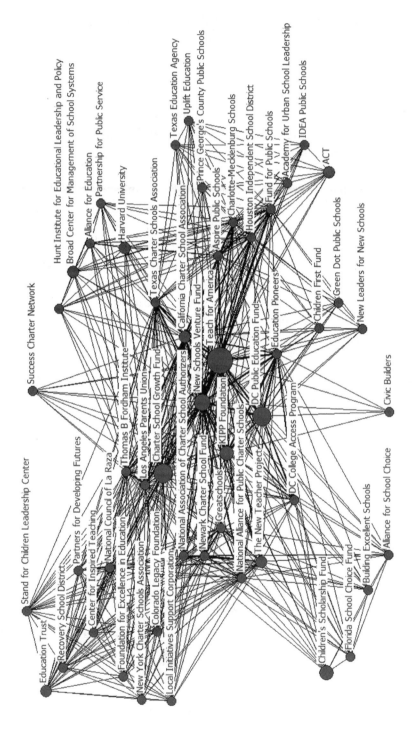

FIGURE 2.7   New foundation grantee networks, 2010

2005 network, the movement of these types of groups into the 2010 network's center indicates a clearer shared focus on these issues than in years past. Funds flowing to grantees more near the peripheries of 2010's new foundation network similarly supported nontraditional education organizations and reforms. More than any other evidence, the 2010 new foundation network clearly exhibits the increased and shared granting priority given by new foundations to organizations and reforms outside traditional education systems.

CONCLUSION

Breaking foundations into these two groups reveals three things. First, old foundations maintained their focus on traditional education organizations and those working in support of traditional systems. Compared with possible expectations about how old foundations might (or might not) change as new foundations became dominant education philanthropies, these findings cumulatively provide strong evidence that entrenchment was the norm. Second, these analyses confirm trends seen in other research showing increased granting to nontraditional organizations like charter schools and Teach for America. Furthermore, this chapter more clearly shows that new foundations were primary drivers of this nontraditional funding growth. Third, convergent granting as a method to pursue goals was far more prevalent among new foundations as time passed than it was among older philanthropies. New philanthropies shared clearer priorities and increasingly funded the same organizations in pursuit of these goals.

A potential caveat emerges when considering funding convergence. The 2010 old foundation network included more grantees with more ties than in previous years (see figure 2.6 as compared with old foundation networks in figures 2.3 or 2.4). While still nowhere near as expansive as new foundation grantee networks, this change may hint that old foundations began aligning their funds with the same recipients more than in years past. Although one cannot make strong statements based on this single year, it presents a potential question for future research: Did old foundations continue to embrace convergent grantmaking tactics after 2010? If so, old foundation convergence may more closely resemble new philanthropies in the future.

One of the biggest questions remains about effectiveness. If old foundations continue granting widely to organizations supporting traditional systems, are they likely to make a substantive difference? Critics who labeled the Annenberg Challenge a failure might say no. These critics may suggest that new foundations have been more effective than old foundations, not only due to their bankroll, but because they concentrated on a narrower set of issues and increasingly gave to the same set of grantees to pursue these priorities. One former president of an organization created during the Challenge agreed with a critique along these lines, saying Challenge efforts "would have accomplished more" if it had been more focused.[23]

In contrast, Annenberg Challenge defenders pointed to many outcomes accompanying the Challenge that were not easily measured or quickly realized.[24] These defenders might likewise support the old foundation priorities and tactics outlined in this chapter because they did not narrow education issues, instead continuing to focus on a variety of issues thought to benefit students and education systems. Finally, a third group might argue that neither old nor new foundations influenced schools as much as they could because they did not effectively direct public policy.[25] A full consideration of these three perspectives would require more discussion than is possible in this chapter and largely falls beyond the scope of this chapter's data. However, such a debate undoubtedly requires continued investigation as education philanthropy evolves.

When all is said and done, philanthropies give in ways they believe improve school contexts, and granting patterns over time show whether they view their efforts as effective or ineffective. Grants shed light on how foundations view themselves—changes in priorities or tactics may indicate a foundation's reevaluation of its success and attempts to become more successful. Although a specter of "failure" hung above the Annenberg Challenge, old foundation grantmaking tended to align with their past initiatives. This shows that traditional foundations saw the Challenge's effectiveness differently than critics and that they will continue granting in areas where success may not be readily apparent. Meanwhile, in efforts to create greater change than previously seen, that same shadow of failure may have driven intense new foundation convergence around nontraditional priorities. This new foundation demand for visible social returns may also lead to rapid changes in focus. For example, Gates believed its small schools initiatives were not successful enough, so it dialed back funding in this area. However, research completed after disinvestment showed small school redesigns had greater positive effects than had been found in earlier studies and may cause some to criticize quick priority shifts.[26] Thus, gadflies will dig up reasons to find fault with both old and new foundations. Some will say old foundations continue to support traditional systems in broadly focused ways that do not show dramatic results. Others will claim new foundations place too much emphasis on a narrow set of nontraditional actors and overemphasize quickly seen results over other long-term successes. As the K–12 philanthropy sector continues to evolve, foundation grants will continue to show both how they view their efforts and whether they change their approaches. Will new or traditional philanthropies listen to their critics and alter their priorities, use of convergent tactics, or other unique characteristics of their granting? Although they might as the sector develops, evidence from 2000 to 2010 makes it seem unlikely.

3

"Singing from the Same Hymnbook" at Gates and Broad

Sarah Reckhow and Megan Tompkins-Stange

The Broad Foundation's 2009–2010 Annual Report offered a sunny forecast for a federal education agenda that was increasingly supportive of the foundation's goals:

> In many ways, we feel the stars have finally aligned. With an agenda that echoes our decade of investments—charter schools, performance pay for teachers, accountability, expanded learning time and national standards— the Obama administration is poised to cultivate and bring to fruition the seeds we and other reformers have planted.[1]

These "other reformers" included the Gates Foundation, Broad's partner in spearheading major philanthropic initiatives in education reform over the last fifteen years. Gates and Broad supported systemic reforms focused on leveraging education policy change through accountability mechanisms, notably teacher evaluation and national standards–based assessments. After 2008, these reforms emerged as central in the federal education policy agenda, a development that many attributed to Gates's and Broad's strategic influence; for example, one foundation official commented, "I am amazed at what they've done. Look at how education is a high-priority item in this country. And it's singularly because of Gates and Broad." While anecdotal evidence of this nature abounds in the field of education reform, questions remain as to how extensive this perceived influence actually is and how Gates and Broad came to be viewed as power players within national education policy contexts.

We address these questions through an examination of Gates's and Broad's advocacy grantmaking regarding teacher quality, a funding priority for both foundations. We primarily focus on teacher quality because the publicly available documentation for this issue (particularly within congressional testimony) is rich; in contrast, there is little in the federal record on the issue of common academic standards. We find that after 2008, Gates and Broad deliberately pursued funding strategies that prioritized federal policy and advocacy initiatives, sometimes in partnership with one another through purposeful convergence.[2] Specifically, we find that since 2008, Gates and Broad shifted funds from local education groups to national advocacy organizations and from discrete project-based initiatives to systemic reform efforts. We also show that congressional testimony on teacher quality by Gates-funded and Broad-funded grantees has increased over time, indicating that these foundations have identified this strategy as a source of significant policy influence.

Finally, we demonstrate that the foundations utilized two distinct strategies within their advocacy funding efforts. First, they closely aligned themselves with high-level officials at the US Department of Education. Second, they funded a broad range of education interest groups that provided testimony to policy makers, disseminated research, and promoted a common set of policy goals.[3] We argue that these targeted strategies led to a dominant narrative emerging within policy debates regarding teacher quality, specifically the concept of "value-added" teacher evaluation. As one Gates official commented, "Anybody who cares to look would find very quickly that all of these organizations suddenly singing from the same hymnbook are getting money from the same organization . . . we fund almost everyone who does advocacy."

Although Broad and Gates took different paths to leadership within the policy realm, their aligned foundation funding for preferred reforms fueled the production of studies and related advocacy work by think tanks and interest groups to amplify these views across organizations on a national stage. Gates and Broad sponsored organizations that publicly endorsed specific approaches to teacher quality as well as think tanks and research organizations that released studies and publications consistently supporting the adoption of similar reforms concerning teacher performance evaluation. These efforts contributed to a watershed shift in education policy. Starting in 2009, the federal government used the Race to the Top program, followed by the No Child Left Behind waiver process, to incentivize states to link teacher evaluations to student test score data. More than two-thirds of states have made significant changes to their methods for evaluating teachers since 2009.[4] Although the widespread adoption of new teacher evaluation systems suggests a significant policy victory—one that our analysis suggests could be partly attributed to the efforts of Gates and Broad—we argue that the declaration of a policy win would be premature. We caution funders who would seek to emulate this model that the absence of robust public debate presents a weakness for policy reforms in the long term, particularly as implementation challenges inevitably arise.

DATA AND METHODS

The goal of our research is to analyze the extent of Gates's and Broad's advocacy activities on teacher quality, specifically as expressed in advocacy-related grants and grantee testimony in Congress. Our research comprises three types of data collection and analysis. First, we collected data on grant distributions at each foundation. Second, we analyzed the testimony of foundation-funded witnesses in congressional hearings. Third, we drew on an original set of interviews with foundation officials, conducted between 2010 and 2012, to contextualize and extend our analysis.

To systematically assess advocacy grantmaking at Gates and Broad, we collected data from each foundation's 2005 and 2010 990-PF tax forms. For each grant that directly funded K–12 education, training and support for K–12 personnel, K–12 policy advocacy or research, or supplementary education services for K–12 students, we recorded the amount of the grant, the recipient, the recipient's location, and the purpose of the grant (if available). We coded each grant recipient based on the grantee's function or role, such as school districts, charter schools, or afterschool programs. We identified all grants that were targeted to support policy advocacy and/or research at the national level. Our definition of national research and advocacy organizations included grants for convening, contacting, or informing policy makers on a national level. We also identified grantees as national advocacy or research organizations based on their websites, organizational purposes indicated on their Form 990 tax documents, and purposes indicated by funders in tax filings. If the grant's purpose indicated support for a grantee to convene, contact, or inform policy makers on a national level, it was included in our set of national advocacy organizations. Additionally, we coded the national advocacy grants based on the issue priority advanced by the grant, using the grantee organization and the grant description to identify issue priority. Our coding scheme included seven major issue priorities advanced by Gates and/or Broad: charter schools/school choice, teacher quality, standards, high school reform, urban education, and principal leadership.

Using ProQuest Congressional, we also gathered data on foundation-funded witnesses who delivered testimony in congressional hearings on teacher quality. We identified ninety-six hearings that contained substantive content on teacher quality. Next, we eliminated all speeches and testimony by members of Congress and federal government officials in order to focus on witnesses from outside the federal government, including school district officials, university researchers, think tank representatives, and advocacy organization leaders. After eliminating federal officials, we had a sample of more than 470 witnesses on teacher quality. We coded these witnesses to identify whether they represented an institution or organization that had received a grant from Gates or Broad in the year they delivered testimony or within the previous two years. We also examined the content of the witness testimony and collected all references to research mentioned in witness testimony. Our tally included references to more than four hundred separate published research items, including academic articles, think tank reports, and government reports. We identified witnesses who referenced the same reports and, using social network analysis, constructed network diagrams to show the shared references to research. References to a shared set of research sources among foundation grantees underscores the similar policy recommendations provided by these individuals.

To contextualize and extend the evidence from our data analysis and coding process, we also drew on an original dataset of semistructured, open-ended interviews with nearly two dozen informants, which allowed us to gain a deeper understanding of how and why foundation insiders elected to engage in advocacy grantmaking as a strategic leverage mechanism. Interview subjects were primarily current and former staff at Gates and Broad, in addition to influential actors in the broader fields of philanthropy and education. Informants were selected to represent roughly structurally equivalent positions, comprising senior staff, program officers, and policy officers in each foundation's education program. Interviews took place over eighteen months between 2010 and 2012, during President Obama's first term in office, and this context emerged in a number of informants' reflections about foundation policy advocacy, as the following sections show.

Because the topic of foundation policy influence is legally sensitive, we risked the possibility that informants would be reluctant to share their views, if they agreed to speak with us at all. In order to address this concern, we determined that we would not identify informants, would attribute all direct quotes anonymously, and, where necessary, would redact background information that might expose informants' identities. Guaranteeing informants' anonymity has drawbacks, including a loss of granularity in our descriptions, but we determined it was necessary to protect informants from any possible risk, given the controversial nature of some of the material that emerged during interviews and the informants' fear of consequences from their employers or damage to the foundations' reputations. Thus, throughout the chapter, all statements made by interviewees are attributed anonymously with general descriptors like "the informant" or "the official."

A GROWING NATIONAL PRESENCE

Gates and Broad share similar origin stories in terms of their founding dates (2000 and 1999, respectively) and involvement in education as a core grant-making priority. The two foundations differ in size (Gates's endowment is currently estimated at about $42 billion, while Broad's assets are around $2 billion) as well as their relative emphases on advocacy as a funding strategy. Whereas informants described Broad as unapologetically involved in policy- and advocacy-related initiatives since its inception, Gates was reticent to pursue any policy-related activities for five to six years after its founding. One Gates informant remarked that a "very strong bias" existed against policy and advocacy during the foundation's early years due to concerns about the legality of lobbying: "They didn't want to call it the 'DC Office' because they were just putting their toes in the water of getting involved in advocacy." Another Gates official attributed this hesitation to a sympathy for progressive politics at Gates, which was viewed as incongruent with a Republican administration prior to 2008: "Our program people were like, 'No, no, no. That's all of that political stuff' . . . Particularly back in the day when people didn't like the Bush administration . . . all federal politics for people in Seattle looked like doing stuff with the Bush administration." After the election of President Obama in 2008, the foundation's focus on policy changed significantly, as one informant explained: "It was much more legitimate to be involved with policy post-2008 with Obama." Similarly, another commented, "[Advocacy] evolved with respect to its place in the organizational food chain. Its change of status was ascendant and rapid."

In contrast to Gates's relatively cautious entrance into policy influence, Broad informants noted that the foundation's benefactor, Eli Broad, had viewed the pursuit of policy as a core element of his vision for the foundation since its inception. One Broad informant told us:

[Our benefactor] had always known that the operating environment in which schools function was a barrier to seeing some of the reforms happen that we initially had started out focusing on as a foundation, and so he really felt like if we could focus on the larger picture by removing policy barriers, that that would probably be the best way to leverage his dollars.

Similarly, another Broad official described changes to the foundation's strategy in 2009 and 2010 that institutionalized policy as a core area of focus:

We recently changed our strategic defining process, and so for the next three years our number-one priority is policy, and we say that we're going to be successful when we see a strong reauthorization of the Elementary and Secondary Education Act.

Another Broad informant confirmed this statement, noting that advocacy funding at Broad assumed a greater percentage of the foundation's overall grantmaking budget after 2009, with the foundation committing more financial resources specifically to advocacy-related initiatives:

Generally speaking, in the past, our policymaking has been important . . . in terms of our involvement in a lot of things, but not in terms of our investment. It's been about 10 to 15 percent. We're looking at trying to do somewhere between 40 and 50 percent of our investments going forward in the policy realm.

Consistent with these statements, our analysis of grants distributed by Gates and Broad showed a shift in funding patterns related to national advocacy from 2005 to 2010. We compared grantmaking by Gates and Broad in 2005 and 2010 across major funding categories (see figure 3.1). We focused on four categories of grants: traditional public schools (including school districts and individual schools), charter schools (including charter management organizations [CMOs] and individual charter schools), local nonprofit organizations (including locally based organizations—not organizations that are part of broader national umbrella groups), and national advocacy (including think tanks and advocacy groups).

Although researchers have documented significant philanthropic investments in charter schools and CMOs,[5] the funding patterns for Gates and Broad from 2005 to 2010 do not show a marked shift away from traditional

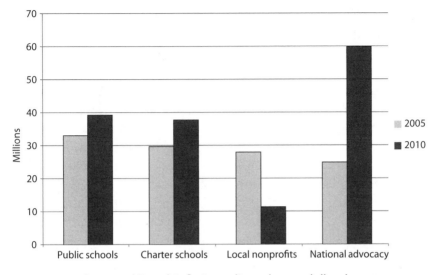

FIGURE 3.1   Gates and Broad: Inflation-adjusted grant dollars by category

public schools and toward charters—in fact, both categories grew in their share of funding from Gates and Broad at relatively comparable levels. Moreover, these foundations provided nearly equivalent levels of support for traditional public schools and charter schools—charter schools and CMOs received $37.8 million from Gates and Broad in 2010, and traditional public schools received $39.3 million—and grant dollars to both types of schools grew by about 2 percent from 2005 to 2010, adjusted for inflation. Rather, the major shift in grantmaking from 2005 to 2010 is from local organizations to national advocacy (see figure 3.1).

Local nonprofits received a declining share of grants from Gates and Broad during this time period. Grant dollars for local nonprofits dropped by 59 percent, adjusted for inflation, while national advocacy funding more than doubled, growing by 140 percent. National advocacy grants reached nearly $60 million in 2010. The types of organizations supported by Gates and Broad funding include key players in national-level education politics, such as major multi-issue think tanks (American Enterprise Institute, Brookings Institution, and Center for American Progress) and organizations focused specifically on education issues (Education Trust, Thomas B. Fordham Institute, and the Hunt Institute). The Gates Foundation also funds organizations that represent racial and ethnic minority groups, including National Council of La Raza, National Urban League, and the National

Indian Education Association; these organizations received grants between $250,000 and $500,000.

As figure 3.1 shows, national advocacy funding grew substantially by 2010. Yet organizational-level funding does not provide the full story of convergence in national advocacy strategies at Gates and Broad. We content-analyzed the purpose and grantee for each national advocacy grant distributed by Gates and Broad in order to identify major issue priorities supported by each grant.[6] In 2005, there was little overlap in the national advocacy issue priorities of Gates and Broad. The dominant issue priority in 2005 was high school reform—31 percent of the national advocacy grant dollars supported this issue. The Gates Foundation exclusively supported this issue; Broad did not provide any grants aligned with high school reform. Broad's issue priorities varied widely, including principal leadership, teacher quality, school choice and charter schools, and urban education.

An example of a high school reform advocacy grant from Gates is a $951,000 grant to the Alliance for Excellent Education to "support an advocacy, communications, and policy development initiative to promote effective federal high school policy reform."[7] Issue alignment was negligible in 2005; both Gates and Broad did provide grants supporting organizations advocating on teacher quality, but these accounted for only 1 percent of the total national advocacy grant dollars in 2005. In contrast, by 2010, both foundations were involved in funding two major issues for national advocacy: common standards and teacher quality. Grants supporting common standards accounted for 26 percent of national advocacy grant dollars from these two foundations, and grants supporting teacher quality accounted for 19 percent of national advocacy grant dollars. For example, in 2010, The Broad Foundation funded the Center for American Progress to support "the Teacher Incentive Fund summit."[8] Gates provided a grant in 2010 to Brookings "to develop criteria for certifying teacher evaluation systems."[9] Both foundations supported the Hunt Institute in 2010 to conduct advocacy related to the Common Core. Thus, the alignment of issue priorities for national advocacy grew stronger across both foundations by 2010.

These data are supported by our interviews, which indicate growing attention to advocacy—particularly at Gates—and a shift toward emphasizing the federal and state levels rather than the local level. Gates officials explained this transition as part of a broader shift at the foundation. From 2000 to 2006, Gates's education program focused predominantly on funding the development of small learning communities and conversion of large comprehensive high schools into smaller schools. This portfolio strategy ceased in 2004–2005, and the foundation began to focus on targeted systemic reform initiatives at a national level in 2005–2006. A Gates informant explained, "[Our staff decided] we can't just be about giving dollars to school districts because we've already seen evidence that we give money and we're not seeing results."

One Gates informant reported that the foundation realized that educational change "involved much more than structure; it needed to involve the context, the policy context, that affected it." With these strategic changes, policy initiatives assumed a new importance after 2006, said another: "Gates had a very explicit theory of action about working at the state level to create a policy environment that would be supportive of the kinds of changes that they wanted to make at the local level." A third summarized this approach in the following way:

> Starting with the governors, we've got to build support at the state level, and once we build support at the state level, then when the dynamics are right, which would have been 2008, and we get an administration—more importantly, an education secretary whose school district benefited from our support—then you've got the ability to drive forward and push it off balance at the federal level.

Under Stefanie Sanford, the foundation's director of policy and advocacy during this period, Gates targeted high-level elected state officials to advance support for desired reforms, with the intention of leveraging state policy wins toward the federal level in the longer term, contingent on favorable political dynamics—which came into sharp focus during the 2008 election.

FEDERAL POLICY: ALIGNMENT WITH HIGH-LEVEL OFFICIALS

The 2008 presidential campaign emerged in our interviews as a pivotal event in the trajectory of national advocacy involvement by Gates and Broad. Both foundations made an initial foray into politics and policy advocacy during the presidential campaign. In 2008, in an unusual instance of explicit philanthropic involvement in a presidential campaign, Gates and Broad teamed up for the ED in '08 campaign, which attempted to situate education as a core issue area in the 2008 election. While journalists have noted that the initiative was unsuccessful in this goal, ED in '08 had a longer-term impact as the first instance of Gates and Broad deliberately collaborating on a national policy-related initiative.[10] Two of the main issue priorities emphasized in the policy documents for ED in '08 were "American education standards"—including a proposal for a fifty-state consortium to develop common standards—and "effective teachers in every classroom"—including recommendations for performance-based compensation.[11]

Soon after the election, both Gates and Broad officials recognized an opportunity for alignment between their policy objectives and the Obama administration on key issues. For example, an informant described the deliberate alignment of Broad's agenda with the federal government, a process that also occurred at Gates:

> So, on the federal level, there are a couple of things that we think are important. One is doing things that can educate policy makers and other opinion leaders about the importance of certain items on the administration's agenda. Things around, for example, national standards, differentiated compensation for educators, expanded learning time, growing the number of high quality public charter schools. All things that we think are important, all things that the administration thinks are important as well. And so it gives us a unique opportunity to align what we believe is important for education change and take advantage of the environment that exists.

This "unique opportunity" yielded the fertile environment for an open policy window that Gates had sought in its original advocacy strategy developed in 2006. Similarly, another Broad official noted the comparable priorities of Broad and the Department of Education:

> One of those is that we have in this administration a secretary of education focused on the issues that Mr. Broad has been pushing through the foundation for the last decade. Those same things I talked about—growth at charter schools . . . quality of charter schools . . . the ESEA authorization that looks at effective teaching, the current standards, common assessments—those are all things that The Broad Foundation had been working on for the first ten years of the foundation. Brand-new is that, rather than doing direct funding, the foundation is now looking at the policies that would create an infrastructure [at] the national level to support those things happening.

This statement was corroborated by Gates officials, who cited the appointment of President Obama's Secretary of Education Arne Duncan—a former Gates grantee in his capacity as superintendent of Chicago Public Schools—as a linchpin in the partnership between Gates and federal policy makers.

Informants noted the similar approaches of the Department of Education and Gates staff, as one Gates informant explained: "[In] 2008, we get an administration that has an education secretary whose school district benefited from our support. When Obama came into office, you got Arne [Duncan], who says, 'Yeah, they're right, we need to do this.'" Another informant commented, "The support that the foundation gave to the department either directly or indirectly, both financially and through intermediaries, greatly affected how some of the early Obama education initiatives were formulated and implemented."

Indeed, numerous Gates officials pointed to the hiring of Obama administration officials as a key factor in amplifying their advocacy funding. For example, several informants mentioned that a number of Secretary Duncan's staff appointments were either former Gates officials or former Gates grantees. One informant noted, "Once Obama was elected, I mean, Gates literally had people sitting at the Department of Education, both formally and informally." These officials included Jim Shelton, assistant deputy secretary for innovation and improvement and former program director of the education program at Gates, and Joanne Weiss, director of the Race to the Top competition and a former partner at the NewSchools Venture Fund, a major Gates grantee that served as an intermediary funder for charter school management organizations. In addition to employing former Gates officials, Department of Education staff continued to engage current Gates officials in key discussions regarding education priorities, as one informant explained: "It gives you a notion of where the field is moving because [Gates staff] have regular sessions . . . or phone conversations between funders and Department of Education officials including [Secretary] Duncan and including [Undersecretary] Jim Shelton."

FEDERAL POLICY: ALIGNMENT THROUGH ADVOCACY GROUPS

In addition to building relationships with high-level officials, both Gates and Broad have focused on funding well-known groups with a track record of involvement in education policy. National advocacy groups can participate in politics and policymaking through a variety of venues, including lobbying legislators and bureaucrats, commenting on rule making, forming coalitions, drafting reports, attempting to inform or persuade the public, and testifying before Congress. Delivering congressional testimony is among the most visible and significant forms of involvement in national policymaking. Groups that testify regularly are recognized as "taken-for-granted" participants in policymaking, and the content of congressional testimony influences policy adoption.[12]

We find that Gates and Broad have supported groups that participated frequently in national policymaking, and that this support grew over time. We examined these groups to identify those that had representatives who testified most frequently before Congress on teacher quality. We then tabulated the amount of grant dollars these organizations received in 2005 and 2010.

Table 3.1 shows the most frequent organizational representatives testifying before Congress on teacher quality.[13] It is important to note that multiple appearances testifying before Congress are very rare; the vast majority of groups had only one opportunity to do so. Many witnesses from groups with multiple appearances represent long-standing and well-established participants in national education policy debates, including the Council of Chief State School Officers and the major teachers' unions (the NEA

TABLE 3.1   Most frequent organizations in congressional hearings on teacher quality, 2000–2012

Witness affiliation	Witness appearances	Advocacy grant $ from Gates and Broad	
		2005*	2010
Council of Chief State School Officers	7	$98,000	$3.2 million
Education Trust	7	$890,000	$4.9 million
National Education Association (NEA)	6	$0	$38,000
Education Leaders Council	5	$0	$0
American Federation of Teachers (AFT)	3	$0	$2.4 million
American School Counselor Association	3	$0	$0
Bill & Melinda Gates Foundation	3	N/A	N/A
Business Roundtable	3	$0	$0
Center on Education Policy	3	$178,000	$580,000
Center for American Progress	3	$0	$785,000
Milken Family Foundation	3	$0	$0
The New Teacher Project	3	$130,000	$2 million
Total	**49**	**$1.3 million**	**$13.9 million**

* Inflation adjusted for 2010 dollars.

and AFT). Other influential actors, such as the Business Roundtable and Education Trust, were also frequent participants. One newer organization, The New Teacher Project, stands out with three appearances, all occurring between 2009 and 2012. Representatives from the Gates Foundation also testified three times.

Overall, a pattern emerged wherein Gates and Broad increased advocacy grant funding to groups that gave frequent testimony—defined as three or more appearances before Congress from 2000 to 2012. Advocacy grant dollars to these groups grew by more than $12 million from 2005 to 2010—well above the overall growth in funding for national advocacy groups. The overall increase in national advocacy funding from Gates and Broad was 140 percent from 2005 to 2010, while the advocacy funding to those who gave frequent testimony (included in table 3.1) increased by tenfold. This funding growth supports new actors, like The New Teacher Project, as well as the establishment groups, like the NEA and AFT. This suggests that Gates and Broad were pursuing a two-pronged funding strategy: diversifying the voices in the debate and extending ties to the education establishment.

Yet support for an organization that delivers testimony is not direct evidence of alignment with the foundation's agenda priorities. In some cases, increased grant support was channeled to organizations that had already shown support for reforms such as using standardized tests to evaluate teachers or implementing performance pay systems. For example, in 2009, The New Teacher Project released *The Widget Effect*, a report supporting a major overhaul of teacher evaluation;[14] since 2009, the Gates Foundation has committed $13.5 million in grants to The New Teacher Project. Representatives from The New Teacher Project testified before Congress in 2009, 2010, and 2012. Meanwhile, the president of the Center for American Progress, John Podesta, testified twice in 2007 in support of linking teacher compensation to evaluation systems. The Broad Foundation began funding the Center for American Progress in 2007 and has since continuously supported the Center for American Progress with almost $1 million in grants, including three grants focused on teacher incentives or pay for performance.

The AFT has not been traditionally associated with vocal support for overhauling teacher evaluation or linking evaluations to high-stakes personnel decisions, but in 2010, the Gates Foundation funded the AFT to support teacher development and evaluation programs. Also in 2010, AFT president Randi Weingarten provided congressional testimony that was relatively supportive of a new approach to teacher evaluation. Weingarten testified in favor of evaluation systems that include inputs and outputs—with outputs including test data. Moreover, her written testimony included the following: "We know that a natural outgrowth of teacher evaluation systems will be differentiated compensation systems. We know from the first-hand experience of our affiliates that differentiated compensation systems developed and implemented with the full support and collaboration of teachers can succeed."[15]

Weingarten remained strongly committed to the collective bargaining process, but she also signaled a willingness to negotiate pay-for-performance systems. Weingarten's fellow panelists at the hearing were eager to note their alignment with the union leader. For example, Tim Daly of The New Teacher Project observed, "Secretary Duncan and some of my fellow panelists, including Randi Weingarten, are among those calling for more rigorous evaluation systems that recognize these differences."[16] Shortly after Daly's testimony, Professor Thomas Kane of Harvard University (and lead researcher on the Gates-funded Measures of Effective Teaching project), commented on Weingarten's cooperation with Measures of Effective Teaching: "Randi Weingarten deserves a lot of credit for supporting that effort, even when it was not easy."[17] Thus, the content of the congressional testimony suggests that organizations appearing frequently before Congress and receiving foundation funds often provided aligned recommendations and perspectives on the issue of teacher quality—views that also aligned with Gates's and Broad's priorities.

In order to determine the extent of philanthropic funding for witnesses on teacher quality, we coded all of the witnesses who testified in the teacher quality and charter school hearings to determine whether they were affiliated with an organization or institution that had received a grant from Gates or Broad in the year they delivered testimony or within the two previous years. The results of our analysis show that the share of Gates and Broad grantees among hearing witnesses has grown. Figure 3.2 shows the proportion of grantee witnesses in the teacher quality hearings.[18] As early as 2004, Broad was funding more than one in five of the groups with affiliated witnesses who testified on teacher quality. Yet Gates has provided long-standing support to groups involved in this issue, with recent and substantial growth shown in 2011 and 2012. Each of the four teacher quality hearings in 2011 included at least one witness with both Gates and Broad funding. At a 2011 House committee hearing titled "Education Reforms: Exploring

Teacher Quality Initiatives," three of the four witnesses represented entities that recently received Gates grants.[19]

Overall, our data show greater support from Gates and Broad for frequent congressional witnesses who represent both traditional and newly emerging education interests. We also show that organizations and institutions receiving Gates or Broad funding compose a growing overall share of the witnesses who testify on teacher quality. These data underscore Gates's and Broad's strategy of influencing policy through providing funding for a wide variety of advocacy groups that participate actively in federal policy debates.

POLICY RESEARCH AND ADVOCACY

Foundations that seek to influence policy often commission intermediaries, including think tanks, academics, and advocacy organizations, to produce reports that frame empirical evidence in an accessible way and to share these reports with policy makers in order to highlight the nature of a problem or the potential impact of proposed solutions. At both Gates and Broad, program officers spoke of concerted undertakings to pair their advocacy efforts with support for research. One Broad program officer explained:

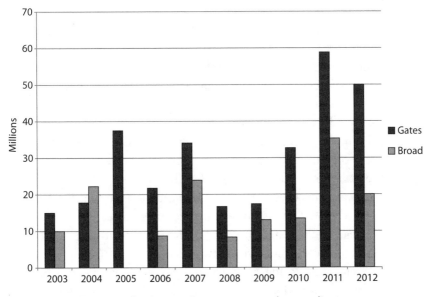

FIGURE 3.2   Percent of grantee witnesses on teacher quality

It's not just about doing good research; it's about doing good research and putting it together in a way that's going to have impact. As you know, there is no shortage of white papers in education.

A Gates official described the following process for producing reports that would be used to influence policy:

It's within [a] sort of fairly narrow orbit that you manufacture the [research] reports. You hire somebody to write a report. There's going to be a commission, there's going to be a lot of research, there's going to be a lot of vetting and so forth and so on, but you pretty much know what the report is going to say before you go through the exercise.

To systematically examine the content of the congressional hearings on teacher quality, we compiled the research and policy reports that witnesses referenced, with attention to the types of reform proposals supported by these reports and their endorsement of particular views or initiatives related to teacher quality. We examined all references to research and policy reports from the witnesses in the teacher-quality hearings. Our content analysis uncovered references to more than four hundred separate published items, including academic articles, government reports, think tank studies, and advocacy reports. We then identified instances in which witnesses referenced the same report.

Based on references to the same reports across multiple congressional witnesses, we constructed affiliation networks of witnesses who referenced the same study or report in their testimony. The network (figure 3.3) shows links between witnesses who share a reference to the same report. The witnesses are labeled in the network with their organizational or institutional affiliation. A circle represents testimony provided by an organizational representative, and a line between two circles indicates references to the same report. Some organizations appear more than once because they had multiple witnesses who testified. We also identified witnesses who were affiliated with groups that had recently received foundation funding. Black circles indicate organizations or institutions that received Gates or Broad grants within two years of the testimony; gray circles indicate groups that did not receive Gates or Broad grants within two years of the testimony.

Overall, references to the same articles or reports are rare in congressional testimony; more than one witness cited only 33 out of 406 reports. Thus, instances of shared citations represent a significant and rare degree

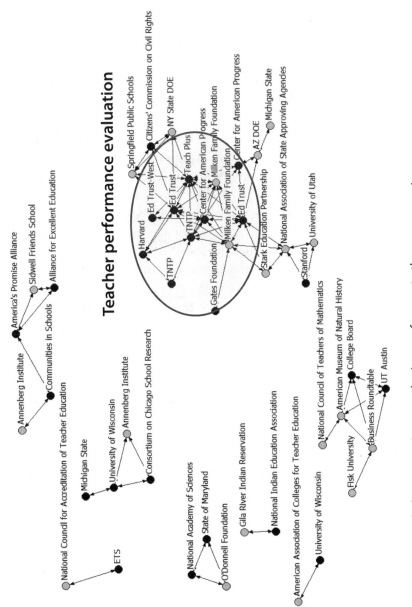

FIGURE 3.3   Links between witnesses sharing a reference to the same report

of common ground between witnesses. By far the most cited study in the teacher quality hearings is "Teachers, Schools, and Academic Achievement" by Rivkin, Hanushek, and Kain; seven different witnesses cited this academic research article. This article emphasizes the importance of teacher quality for student achievement and concludes with the following recommendation: "[T]here is strong reason to believe that a closer link between rewards and performance would improve the stock of teachers."[20]

In the network, there is one large cluster of witnesses with many shared citations. It includes major Gates and Broad grantees such as Education Trust, The New Teacher Project (TNTP), and the Center for American Progress. This cluster is labeled with a common policy recommendation shared among the witnesses: "Teacher performance evaluation." The witnesses in this cluster exhibit remarkable consistency in the content of their testimony—both over time and across organizations. For example, 2004 testimony delivered by Ross Wiener of Education Trust includes the recommendation "Support value-added data systems."[21] In 2007, Amy Wilkins of Education Trust testified, "We think that the States need to move to value-added systems to look at the effectiveness of their teachers."[22] Also in 2007, John Podesta from the Center for American Progress testified, "To effectively determine advancements, expanded compensation for teachers and principals should be coupled with a meaningful evaluation system for them."[23] And in 2010, Timothy Daly of The New Teacher Project testified, "In many cases, greater outcomes will result from mandating the public reporting of teacher effectiveness data."[24]

These witnesses primarily share references to the Rivkin, Hanushek, and Kain article, as well as to the reports by Education Trust, Brookings, and The New Teacher Project. Among the institutions and think tanks that produce reports, Education Trust has the largest number of multiple citation reports (four reports), and Brookings has the second-largest number (two reports). The Brookings and Education Trust reports draw heavily on the perspective advanced by Rivkin, Hanushek, and Kain—emphasizing the importance of teacher quality for student achievement and demonstrating how high-quality teachers could be identified more effectively through measurement of student achievement. These think tank reports also advance specific policy recommendations. For example, the 2006 Brookings report *Identifying Effective Teachers Using Performance on the Job* provides five specific policy recommendations, including "Provide federal grants to help states that link student performance with the effectiveness of individual teachers over time."[25]

The most recently published report with multiple citations in congressional testimony is *The Widget Effect*, released by The New Teacher Project in 2009. This report is referenced three times. The report critiques existing approaches to teacher evaluation by examining assessment practices in twelve school districts and four states, and it uses the resulting data to advocate for specific policy reforms, including "Use performance evaluations to inform key decisions such as teacher assignment, professional development, compensation, retention, and dismissal."[26] Several national foundations, including the Gates Foundation, the Walton Family Foundation, the Robertson Foundation, and the Joyce Foundation, funded the report.

In other parts of the network, there are links to reports with alternative perspectives, but none share the level of cross-referencing that appears in the group emphasizing performance measurement and evaluation of teachers. One example of an alternate perspective is the publication cited by the witnesses from University of Wisconsin and the American Association of Colleges for Teacher Education. These two witnesses both cited Linda Darling-Hammond's 2007 article "A Marshall Plan for Teaching," which recommends policies related to teacher preparation and mentorship.[27] Another study with multiple references (from witnesses representing the University of Wisconsin and the Consortium on Chicago Schools Research) is *Organizing Schools for Improvement: Lessons from Chicago*.[28] This book provides comprehensive recommendations for school improvement rather than focusing specifically on teacher quality or performance evaluation as a single lever for improvement. Within these smaller clusters, many of the witnesses are university-based scholars or researchers affiliated with academia rather than think tank or philanthropic organization representatives.

Among the cluster of witnesses sharing references to reports on teacher performance evaluation, there are common recommendations that teacher quality should be measured with test scores, reported, used to structure professional development, and applied to high-stakes personnel decisions. The majority of these witnesses also represent organizations with substantial funding from Gates and Broad. A Gates informant elaborated on this dynamic: "For organizations with our size . . . and with our resources . . . you can make grants to lots of organizations to promote a certain message not just . . . with government but also with business and with the public."

This alignment has generated concerns that ideas endorsed by Gates and Broad may be taken for granted without due critique or rigorous evaluation, for fear of alienating potential funders. The example of "value-added" teacher evaluation as a dominant approach was highlighted in a conversation with one Gates official:

> You've got a relatively small number of pretty bright and committed people who usually base [decisions] on evidence that, if you look at it carefully, it's dubious . . . So take "value-added" . . . as people get away from technical appendices and the caveats . . . and distill those into summaries and into PowerPoints . . . all that gets washed away and comes back down to . . . the presupposition you began with, which is, "Value-added is the way to evaluate and pay teachers."

Within a small orbit of think tanks, some university-based researchers, advocacy groups, and philanthropic funders, an argument favoring new evaluation systems and pay for performance to transform teacher quality was widely shared and transmitted in national policy arenas. Our analysis of congressional testimony suggests that alternate perspectives did not share the same level of coherence and cross-referencing among a broad set of actors. Thus, Gates and Broad were able to amplify a message regarding teacher performance evaluation that did not face a rigorous and coordinated critique at the federal level. As states begin to implement these new evaluation systems, the opportunity for more scrutiny is emerging as implementation challenges arise—but only after federal policy has led states to make significant investments in assessments and systems for evaluation.

IMPLICATIONS FOR POLICY AND PHILANTHROPY

Our study of Gates's and Broad's education grantmaking revealed two main aspects of their strategic approach toward policy influence: cultivating direct relationships with high-level officials and supporting widely recognized and influential organizations in education, from both traditional and reform contexts, to engage in advocacy activities at the federal level. These activities engendered a shift in funding from the local level to the national level, and accordingly, grantees were frequent witnesses in congressional testimony on teacher quality, particularly as Gates's and Broad's support for advocacy increased over the course of the last several years. In particular, Gates's and

Broad's purposeful convergence on advancing similar policy issues and organizations emerged as a key factor in marshaling their resources toward their desired outcomes.

As a caveat, our study does not claim to make a causal argument regarding foundation funding of advocacy, as it is impossible to link policy outcomes definitively to grants in this case. Furthermore, we do not assume that foundations necessarily dictate what their grantees testify, or that witnesses' testimony is similar *because* they received grants from Gates and Broad. In fact, it is likely that Gates and Broad sought out organizations already engaged in reform initiatives that resonated with their philanthropic objectives. Rather, we emphasize that the strategic and purposeful alignment of foundation funding focused and accelerated the volume of grantees' advocacy work on key issues, which subsequently had the effect of saturating the market of policy-relevant ideas related to teacher quality and propelling the foundations' preferred models of reform onto a national stage. Our findings are similar to the conclusions of Scott and Jabbar, who have studied foundation involvement in the promotion of research evidence; they argue that "foundations can be critical in determining which ideas or initiatives move ahead, which organizations are high quality and worthy of private and public investment, and which stall."[29] In the field of teacher quality, Gates and Broad legitimated and diffused some approaches to teacher quality over others, illustrating the power of foundations to anoint exemplars within a field of organizations.[30]

While other foundations may seek to replicate the actions of Gates and Broad in the policy realm, these strategies should not be interpreted as a recipe for policy success, as the long-term outcomes of foundation-sponsored education reforms remain unknown. In fact, several of Broad's and Gates's flagship efforts in areas such as the Common Core have been met with significant political backlash from states, localities, school districts, and nonprofit organizations. These foundations have also begun to face increased criticism about the legitimacy of privately funded and managed policy actions in the context of a liberal democracy, even at times from those foundation officials who pushed the reforms. For example, one Gates official commented on the similarity between the federal government's plan and the foundation's agenda:

There was a twinkle in the eye of one of our US advocacy directors when the Obama administration's . . . education policy framework came out . . . this person said . . . "Aren't we lucky that the Obama Administration's education agenda is so compatible with ours, you know?" . . . We wouldn't take credit . . . out loud even amongst ourselves . . . But, you know, the twinkle . . .

From a normative perspective, the notion of a "twinkle"—rather than claiming credit more openly—highlights one of the more problematic aspects of the concentrated influence of Gates, Broad, and other foundations in the policy realm. While these foundations advocate for specific reforms, often defined by elite experts without significant democratic input,[31] they avoid claiming credit for their policy wins or even publicly acknowledging an advocacy role. For example, in a 2014 *Washington Post* interview, Bill Gates "grew irritated" when discussing the foundation's advocacy work on the Common Core, describing his foundation's role as funding "the research and development of new tools and offer[ing] them to decision-makers" and arguing, "These are not political things . . . We don't fund people to say, 'Okay, we'll pay you this if you say you like the Common Core.'"[32]

This avoidance of attribution and depiction of grants as apolitical has the effect of limiting authentic democratic debate about the issues that philanthropists support. One Gates informant offered this critique: "We have this enormous power to sway the public conversations about things like effective teaching or standards and mobilizing lots of resources in their favor without real robust debate . . . I mean, it's striking to me, really." In the case of teacher quality, the development of sophisticated methods to measure teacher impacts on student learning by statisticians and econometricians presented a useful opportunity to examine the best approaches for using this data to motivate continuous improvement in teaching. Yet the policy recommendations that were advanced, amplified, and repeated to an audience of federal policy makers, particularly in reports cited by foundation grantees, focused heavily on using evaluations to drive decisions about merit pay, firing, and tenure; this may have limited the scope of debate about alternative uses of teacher performance data.

The circumvention of public debate is often accomplished by framing desired reforms as "evidence-based"; that is, as unbiased and politically neutral because of their empirical legitimacy.[33] Reckhow argues that this framing can result in the "sidelining" of stakeholders outside of an elite, expert-driven network.[34] However, foundations also have the power to facilitate democratic debate through their unique ability to foster pluralism and support competing views as well as different visions of social order. One informant commented on the ideal role of foundations in policy contexts:

I think what's valuable [about] a foundation's role . . . is [that] they're funding just zillions of different models, in real settings that really have value because they're worked out in communities where a lot of real social change and innovation does happen and they could provide tremendous value in learning for policy making.

Thus, we argue that foundations seeking to influence education policy would be advised to purposefully facilitate this robust democratic debate that reflects a wide variety of approaches, rather than the same hymnbook.

4

Philanthropy Goes to College

Andrew P. Kelly and Kevin J. James

U nlike K–12 education, which has been the subject of a well-financed reform movement for the past decade and a half, higher education has largely flown below the reformers' radar, viewed as a lone bright spot in America's otherwise troubled education system. At the K–12 level, while Americans tend to give their local schools high marks, they are far more skeptical about the quality of the public school system as a whole.[1] In contrast, the US higher education system has traditionally been viewed as the best in the world, and Americans think much more highly of their colleges and universities than they do of their public schools.[2] Even though policy makers and the public often gripe about tuition increases, few have asked serious questions about whether the system performs as well as it should. If the K–12 schools are America's problem children, colleges and universities are their overachieving older siblings.

Private donors, too, have tended to view colleges very differently than elementary and secondary schools. In K–12, philanthropic money has generally sought to change and improve schools, first by providing additional resources to particular schools and districts and more recently by changing the policies that govern them. In higher education, however, grants have traditionally subsidized colleges to do more of what they were already doing—more research, more fields of study, new curricula, and more physical space—while also providing scholarships to help more students access those things. These investments help colleges accomplish their goals, but do little to change the way students are educated or financed.[3]

More recently, however, elites' rosy view of American higher education has increasingly come into question, and higher education philanthropy has changed with it. According to data collected by the Organisation for

Economic Co-operation and Development (OECD), while the United States ranks fourth in overall degree attainment for adults ages twenty-five to sixty-four, the country ranks twelfth among the youngest cohort of workers (twenty-five- to thirty-four-year-olds).[4] College enrollments are up, but graduation rates have remained stagnant, hovering around 60 percent at four-year colleges and 30 percent in two-year schools.[5] Student debt has ballooned past $1 trillion, and labor market data suggest that nearly 45 percent of college graduates are underemployed—working jobs that do not require a college degree.[6]

In light of this evidence, policy makers on the left and right have started asking tough questions of colleges and universities. In 2006, George W. Bush's Secretary of Education Margaret Spellings commissioned a hard-hitting report on the shortcomings of our higher education system, stating that "higher education has become . . . increasingly risk-averse, at times self-satisfied, and unduly expensive."[7] President Obama has been similarly critical, warning in his first State of the Union address that the "countries that out-teach us today will out-compete us tomorrow" and setting a bold goal that America would once again be the most educated nation in the world.[8] By 2012, the president put colleges "on notice" for failing to keep tuition prices affordable.[9] In 2013, he proposed a set of reforms that would "shake up the current system, create better incentives for colleges to do more with less, and deliver better value for students and their families."[10] A far cry from the "best in the world" talk to which US colleges are accustomed.

These changes did not occur in a vacuum. As we show in our data analysis, this change in the perception of higher education has paralleled a shift in higher education philanthropy toward a policy- and advocacy-oriented approach. This shift toward advocacy philanthropy mirrors earlier changes in the contours of K–12 giving (outlined in chapter 2 by Jeffrey W. Snyder and in chapter 3 by Sarah Reckhow and Megan Tompkins-Stange). Led by the Bill & Melinda Gates and Lumina Foundations, a loose coalition of grantees has promoted a "completion agenda" focused on the need to improve student success at American colleges—and not just at elite schools, but at the thousands of institutions where the bulk of American students enroll. Both organizations have set ambitious attainment goals—Gates aims to double the number of young, low-income Americans with a postsecondary credential, while Lumina aims to reach a 60 percent college attainment rate by 2025.[11] In contrast to the access agenda that has dominated higher education policy for the past half-century, this emphasis on completion has entailed far more criticism of colleges—and the public policies that govern them—than has been the norm.

Other scholars and journalists have already charted the rise of advocacy philanthropy in higher education, noting that it reflects a very different conception of American colleges than foundations have espoused in the past.[12] Rather than seeing America's institutions as the "best in the world," these new funders view traditional higher education (and the policies that govern it) as a sector that is organized to serve the interests of administrators and faculty over those of students and taxpayers and, as a result, is poorly designed to meet the needs of a changing student body. And, as scholars Cassie Hall and Scott Thomas argued in a 2012 paper, this perception is coupled with "distrust that higher education institutions can successfully enact reforms" on their own.[13]

In this chapter, we explore the evolution of this world view and illustrate how it has driven Gates and Lumina to adopt a very different strategy of giving than other higher education philanthropies, one focused on making a public case for reform and empowering outside organizations to serve as a counterpoint to the higher education establishment. We start by discussing the traditional approach to higher education philanthropy and the changing politics of higher education. We then analyze grant data from fifteen large foundations that give to higher education, providing an empirical snapshot of the landscape that highlights the different approaches. We move on to discuss the pushback that advocacy philanthropy has catalyzed and conclude with a discussion of whether the new approach is "good" for American higher education.

TRADITIONAL APPROACH TO HIGHER EDUCATION PHILANTHROPY: SUBSIDIZING MORE COLLEGE

In chapter 1, Jay P. Greene points out that effective philanthropists must recognize that they "do not have enough money to buy the broader change they want. Instead, they have to redirect how public funds are used by changing public policy and practice." We argue here that much of the philanthropic activity in higher education before the emergence of Gates and Lumina falls well short of Greene's standard of "high-leverage" giving. Why might that be the case? Below we highlight the key characteristics of higher education that likely tilt the scale in favor of low-leverage giving (even more so than in K–12).

Colleges Are Held in High Esteem

The first and most important difference is the one we started with in the introduction: colleges and universities occupy a very different—and more revered—place in the hierarchy of American institutions than the public schools. American universities dominate international rankings of research institutions, making up fifteen of the top twenty schools on the *Times Higher Education* World University Rankings and eight of the top ten on the Shanghai Jiao Tong World University Rankings.[14] And each year, the world's top students flock to these campuses to seek what many in the global elite believe is the best undergraduate education money can buy.

Americans themselves have largely internalized this view of colleges and universities. In a 2010 poll, nearly three-quarters of respondents rated the quality of education at four-year colleges as being good or excellent. Asked how good a job their state's public colleges were doing in providing a high-quality education, 72 percent said good or excellent. Even more telling: when asked "Who is to blame for low graduation rates on college campuses?" 70 percent blamed students themselves, and nearly 40 percent opined that students deserved a great deal of the blame. Just 32 percent placed a "great deal" (14 percent) or "a lot" (18 percent) of the blame on professors, and the responses were nearly the same when asked about the culpability of state education officials.[15]

Contrast that with the public's view of the K–12 public schools. Asked how well their local public schools were doing preparing students for college, 49 percent said "good" or "excellent." Perceptions of who is to blame for "problems facing the country's public schools" were also quite different. The proportion of respondents blaming students dropped to 46 percent, while fully 65 percent and 59 percent placed a great deal or a lot of the blame on state and federal education officials, respectively. When it comes to perceptions of the public school system as a whole, Americans are even less enthusiastic. One annual survey consistently finds that, while about half of respondents give their local schools an A or B, less than one-fifth assign an A or a B to the nation's public schools.[16] In short, the public not only views the K–12 system as being in need of reform, but they also place the lion's share of blame on state and federal policy makers for its problems.

In comparison, because the higher education system is held in such high esteem, the natural inclination is to subsidize more of what colleges already do—more access to college, more physical space to accommodate students, and more services and enrichment opportunities for students once they arrive on campus. This is essentially the approach the federal government has taken for the past half-century, providing grants and loans to students to facilitate access but otherwise demanding little in return from colleges.[17] And, as our analysis shows, philanthropists have typically taken this approach as well.

Higher Education Is a Fee-for-Service Market

In contrast to the K–12 sector where most students attend a free public option, higher education is a fee-for-service market. To get access, students must pay tuition through some combination of grants, loans, and private resources. This creates a natural opportunity for philanthropists who simply want to increase access to college: funding scholarships. One study estimated that between $3.1 and $3.3 billion in private scholarship aid was given out in 2003, and that foundations and scholarship funds were the second most common source of scholarships.[18]

Scholarships help individual students gain access to a campus, but they do not change colleges themselves. To the extent they subsidize high-achieving students who would have gone to college anyway, they may not change much at all.

An Insatiable Demand for Expansion

In the 1970s, higher education economist and college president Howard Bowen argued that the pursuit of prestige drives colleges to "raise all the money they can, and spend all the money they raise."[19] In order to produce more education and research, colleges tend to build more space on campus and hire more employees, investments that entail expensive capital projects and new spending commitments. And unlike K–12 public schools, where buildings are usually financed by the locality, new buildings on college campuses are often privately funded (and often bear the name of the funder).

Historically, capacity investments have played a significant role in the sector's development. In their history of higher education philanthropy, historians John Thelin and Richard Trollinger show how, in the 1910s, the Carnegie Foundation for the Advancement of Teaching used the "carrot" of faculty pension funding to encourage colleges to raise their admissions standards and serve more students.[20] In addition, the Ford Foundation, whose $12 billion in assets in 1960 would make it three times larger than the Gates

Foundation today, created the Fund for the Advancement of Education in 1951. The fund emphasized moving beyond "business as usual," which translated to changing curricula on grantee campuses.[21] In 1955, the Foundation made a $210 million gift ($1.85 billion today) to a set of 630 private liberal arts colleges to raise faculty salaries at those institutions.

Colleges' Core Business Is Insulated from Outside Influence

Unlike the K–12 system, where multiple layers of government directly shape what goes on in schools and classrooms, the day-to-day operations of colleges are only loosely affected by government policy. This is especially true of private nonprofit and private for-profit colleges, which together enroll about one-quarter of students.[22] To be sure, states have some control over their public institutions via the appropriations process, state coordinating boards, and accountability systems, but the level of oversight varies dramatically across states. Likewise, while federal money picks up a large fraction of the higher education tab, federal policy says little about what should happen on campus and in classrooms.[23] Regulation of academic quality is left to accreditation agencies. In addition, strong traditions of autonomy and academic freedom insulate college departments and classrooms from outside influence.

This insulation makes it far more difficult for outsiders like philanthropists to affect the way colleges provide education. Thus, while a large proportion of philanthropic activity in K–12 has focused on improving teaching and learning through research, policy reform, and direct intervention, there are fewer direct routes for private money to influence more than a handful of campuses that are interested in changing the way they provide education.

Alumni Giving Reinforces the Status Quo

In addition to foundation dollars, colleges are awash in tax-deductible donations from their alumni. In 2014, for instance, a survey of over three thousand colleges found that alumni gave nearly $8.7 billion in donations to their alma maters. Big name schools like Stanford ($271 million), MIT ($153 million), and Princeton ($117 million) top the list. But even smaller, less prestigious institutions like Kalamazoo University, John Carroll University, and Heidelberg University each rake in more than $5 million a year. It seems reasonable to assume that most of this money goes toward expanding a college's existing offerings rather than changing the way it operates. In other words, alumni gifts likely reinforce the status quo.[24]

In sum, there are a number of reasons why philanthropists with an interest in higher education would be predisposed to low-leverage giving, foremost among them the perception that American colleges are the best in the world. As the next section describes, however, elites' perception of higher education has begun to change, and higher education philanthropy has changed along with it.

AN ALTERNATIVE APPROACH: CHANGING PERCEPTIONS AND THE RISE OF "ADVOCACY PHILANTHROPY"

Not everybody shares the opinion that American colleges are the best in the world. In June 2014, Kevin Carey, the director of the education policy program at the New America Foundation, wrote an op-ed in the *New York Times* that summed up the disconnect between the American public's views of higher education and mounting evidence of mediocrity:

> Americans have a split vision of education. Conventional wisdom has long held that our K–12 schools are mediocre or worse, while our colleges and universities are world class. While policy wonks hotly debate K–12 reform ideas like vouchers and the Common Core state standards, higher education is largely left to its own devices. Many families are worried about how to get into and pay for increasingly expensive colleges. But the stellar quality of those institutions is assumed.[25]

Carey goes on to document how that assumption is flawed using results from the OECD's Programme for the International Assessment of Adult Competencies (PIACC), a standardized test that measured literacy, numeracy, and problem solving across thirty-three countries. American college graduates performed below international averages, lagging behind high school–age test-takers in some countries. Like the OECD's international rankings of educational attainment, these results suggest that American colleges may not be equipping students to compete in a global economy.

The international comparisons are just one indicator of trouble. One study found that more than one-third of undergraduates at a subset of four-year schools did not make meaningful gains in critical thinking over four years in college.[26] Meanwhile, inflation-adjusted tuition at public four-year colleges has nearly quadrupled since the early 1980s, requiring students and families to pay, and borrow, far more than ever before.[27]

As a result, the American public's traditional confidence in colleges has developed some cracks. A 2011 Pew poll found that 57 percent of Americans thought colleges do not provide good value for the money, and 75 percent felt that college is too expensive for most Americans to afford.[28] A year later, a survey from *Time* magazine and the Carnegie Corporation of New York found that fully 89 percent of Americans viewed higher education as being "in crisis," and more than half thought higher education to be on the "wrong track."[29]

This change in the perception of American higher education has paralleled—and arguably been influenced by—the rise of a new, aggressive style of philanthropy in higher education. In August 2010, the *Chronicle of Higher Education* ran an article about the rapidly growing influence of major foundations in this arena, most notably the Gates Foundation.[30] In contrast to foundations that have traditionally funded higher education, Gates (and Lumina) has employed a more aggressive strategy to reshape the sector through changes in public policy. As Terry W. Hartle of the American Council on Education argued in the article, "I think that Gates and a couple [of] foundations, primarily Lumina, are pioneering a new approach that wouldn't have been used in the past. Let's call it 'advocacy philanthropy.'"

For their part, leaders at Gates and Lumina have made no secret of their desire to use their resources to shift the public debate about higher education. Hilary Pennington, the former leader of Gates's postsecondary strategy who is now at the Ford Foundation, summed up this new role:

> The question confronting us now: what innovative practices and public policy changes are needed to quickly advance this agenda? At the foundation, we believe fresh thinking on this question requires a new angle of vision. Too often the debate is framed by the perspectives of higher education institutions rather than by the needs of . . . their students."[31]

Jamie Merisotis, CEO of Lumina, voiced a similar sentiment in 2013:

> If you think about the fact that national college-attainment rates have been hovering for decades around 40 percent . . . and with experts predicting that nearly two-thirds of jobs will require some level of college-level learning

by the end of this decade . . . it's clear that college attainment must increase dramatically . . . The status quo is simply not an option.[32]

Hall and Thomas examined the rise of advocacy philanthropy in higher education more closely.[33] They concluded that "the Bill & Melinda Gates Foundation and the Lumina Foundation for Education have taken up a set of methods—strategic grantmaking, public policy advocacy, the funding of intermediaries, and collaboration with government—that illustrate their direct and unapologetic desire to influence policy and practice in numerous higher education arenas." In July 2013, the *Chronicle of Higher Education* published a six-part series, "The Gates Effect," which documents how the Gates Foundation has spent almost half a billion dollars, most of it since 2008, with the goal of "changing how [higher education] is delivered, financed, and regulated."[34]

What are these foundations advocating for? At the risk of oversimplifying, the completion agenda is built on three beliefs. First, some form of postsecondary education is more important than ever before to economic success. Second, access to postsecondary education is not enough; to reap its benefits, students must finish a credential with labor market value. That means figuring out how to encourage degree completion. Third, colleges themselves can have a direct effect on student success and must do more to promote it. However, most institutions have little incentive to focus on this outcome in the absence of changes to policy.[35]

How do the foundations advocate for their ideas? In chapter 1, Jay P. Greene argues that foundations must leverage their money by working to change the rules that govern the flow of public dollars. That means funding the kind of research, advocacy, and coalition-building activity that can foment policy change. It also means funding the kinds of organizations that do this type of work—advocacy groups, think tanks, and other nonprofits outside of the academy. As we show in the next section, Gates and Lumina have done both.

AN EMPIRICAL SNAPSHOT OF CONTEMPORARY HIGHER EDUCATION PHILANTHROPY

What does the distribution of higher education philanthropy look like today, and how different are Gates and Lumina? In this section, we look at a snapshot of higher education giving by fifteen foundations that were among the most active in funding higher education in 2012. The intent is to describe differences in the distribution of grants—who gets them and what they pay for—across the largest funders.

Data

Generating a list of the top higher education funders is not as simple as it seems. First, the most common source of data—the Foundation Center's Foundation Directory Online—tends to code any grant that flows to a college or university as "higher education, university." But it is important to distinguish between two very different varieties of grantmaking to higher education. One category of giving is broadly designed to affect higher education itself: scholarships; curriculum development; interventions to boost student success; research funding to study various aspects of higher education; and assorted projects that expose students and faculty to new ideas, fields of study, and cultural opportunities. This category includes efforts to improve individual campuses through capital projects (new buildings).

A second category of grants leverages universities' research capacity to improve the world in ways that may be unrelated to education, such as through medical research, the development of new technology, and the preservation of the past. These research grants account for a substantial proportion of the philanthropic money flowing to higher education every year but are clearly distinct from the first category in that they do not seek to affect education directly. Since our focus is on education, we explore only the first category in the analysis below.

Unfortunately, this murkiness also makes the task of coming up with the top fifteen funders more difficult. As we found when we set out to do this study, many foundations give millions to universities for research but do not even name "higher education" as a primary focus on their websites. By the Foundation Directory's method, these funders would qualify as top funders of "higher education" even though they do not focus on education at all.

To generate our list of the top fifteen funders, then, we started with the fourteen foundations that Hall and Thomas identified as the most prominent higher education grant makers during the decade from 2000 to 2009.[36] We then downloaded 2012 grant-level data—the most recent available at the time the project began—for each of these foundations and coded the grants to determine which fell into the first category: funding designed to affect higher education itself. After coding the grants, we summed up the totals dedicated to higher education to get a sense of how much each of the fourteen foundations spent in 2012. We found that one foundation on this list—the John D. and Catherine T. MacArthur Foundation—had invested only $4 million in grants related to higher education itself in 2012, far less than the others. Therefore, we decided to drop MacArthur and add two other funders to round out a list of fifteen.

To find the two additional funders, we consulted the Foundation Center's ranking of the fifty biggest education funders in 2012 and, working down the list, chose the first two foundations that mentioned higher education as a priority on their profile that were not already included.[37] That led us to add the Robert W. Woodruff Foundation ($75.5 million to higher education) and the Foundation to Promote an Open Society ($49.1 million to higher education). There are certainly other ways to come up with a list of the most prominent higher education funders, but we doubt that a different method would dramatically change the findings we discuss below. Table 4.1 displays

TABLE 4.1   Top fifteen foundations' spending on higher education, 2012

	Higher education grants, 2012	Higher education funding, 2012
Andrew W. Mellon Foundation	166	$81,282,052
Alfred P. Sloan Foundation	42	$11,151,444
Bill & Melinda Gates Foundation	108	$75,737,615
Carnegie Corporation of New York	35	$9,829,900
Duke Endowment	16	$66,713,874
Ford Foundation	42	$27,225,309
Foundation to Promote Open Society	72	$49,071,252
Kresge Foundation	61	$27,862,452
Lilly Endowment Inc.	69	$58,393,587
Lumina Foundation	165	$51,451,725
Robert Wood Johnson Foundation	68	$13,243,427
Robert W. Woodruff Foundation, Inc.	12	$75,460,011
Starr Foundation	17	$35,610,000
William and Flora Hewlett Foundation	38	$9,898,737
W. K. Kellogg Foundation	36	$13,496,884

Source: Authors' calculations.

the fifteen foundations in our set, as well as the number of grants and the total amount they gave to promote higher education improvement in 2012.

As you can see from the table, some foundations gave few grants that were very large (Robert W. Woodruff and the Duke Endowment), while others gave many grants that were comparatively smaller. The total amount given to improve higher education ranged from just over $81 million from the Mellon Foundation to just under $10 million from the Hewlett Foundation and Carnegie Corporation. Gates and Lumina are near the top of the list in terms of both the number of grants and the amount spent, an indication of how active they are in this area.

After identifying the top fifteen, we then coded each grant based on the type of recipient (institution of higher education, membership organization, etc.) and the grant purpose (scholarships, general support, research, direct services). In all, we coded over twenty-five hundred grants from the 2012 cycle. In describing the results, we generally disaggregate the data for Gates and Lumina to compare them with the rest of the funders in the set.

Results: Who Gets Money?

What does the distribution of recipients look like across funders? Traditional, low-leverage giving should be heavily weighted toward institutions of higher education and scholarships—grants that subsidize more college. Reform-oriented philanthropy, which emphasizes policy change, should make grants to a broader array of organizations, including advocacy groups, think tanks, membership groups, and even government agencies.

Other observers have already noted how Gates and Lumina have invested heavily in advocacy and policy work, and we find a similar pattern. But how does this compare to other higher education funders? Figure 4.1 shows the distribution grant dollars to different types of recipients across all fifteen funders and disaggregates the results for Gates and Lumina.

A few important patterns jump out immediately, each of which crystallizes the difference between Gates and Lumina's new model of advocacy philanthropy and the traditional approach. First, Gates and Lumina gave far less of their funding for higher education to colleges and universities themselves. Whereas other foundations in our set gave 66 percent of their funding to institutions, Gates and Lumina gave just under half and less than a quarter, respectively, to colleges and universities. This investment pattern jibes with one of the lessons that Hall and Thomas note in their 2012 study: reform-minded foundations are skeptical that higher education

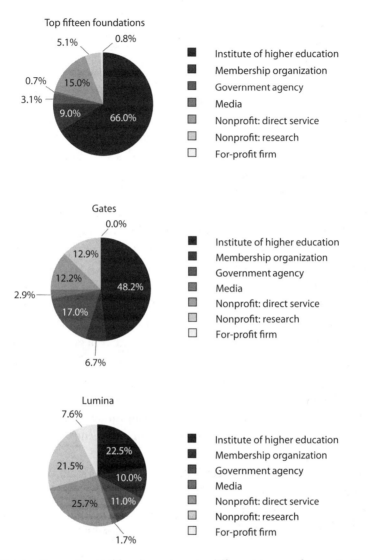

FIGURE 4.1   Percentage of funding given to different types of organizations, 2012

institutions can reform themselves from the inside to accomplish the foundations' goals.[38]

Second, Gates and Lumina both invest far more than other foundations in nonprofit research organizations—think tanks, contract research firms, and nonprofit consultancies. If you exclude Gates and Lumina from the calculations, just over 2 percent of the grant money from the other thirteen foundations goes to nonprofit research organizations not affiliated with universities (not pictured). In contrast, Lumina invested more than 20 percent of its grant money in research nonprofits. At Gates, about 13 percent went to nonprofit research organizations.[39]

Third, the new higher education philanthropists invested a much larger portion of their grant money in government and quasi-government agencies—a somewhat broad category that includes state boards of regents as well as interstate compacts like the Southern Regional Education Board (SREB) and the Western Interstate Cooperative for Higher Education. Gates stands out here, dedicating 17 percent of its 2012 higher education grants to government or quasi-government agencies. Finally, Gates and Lumina each give a nontrivial slice of money to media organizations, while only a trace of grant money from other foundations flows to such groups.

These patterns point toward a high-leverage, policy-oriented strategy. Funders with a more traditional approach spent about 96 percent of their higher education dollars on institutions, direct service providers, and the membership organizations that often represent colleges. In other words, the majority of those dollars are going to produce more of what traditional colleges offer. To be sure, Gates and Lumina spend quite a bit on direct services—which could qualify as low-leverage investments—but most of their grant money flowed to organizations that can influence policy and public sentiment—nonprofit research organizations, government agencies, and the media.

Grant destinations also reflect Gates's and Lumina's focus on policy. Consider that 40 percent of Lumina's 2012 grants went to groups based in Washington, DC—organizations that are designed to influence federal higher education policies. While Gates was somewhat less focused on DC groups, dedicating about 12 percent of its money inside the Beltway, the other foundations invested just 6 percent of their grant funding to organizations in the nation's capital.

What types of colleges do foundations fund? Because the completion agenda focuses on raising attainment rates, we might expect the new class of funders to target resources where the students are—in nonselective, public two- and four-year colleges. In comparison, more traditional foundations may be more eager to fund high-profile initiatives at elite colleges, which tend to set the tone for the rest of the sector. To get a rough sense of what this looks like, we coded whether an institution of higher education or affiliated organization was a community college, and whether institutions were ranked in the top 50 of the *U.S. News & World Report* rankings. We then calculated the proportion of higher education grant money and higher education grants that went to each category and disaggregated those results across Gates, Lumina, and the thirteen other foundations. Table 4.2 displays the results.

As expected, Gates and Lumina invested a much higher percentage of their funding in community colleges compared with other foundations. Gates stands out again, giving almost a quarter of its 2012 higher education funding to community colleges or affiliated groups. Community colleges enroll about 45 percent of all college students, but they also struggle to retain and graduate them, making them a natural place for the completion agenda to focus.[40]

When it comes to elite colleges, the results again jibe with expectations. The other thirteen foundations invested about 31 percent of their higher education funding in institutions in the top 50 of *U.S. News & World Report*. In contrast, Gates and Lumina each dedicated less than 15 percent of their higher education budgets to projects at elite colleges.

Results: What Does the Money Pay For?

Using the grant descriptions from the Foundation Directory datasets, we also coded the grant's purpose into various categories: research on higher

TABLE 4.2 What percentage of grants goes to elite and community colleges?

	U.S. News top 50	Community colleges
Gates:		
• Proportion of higher ed grant money	13.7%	22.6%
• Proportion of grants	13.9%	16.7%
Lumina:		
• Proportion of higher ed grant money	10.5%	10.0%
• Proportion of grants	5.5%	10.3%
Others:		
• Proportion of higher ed grant money	30.8%	1.8%
• Proportion of grants	28.0%	2.1%

Source: Authors' calculations based on 2012 data.

education, direct services geared toward students or faculty, advocacy and engagement work to affect policy and public opinion, scholarships to help students pay for college, and support to fund campus operations and capital projects like new buildings or renovations. We then disaggregated the grants in the research and direct service categories according to the specific topic they focused on, paying particular attention to grants supporting the cornerstones of the completion agenda: readiness, access, and success.

Figure 4.2 shows the distribution of grants across the major categories for Gates, Lumina, and the other thirteen funders. Gates and Lumina spent nothing on capital projects and very little on general support or scholarships. The others spent nearly a third on capital projects and general support combined; add in scholarships and 62 percent of the other foundations' giving was accounted for. This distribution fits with expectations about low-leverage giving. In contrast, Gates and Lumina spent the majority of their money on direct services and research on higher education topics. Lumina also spent about 13 percent on advocacy and engagement—activities designed to rally support and make a public case for higher education reform.[41] Relative to Lumina, Gates invested less of its money on advocacy and engagement.

What topics did research and direct service projects focus on? We coded those grants into a set of subcategories to take a more detailed look at funder priorities. Table 4.3 ranks the three largest direct service subcategories in terms of the percentage of total higher education giving that was dedicated to each subcategory. It also provides the same information for research.

Table 4.3 shows that for Gates, Lumina, and the thirteen other foundations, direct services to promote readiness, access, and success were the top priority in the direct service category, though Gates and Lumina dedicated much larger percentages of their overall budgets to this category. Among the other thirteen foundations, other campus services—such as study abroad programs, arts, internships, and community service—came in second, followed by faculty development.

Two of Gates and Lumina's respective priorities emerge in the second slot. Gates has made large investments in higher education innovation—including creation of the Next Generation Learning Challenges, support for competency-based education, and promotion of open educational resources.[42] Not surprisingly, technology and innovation emerged as Gates's second priority, accounting for about 25 percent of its overall higher education budget. Likewise, in 2009, Lumina launched a signature productivity initiative, under which the foundation partnered with select states to test new ways to make

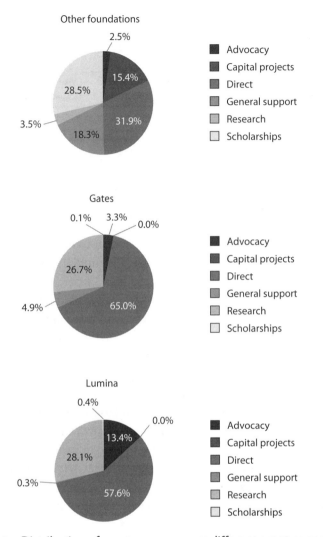

FIGURE 4.2   Distribution of grant money across different grant purposes, 2012

public higher education more cost-effective. In 2012, investments related to cost-effectiveness accounted for about one-sixth of its overall budget.[43]

When it comes to research, studies having to do with readiness, access, and success were again the top category across all three groups (table 4.4). But the proportion of funding dedicated to this kind of research varied dramatically across foundations. In particular, it is worth noting how small a

TABLE 4.3   Top direct service priorities across foundations, 2012

Priority ranking	Others	Gates	Lumina
1	Readiness, access, success: 11.3%	Readiness, access, success: 38.0%	Readiness, access, success: 29.8%
2	Other campus services: 7.1%	Technology and innovation: 24.9%	Cost effectiveness: 17.1%
3	Faculty development: 5.8%	Other campus services: 2.0%	Policy: 6.4%

Source: Authors' calculations.

portion of the overall budget at the thirteen other foundations went to fund research (~3.5 percent across the most heavily funded categories).

In contrast, Gates and Lumina spent about 14 percent and 19 percent of their *total* higher education budgets on readiness, access, and success research. Again, research on technology and innovation ranked as a priority for Gates, as did policy research. Lumina invested about 6 percent of its total budget on policy and cost-effectiveness research.

It does not take a statistician to recognize the important differences between the advocacy philanthropists and other foundations in our study. Of course, we would be remiss if we did not note that some of the other foundations in the group of thirteen are also actively engaged in various facets of higher education reform. On the innovation front, the Hewlett Foundation has led the way on open educational resources since the early 2000s.[44] And Gates's first postsecondary success leader, Hilary Pennington, now oversees higher

TABLE 4.4   Top research priorities across foundations, 2012

Priority ranking	Others	Gates	Lumina
1	Readiness, access, success: 2.3%	Readiness, access, success: 13.6%	Readiness, access, success: 19.4%
2	Policy: 0.8%	Technology and innovation: 6.1%	Policy: 3.0%
3	Financial aid: 0.3%	Policy: 6.0%	Cost-effectiveness: 2.5%

Source: Authors' calculations.

education at the Ford Foundation and will almost certainly focus the foundation's work on college access and completion.[45]

The Kresge Foundation, in particular, seems to have followed Gates and Lumina's lead in adopting a focus on student success.[46] In additional analysis not reported here, we charted Kresge's giving from 2008 to 2012. In 2008, the foundation dedicated fully 91 percent of its giving in higher education to capital projects and general support. It invested no money in advocacy or research on readiness, access, and success. By 2011, this had all changed; Kresge spent just 7 percent of its budget on general support (and funded no capital projects). Instead, it invested one-third of its budget in services designed to promote student success. Another 8 percent went to advocacy and engagement.

We believe that other foundations are following Gates's and Lumina's lead because their brand of advocacy has likely changed higher education policy debates for the foreseeable future. However, as we detail in the next section, that level of influence has made their efforts controversial at times.

PUSHBACK

One measure of the effect that this new style of philanthropy has had on policy debates is the amount of criticism it has catalyzed among skeptics. Critics frequently question both the tactics employed by the insurgent foundations as well as the content of their agenda. More broadly, as Michael Q. McShane and Jenn Hatfield point out in chapter 6, critics have raised questions about the role of foundations in public life, charging that they bring specific agendas to the discussion but face little in the way of accountability—democratic or otherwise—for the reforms they push.

Criticism of Tactics

Much of the criticism of Gates and Lumina has focused on the expanded role they are playing—both directly and via their grantees—in the policy process. Others have criticized what they see as a systematic exclusion of college faculty and administrators and a reliance on researchers and policy wonks with no higher education experience.

Concerns About Democratic Accountability. In general, critics seem most troubled by the fact that the foundations are taking on an increasingly important role in agenda setting and policymaking but are not democratically controlled in any way. Writing in July 2013, sociologist Robin Rogers of the City University of New York aptly summed up these concerns:

> Changes in higher education are necessary; I think we can all agree on that. Philanthropy, however, can become de facto public policy making. The continued existence of an informed, educated, independent citizenry will be possible only if leaders in the philanthropic sector are accountable to the public whose tax money is being leveraged to shape America's future. Philanthropy is no longer, if it ever was, benign and benevolent—it is powerful. This shift of power to the economic elite via philanthropy makes it even more important to our democracy's health that we support a viable public option in higher education that is not determined by the priorities and judgments of the very wealthy, however well-intentioned they may be.[47]

Spencer Foundation president Michael McPherson has argued that the new "advocacy philanthropy" of Gates and Lumina is "in tension with the original spirit of what foundations are designed to do: go off and do their own thing." Spencer fits more squarely into this "original spirit": it funds education research, including doctoral fellowships for graduate students. In contrast, Gates's and Lumina's strategies "[represent] a shift from working at the edges to a concerted effort to change the core, working through political avenues . . . These are people nobody has voted for . . . They hold everybody else accountable but haven't been elected themselves."[48] Observers on the right have levied similar warnings about a lack of accountability for funders. George Leef and Jenna Ashley Robinson, both of the right-leaning John William Pope Center in North Carolina, have asked what happens when philanthropists' ideas don't pan out: "Unlike business capital, which can be lost when executives back bad products, foundations lose nothing when their executives back bad ideas."[49]

Concerns About the Exclusion of Stakeholders Within Higher Education. Some within higher education also feel that Gates and Lumina have purposefully excluded practitioners from their reform strategy. As one veteran college lobbyist explained to the *Chronicle of Higher Education*, these foundations' mistrust of the establishment has led them to create an "impenetrable cluster" of wonks and policy professionals: "They've locked out practitioners in favor of those with no hands-on experience or responsibility to students."[50] Educators have leveled an almost identical complaint against K–12 reformers,

often arguing that public school teachers and school leaders are systematically excluded from education reform conversations in favor of consultants,
businesspeople, and professional advocates.[51]

Criticism of Content

Observers have also leveled criticism at the content of foundation reform
agendas, particularly the emphasis on completion and cost-effectiveness, the
focus on the economic value of degrees, and the potential for reform ideas
to stretch the limits of what current research might support.

The Risks of Focusing on Degree Completion. First, critics worry that focusing on degree completion will lead to unintended consequences, like the
dumbing down of standards, more selective admissions, and, over time, a
cheapening of the value of a college degree. Veteran higher education ana-
lyst Arthur Hauptman has been among the most vociferous critics of the
focus on completion, warning in 2011 that emphasizing completion rates—
as opposed to the number of degrees produced—would lead colleges to
become more selective and to limit capacity. With regard to goals set out
by Gates, Lumina, and President Obama, Hauptman stated, "I don't think
it helps to have broad, unrealistic goals that will never be met."[52]

Faculty have also often bristled at the suggestion that institutions increase
their completion rates—particularly in the context of performance-based
funding, a priority for both Gates and Lumina. In response to reforms
emphasizing completion, for instance, the California Faculty Association
warned that "most obviously, one way to improve graduation rates is to
exclude students who face greater challenges to graduating."[53] Writing about
the "graduation rate craze," Susan Meisenhelder, a professor at California
State University, San Bernardino, cautioned that emphasizing one outcome—
graduation—could actually leave us with less-well-educated students, as
colleges would start to place "insufficient focus on quality and academic
rigor." In her view, "facilitating graduation" could quickly become a "plain
old cheapening of degrees."[54]

Still others have railed against the assumption that the country needs
more college degrees. In 2011, conservative writer George Leef took exception to one Lumina Foundation vice president's suggestion that "there's no
real debate here that more people need college degrees." "Sorry," Leef wrote,
"but there *is* a great debate over that, and apparently Lumina continues to
shut its ears to it."[55]

College Is About More Than Economic Returns. Both Lumina and Gates emphasize "labor market value" in their higher education attainment goals, and each has invested in efforts to collect and report better data on the economic returns to higher education. This emphasis on value helps to deflect criticism that the completion agenda will lead to diploma mills printing useless degrees. It also serves as a key rationale for raising the country's attainment rate.

Whatever the benefits, however, Gates and Lumina have faced a steady stream of criticism on this front. Many critics have expressed a fear that emphasizing workforce outcomes could incentivize institutions to give short shrift to aspects of higher education that aren't as valuable for career success but benefit the student and society. Education historian Diane Ravitch, a frequent critic of the Gates Foundation, expressed this view succinctly in July 2013: "Can anyone speak honestly to Bill Gates before he turns American higher education into a giant industry committed to building skills and competencies instead of fostering intelligence, ambition, and innovation?"[56]

Foundations' Preferred Policy Solutions Go Beyond the Research Base. A distinct criticism relates to whether the solutions pushed by the new higher education philanthropy are "evidence-based," including whether the foundations invest enough in the basic research needed to test their ideas. In particular, critics have charged that foundation efforts to promote performance-based funding, financial aid reform, and innovations like massive open online courses and competency-based education have outstripped the base of available research.

For instance, the most recent large-scale studies of performance-based funding produced null effects, suggesting that this central policy reform of the completion agenda may not produce the expected effects.[57] When asked why states were still adopting performance-based systems, an author of the most recent studies responded: "There is no meaningful evidence of effectiveness, but we see a rush toward adoption . . . It seems as though there is something other than evidence at work here."[58] Similarly, when the Gates Foundation funded sixteen grants to explore options for redesigning federal aid programs to promote degree completion, William Goggin, director of the congressionally appointed Advisory Committee on Student Financial Assistance, argued that this goal flies in the face of existing research on student aid. "The burden of proof," Goggin went on, "should be on those who say you can redistribute and come out ahead."[59]

Some see this as a chronic problem inherent in setting strategic goals on relatively tight timelines. The University of Wisconsin's Sara Goldrick-Rab, a grantee of both Lumina and Gates but also one of their strongest critics, has argued that both place "small emphasis on peer review and high priority on strategic goals that often do not seem to align with research evidence."[60] In their look at advocacy philanthropy, Cassie Hall and Scott Thomas reported one anonymous policy expert's view that Gates and Lumina "have not defined the issues they are addressing as research problems but, rather, as implementation problems," leaving less foundation money to examine the actual impacts of reform initiatives.[61]

CONCLUSION

This pushback has raised important concerns that bear on this volume's overarching question: is the new philanthropy "good" for higher education? To conclude, we provide an appraisal of some of the pros and cons for both education and democratic governance, as well as what to watch for in the future.

Is the New Higher Education Philanthropy Good for Higher Education?

The new philanthropists have successfully placed the problems in American higher education on the agenda. They have shifted the discussion from one focused on access at all costs to one in which student success has taken center stage. The access agenda paid dividends, but it also had many casualties—students who enrolled in programs that were not worth the time or money and wound up dropping out. Pushing the debate to focus on access *and* success has been a positive development.

The foundations have also drawn attention to where it was previously lacking, most notably to the nonelite institutions that serve the bulk of America's postsecondary students and to the growing number of nontraditional students who are trying to juggle work, family, and college. These institutions often have lackluster outcomes, and nontraditional students are often left searching for an option that works with their schedule and budget constraints. Shifting our focus from elite institutions and traditional undergraduates to the schools most students attend and the needs of nontraditional students are both positive steps.

Likewise, funding from Gates, Lumina, and other foundations has cultivated a base of researchers and organizations that are independent of the higher education establishment. In light of the dominant role that traditional higher education and its trade associations have played in federal and state policy for decades, the emergence of these independent organizations is an important counterweight to the sector's views on what is best for students.

Skeptics will criticize this as another instance of moneyed interests driving policy. But it helps to take a step back. Reform movements often make headlines for their efforts to shape policy, but the truth is that established interests tend to have more political power and more resources at their disposal than do the reformers. They can use these assets to play defense, quietly using their agenda-setting power and existing political resources to stunt any effort to change policy. While this may not look like usurping democracy, these organizations—trade and professional associations—are often as unaccountable to the public as private foundations. That does not wish away the problems of political accountability, but it does suggest that critics of education foundations may only be seeing the tip of the iceberg.

There is also a tendency among critics to cast foundation funding of policy work as the kind of quid pro quo lobbying that good government types despise. But the notion that existing organizations are willing to change their preferences at the first hint of foundation dollars, and to do so in this polarized political climate, is rooted in a misconception of interest group politics. Instead, political scientists have argued that most lobbying functions as a "legislative subsidy," providing information and expertise that loosens the budget constraint of sympathetic congressional offices and allows them to spend more time on the interest group's key issue.[62] Likewise, most of the new philanthropy operates more like a subsidy than a bribe, loosening the budget constraints of like-minded grantees so that they can focus on issues of interest to both them and the foundations. In this way, foundation money *amplifies* perspectives rather than *changing* them. In higher education, this amplification has helped to develop a stock of intellectual capital and research that is independent of the college lobby. On balance, this is a good thing for students.

That's not to say, however, that the foundations have no blind spots. For example, a strategy focused solely on the incentives facing existing institutions may not pay sufficient attention to increasing the supply of seats available. As one of the authors of this chapter wrote in 2013 about innovation in higher education, "efforts to improve existing institutions make good sense . . . But this approach . . . overestimates the ability of existing players to reinvent themselves. Established routines, structures, and hierarchies make it inordinately difficult for organizations to rethink their cost structures and business models."[63] Foundations, therefore, should balance their work with existing institutions with efforts to foster new institutions, built from scratch and therefore free of the organizational inertia that can bog down reform initiatives. After all, many of the nation's most well-known universities—such as the University of Virginia and Johns Hopkins—and hundreds of community colleges came about in response to existing institutions' failure to adapt to the changing needs of the country.[64] It is true that the new philanthropists have not ignored new actors—the Gates Foundation, for example, has funded efforts to leverage Massive Open Online Courses (MOOCs) for credit.[65] But it's also fair to say that a focus on changing the incentives facing existing institutions has held a higher place on the reform agenda than breaking down barriers to entry for new ones.

Finally, while a passion to improve the system can be an important driver of reform, it can also lead foundation leaders and trusted grantees to ignore warning signs about potential flaws in preferred policies. For instance, translating a high-level vision of performance-based accountability into a policy that works on the ground is fraught with potential problems. Reformers are often quick to dismiss any opposition from the establishment as merely self-serving or ideologically obstinate, but that opposition often contains reasonable criticisms that should help guide policy. Prudent reform requires that those pushing for change listen closely to critics so they can identify true pitfalls that stand in their way.

At the beginning of this chapter, we suggested that the new approaches to K–12 philanthropy that emerged in the first decade of the 2000s eventually made their way, with a lag, to higher education. Observing the evolution of philanthropy in both sectors at this moment, however, it's hard not to notice significant differences in their trajectories. In higher education, the Obama administration's recent proposal to rate colleges and universities reflects the kind of technocratic fervor that many in the education reform community—including funders—have been quick to adopt. In some ways, the ratings proposal indicates that the "completion agenda" has reached the highest levels of the policymaking apparatus (if it had not already).

But, if K–12 reform is a guide, this success could also serve as something of a warning. Parts of the reform agenda in K–12 are now under assault as policy makers retreat from the perceived excesses of No Child Left Behind, prescriptive federal mandates around teacher evaluation, and the Common Core State Standards. The point here is not to weigh in on the merits of those ideas; rather, it's to point out the potential pitfalls of aggressive, no-holds-barred attempts to push prescriptive reforms onto established institutions. Such efforts are fraught with policy and political difficulties, and those difficulties can create a backlash that sets reformers' original goals back instead of moving them forward.

The new higher education philanthropists have imported many lessons from the K–12 sector. But learning from past mistakes may be the most important of all.

5

Advocacy and Assumptions in Foundation-Sponsored Research

Dana Goldstein

I n January 2013, the Bill & Melinda Gates Foundation released findings from an unprecedented research project it had funded called Measures of Effective Teaching, or MET. The core of the study entailed collecting videotaped lessons from three thousand volunteer teachers in six urban school districts. Nine hundred trained observers used five different classroom observation tools to rate the lessons, and those ratings were then compared with how well the students of those teachers performed on standardized tests, and also to how 44,500 of those students rated their teachers on surveys. Unlike most education research, the MET project included a randomized controlled trial. During the study's second year, some of the participating schools randomly assigned students to teachers who had volunteered for the study—theoretically removing the bias that can occur when principals choose to assign the toughest students to either the weakest or strongest teachers or when the most involved, affluent parents successfully demand the best teachers for their children.

The MET project took place in a climate of red-hot policy debate, legislating, and media attention on the question of how best to judge the performance of public school teachers. The Gates Foundation had a clear position, as reflected in its funding priorities since 2007: it believed in evaluating teachers based on whether they raised students' scores on standardized tests and in weakening teacher job protections so that ineffective educators could be terminated. Teachers' unions responded that student test scores were an incomplete and unreliable measure of teachers' effectiveness, and that tenure—which had existed since 1909—was crucial in protecting teachers' academic freedom and insulating them from the whims of incompetent administrators. The Obama administration chose a clear side in this battle when, in 2009, it asked states to tie teacher evaluation and tenure to student test scores.

Perhaps the most potent critique of the Obama administration and Gates Foundation's shared agenda on teacher reform was that, as much as it focused on changing human resources policies, it paid scant attention to how to improve teachers' actual classroom practice—the words they spoke, the materials they used, and the assignments they gave. The MET project was clearly an attempt to respond to that critique. And when MET launched in 2010, it immediately garnered media attention. Publications including the *New York Times, Fast Company*, and NPR covered the massive data-gathering effort, often focusing on the novelty and controversy of videotaping teachers at work.[1] Three years later, the media reaction to the announcement of MET's findings was less coherent. The *Washington Post* characterized the study as having "figured out what makes a good teacher . . . Researchers found that multiple classroom observations of teachers by several people—a principal, a peer, an outside expert—result in the most accurate assessments."[2]

In contrast, the *Huffington Post* declared that MET had found "teacher observation less reliable than test scores."[3] The *Pittsburgh Post-Gazette* had a similar take, noting that MET "concludes that testing data give teachers better feedback for improving their practice" than other types of evaluations.[4]

None of the journalists who wrote these stories were necessarily wrong. The hundreds of pages of MET project documents could credibly be used to support all these contentions. The conflicting media reaction—had the findings of MET ultimately supported or criticized the usefulness of classroom observation?—was a function of the complexity of the research. And yet much of that complexity remained obscure to the public. Little of the media coverage, with the exception of that by *Education Week*, a trade publication, explained the study's key methodology of judging all modes of evaluating teachers based on whether they predicted growth in state standardized test scores.[5] Nor did media outlets typically point out the small correlations between student achievement and the various teacher evaluation strategies tested in the study.

How is research received by scholars, policy makers, and practitioners when the sponsor of that research—and political allies including the president of the United States—have already embraced the reforms being studied? And is anyone paying attention when the conclusions of such research appear to contradict, or at least to complicate, some of the core assumptions of that reform agenda?

Relying on interviews, past scholarship, and an examination of foundation financial data, in this chapter I will trace the history of the Gates Foundation's MET project, which exists within a century-long tradition of foundation-funded research closely tied to advocacy and policy change. MET is unique, however, in that it was released during a time of profound and quick-moving policy change on the very reforms being studied. Those changes were driven, in part, by close ties between the Gates Foundation and the Obama administration.

A BRIEF HISTORY OF FOUNDATION-FUNDED RESEARCH AND ADVOCACY ON TEACHING

There is nothing new about corporate philanthropists playing a major role not only in reforming the teaching profession, but also in conducting and promoting research they hope will drive policy change. Andrew Carnegie was, in many ways, Bill Gates's antecedent in tactics and influence, although their policy prescriptions were quite different. Carnegie supported vocational education and was skeptical about the liberal arts. In 1920, the Carnegie Foundation for the Advancement of Teaching, which is still active today, researched a group of normal schools in Missouri and then published a report that called for teachers to spend all four years of their preservice training absorbing a "professionalized" curriculum in pedagogy rather than focusing on more prestigious academic training in math, literature, history, or the sciences. Such ideas cemented teacher education as a lower-status corner of American higher education.[6]

In 1983, the Reagan administration published *A Nation at Risk*, which condemned America's teachers as academic laggards producing a generation of students unable to compete in math, sciences, and foreign languages with their counterparts in the USSR and Japan. In response, the Carnegie Foundation released *A Nation Prepared*, which shifted the foundation away from its earlier views on teacher preparation. The report concluded that teachers should earn subject-matter bachelor's degrees, such as in biology or history, and then earn master's degrees in teaching.[7]

As documented by Sarah Reckhow in *Follow the Money*, the new venture philanthropies founded by Bill and Melinda Gates, the Walton family, and Eli and Edythe Broad have since surpassed Carnegie and its older peers, like

Ford and Annenberg, in education giving, political influence, and giving to research.[8] In 2002, the Gates Foundation, by far the largest of the venture philanthropies, spent $13 million, or 5 percent of its total education budget, on research and advocacy combined.[9] According to Gates Foundation internal estimates, in 2013 and 2014 it spent $50 million on research alone—which includes research development, evaluation, technical assistance, and dissemination of research findings.[10] Annualized, this accounts for roughly 6 percent of the foundation's $423.3 million education budget.[11] In comparison, the Carnegie Foundation had a total budget of just $12 million in 2013, less than half of Gates's research budget.[12] The Walton Foundation, a peer of the Gates Foundation in the venture philanthropy space, reported in 2013 that it spent $1.1 million on "research and evaluation," less than 1 percent of Walton's total education budget.[13] The Spencer Foundation, which focuses almost exclusively on education research, had a total budget of $15.3 million in 2013, still less than the Gates Foundation spent on research alone.[14]

THE HISTORY OF VALUE-ADDED MEASUREMENT AND THE ORIGINS OF MET

Value-added measurement (VAM) is a statistical technique for using student test scores to evaluate teachers. Each student's past scores on standardized tests are used to predict his or her future scores. Teachers are then evaluated on whether their students' test scores turn out as expected, lower than expected, or higher than expected. Most value-added formulas control for student demographic factors, such as family income, in recognition of the fact that disadvantaged children tend to experience slower learning gains regardless of whether they start out with low, average, or high test scores.

Value-added measurement first entered the national school reform debate in the mid-1990s, largely through the work of William Sanders, a Tennessee statistician whose expertise was in agricultural processes. The Education Trust (EdTrust), a Washington-based think tank funded by almost every major education foundation, publicized Sanders's findings through congressional hearings, white papers, and statements to the media. During the political debate on how to reauthorize No Child Left Behind, EdTrust founder Kati Haycock promoted Sanders's theory—which remains untested in real-world conditions—that a child with a continuous sequence of high-value-added teachers could make up to 50 points of gains on a standardized test. Haycock argued that NCLB should thus be overhauled to hold individual teachers, not just schools, responsible for raising student test scores.[15]

Congress never reauthorized NCLB. But in the meantime, more and more scholarship appeared using value-added measurement of teachers, much of it produced by labor economists. Thomas Kane, Douglas Staiger, and Robert Gordon's 2006 discussion paper for the Brookings Institution, "Identifying Effective Teachers Using Performance on the Job," was particularly foundational.[16] Based on panel data on 150,000 Los Angeles public school students and their teachers, the researchers showed that teachers' pathways into the profession—whether through a traditional education college or an alternative pathway like Teach for America—did not seem to impact student performance on standardized tests. Yet students assigned to top-quartile teachers as measured by value-added demonstrated 10 additional points of achievement gains in math compared to students of bottom-quartile teachers. Because their study found that teachers' past value-added performance predicted their future value-added performance, the researchers advocated for firing the bottom quartile of first-year teachers annually, on the theory that they were unlikely to improve.

In 2007, Vicki Phillips left her job as schools superintendent in Portland, Oregon, where she was known as a hard-charging reformer intent on lifting test scores. She became director of the Gates Foundation's K–12 education program. Phillips had read the Brookings paper and quickly set up a meeting between Bill Gates, Thomas Kane, and Douglas Staiger in New York City that October. David Coleman, who was just beginning his work as a chief architect of the Common Core State Standards in English and math, and who would go on to become the president of the College Board, also attended. "[Bill Gates] came in and he had clearly read it and had a very marked-up copy of the paper," Kane says. "We spent a couple hours talking about it."[17]

It was a time of transition for the Gates Foundation's education agenda. Since 2000, the foundation had spent $2 billion creating new, small high schools and breaking large high schools up into smaller ones.[18] Simultaneously, it had funded research to see if the model worked. A 2006 evaluation of the small schools program prepared for the foundation by the American Institutes for Research (AIR) and SRI International found that although student-teacher relationships were stronger in the new Gates-funded small schools, fewer than 40 percent of those small schools had English test scores higher than district averages, and fewer than 30 percent had math scores higher than average.[19] Those numbers were a disappointment to the resolutely data-driven Bill Gates.

Driven by Phillips and the growing body of value-added research, the Gates Foundation began to shift its focus to teacher effectiveness, with a clear interest in redesigning the traditional teacher career ladder that had been protected by unions since the early twentieth century. Under that system, pay is determined by seniority, not performance; tenure is typically awarded after a few years on the job; and tenured teachers are difficult to fire. In many large school districts, 99 percent of teachers receive a satisfactory evaluation each year, with three-quarters hearing no actionable feedback on how to improve their practice.[20]

In July 2007, Gates began making grants on teacher quality. It provided AIR with $881,000 to work on alternative human resources models for schools. Teach For America, a strong supporter of using student test data to drive teaching practice, received $1 million for its expansion in New Orleans. Gates gave $1.3 million to the National Council on Teacher Quality, a Washington-based advocacy organization critical of teachers' unions.[21]

Meanwhile, Kane and Staiger continued to publish research on teachers in Los Angeles. Several weeks after the meeting with Gates, they released the first draft of a study that entailed randomly assigning students to pairs of teachers.[22] Commissioned by the National Board of Professional Teaching Standards (NBPTS) and funded by the Spencer Foundation and the US Department of Education, it tested whether teachers who had participated in the complex NBPTS certification process—consisting of videotaped lessons, timed essay tests of teachers' content knowledge, and portfolios of student work—produced larger student gains on the Stanford 9 achievement test than their peer teachers who were not NBPTS certified. The results indicated that much of the NBPTS process bore little relation to student achievement. But Kane and Staiger, writing with Steve Fullerton of Harvard and Los Angeles Unified School District chief research scientist Steven Cantrell, found that observers' ratings of videotaped lessons did seem to hold predictive power when it came to students' test scores.[23] That insight would later become central to the design of MET.

In March 2008, Cantrell joined the Gates Foundation as a senior program officer in charge of research. Within a year, planning for the MET project, to be led by Kane, was underway. Kane explained the team's thinking:

Let's test a bunch of different [teacher evaluation tools]: the power of classroom observations, student surveys. Let's look at achievement gains, but let's also try to answer the question of if achievement gains on the state test are related to achievement gains on other types of tests. The MET project was deeply connected with the other big initial push of the foundation to provide grants to districts to reinvent their human resource programs, and that also explains the speed with which we carried it out. I had promised Vicki we'd do this within two years. [Laughter] So it was a very practical reason that drove the timing of it. We've got to provide some tools to these districts that are about to implement this.[24]

Time was of the essence because states were in the midst of rewriting their teacher evaluation laws and procedures in response to federal incentives. When the Obama administration came into office in January 2009, Secretary of Education Arne Duncan chose Jim Shelton, a Gates Foundation program director for education, as one of his chief deputies. Duncan also hired Joanne Weiss of the NewSchools Venture Fund, another West Coast venture philanthropy outfit committed to teacher accountability tied to student achievement data. Weiss would oversee Race to the Top, Obama's signature education program. Race to the Top initially passed through Congress as part of the 2009 economic stimulus, and it was the first federal school reform effort to focus on the performance of individual teachers. It offered $4 billion in grants to states that agreed to evaluate, pay, and grant tenure according to how effectively a teacher grew student achievement in measurable ways— which, in most cases, meant standardized test scores. Other Department of Education grant programs, as well as the No Child Left Behind waiver process announced in 2011, adopted similar priorities on teacher accountability. The entire federal education reform agenda was thus tightly aligned with the philanthropic agenda of the Gates Foundation, and the confluence produced real policy change. Two-thirds of the states changed their teacher work laws, with half declaring that student achievement would be factored into teacher evaluation scores and eleven states weakening teacher seniority protections. Florida and North Carolina ended teacher tenure, while Wisconsin, Michigan, Indiana, and Massachusetts limited the scope of issues that teachers' unions could address through collective bargaining.[25]

In the fall of 2009, as state legislatures debated these changes, the MET project began to recruit volunteer teachers in Charlotte-Mecklenburg, Dallas,

Denver, Hillsborough County (Tampa), Memphis, and New York City who were willing to videotape their lessons and have their practice researched alongside their value-added scores. Crucially, the two-year time frame of the MET project did not coincide, in any of the study districts, with a period in which teachers' value-added scores were used to make high-stakes human resources decisions. This is a key limitation of the MET study, yet it was almost totally unacknowledged in the media and policy discourse around the project's findings. Teachers in the MET study were *not* being evaluated, paid, promoted, or fired based on test scores. The MET study is therefore not a test of the high-stakes teacher accountability policies that have rolled out across the country during the Obama era.

Thomas Kane defends the Gates Foundation's decision to fund high-stakes teacher evaluation changes at the district level before the results of MET were actually available:

> Let's go back to how MET got started. It was based on the fact that for decades we had evidence that a huge share of the action [on improving student achievement] was at the individual teacher level. That, mixed with the fact that current teacher evaluation systems were completely a joke . . . Now do you say, okay, the right thing to do is to wait for individual researchers applying to the Spencer Foundation and to the William T. Grant Foundation to fill that hole? Or does it take a large foundation like the Gates Foundation to say that, yes, we're advocating for the fact that this is a very big problem, that the evaluation system is broken and needs to be fixed? Yes, they had decided that, but I think there was tons of evidence. That wasn't made up. Teacher evaluations were completely perfunctory.[26]

Other scholars, however, note that because of the convergence between the Gates Foundation's and the Obama administration's agendas, widespread changes in teacher evaluation rolled out before research results were available on how high-stakes teacher accountability affects student outcomes. Jesse Rothstein, an economist at the University of California, Berkeley, who has been critical of the MET project and the federal push on teacher accountability, says, "One of the problems is that when we're rolling out these policies, we're not rolling them out as an interesting new pilot that we're not sure about whether it works, but we're going to learn. We're doing it everywhere all at the same time."[27]

MET METHODOLOGY AND FINDINGS

Robert Pianta, dean of the Curry School of Education at the University of Virginia, first learned about the nascent MET project at a Stanford conference on classroom observation, where he spoke with Steven Cantrell. Pianta was initially skeptical. The project "tilted at the early stages quite heavily toward a model of teacher evaluation that was driven around selection, retention, and tenure—the structural features of human resources," he said in an interview. "Value-added measurement was the privileged indicator," with classroom observation, Pianta's specialty, playing a secondary role. Yet it was classroom observation, Pianta felt, that provided teachers with detailed information on how to improve their instruction in ways that benefited kids.[28]

But as the Gates Foundation talked more to Pianta about using his own observation system, CLASS (Classroom Assessment Scoring System), within the MET project, Pianta became more involved. He accepted a grant from Gates to assist with certifying MET observers in using CLASS, reviewing the various project reports, and eventually co-editing MET's capstone book. Ultimately, the Gates Foundation and Kane recruited twenty-four lead research partners. They included Pianta and other classroom observation experts, like Charlotte Danielson, who have expressed skepticism of the heavy weight given to value-added measurement in new teacher evaluation systems.

Some of those partner scholars helped move MET toward a conception of using evaluation not just to reward and punish teachers, but also to help them improve. Yet the presence of Pianta, Danielson, and other experts on instruction did not change VAM's "privileged" position within the study's methodology; other forms of teacher evaluation were used to validate VAM, seemingly under the assumption that measures that did not validate VAM were less legitimate. MET tested whether a host of more holistic performance indicators predicted teachers' value-added scores on state standardized tests. Those indicators included teachers' previous year value-added scores; student achievement gains on exams more rigorous than state tests; student perceptions of their teachers as measured by surveys; tests of teachers' content knowledge; a survey of teachers meant to evaluate working conditions; and five different classroom observation tools. For the classroom observation element of the study, more than nine hundred observers, 75 percent of whom had six or more years of classroom teaching experience, were trained through Educational Testing Services and Teachscape to use the various tools.

Academics interviewed for this chapter agreed that the MET project had a strong research design. Doug Harris, an economist at Tulane University and director of the Education Research Alliance for New Orleans, has a reputation as a scholar who uses value-added measurement without sugarcoating its limitations. "MET was clever, smart, ambitious, and very well done," he said. "It gives us more confidence in value-added measures than we had before the MET study." Harris added that the economists Raj Chetty, John Friedman, and Jonah Rockoff have also claimed to validate VAM with their study showing that students assigned to teachers with value-added scores one standard deviation above the norm experienced slightly higher incomes and college enrollment rates as young adults. Yet that study was an "indirect test of validity," Harris said, because it used longitudinal data. "MET's randomized controlled trial is more convincing" because it was able to partially control how students were assigned to teachers.[29]

The Gates Foundation released the findings from the MET project in four waves of increasing complexity between 2010 and 2014. Below I will highlight major findings.[30]

Student Surveys

The Gates Foundation announced that both student survey ratings of teachers and teachers' previous year VAM scores predicted future VAM scores. The bulk of the student survey was drawn from Ron Ferguson's Tripod method, which asks students questions about their teachers that test for the "7 Cs": care about students, control behavior, clarify lessons, challenge students, captivate students, confer with students, and consolidate knowledge. In addition, a student's self-reported enjoyment of class was positively correlated with achievement gains.

Other survey questions based on much-touted indicators of social-emotional growth were *not* correlated with measurable student achievement gains. Those indicators included Angela Duckworth's measure of "grit," or a student's ability to persevere in a challenging task, and Carol Dweck's measure of whether students believe success is a result of effort rather than fixed ability (the idea that "the mind is a muscle" that can be developed through practice).

Testing and Test Prep

According to MET, teachers with high value-added as measured by state standardized tests also helped their students perform better on more rigorous exams. Teachers whose students reported spending a lot of time in class practicing for the state test did produce test score gains, but those gains were not as large as those produced by teachers who did *not* explicitly prep for tests and focused instead on broader concepts from the curriculum.

Classroom Observation

The clearest takeaway from three MET papers released in 2012 was that observation scores best matched VAM scores when multiple trained observers visited each teacher's classroom on multiple occasions and the overall observation score was the average of the scores from each visit. Although all five of the tested observation tools were individually correlated with student achievement gains, the Gates Foundation described the size of that correlation as only "modest"—a finding that critics would use to argue against investing further resources in improving teacher observation.

The 7,491 lessons videotaped and assessed for this phase of MET offered the largest-ever snapshot of teaching practices across the country. One of the most fascinating findings was that the lessons, when assessed as a group, rated highest on classroom control and behavior management and lowest on measures of intellectual rigor such as quality of teacher feedback, conceptual questioning of students, and quality of student participation in class discussions. One implication was that, beyond mere teaching practice, the curriculum being presented to students was perhaps subpar, or perhaps many teachers lacked the training and intellectual sophistication to dive deeper with their students.

Another finding highlighted in MET research papers, but not in Gates's 2012 four-page media brief on classroom observation, was that only 14 to 37 percent of the variance in classroom observation scores was due to persistent differences between teachers; the rest of the variation appeared to be due to differences in raters' perceptions, day-to-day fluctuations in teachers' performance, and differences in the student demographics of each classroom. Indeed, teachers with poorer students consistently earned lower observation scores regardless of their performance, which seemed to call into question the entire premise that observation is fair. Yet classroom observation remained important, the Gates Foundation concluded, because it "provides diagnostic feedback that a teacher can use to improve."

How to Build Teacher Evaluation Systems

MET found that observers rating their colleagues—such as a principal judging the work of his own teaching staff—offered a "home field advantage," so the Gates Foundation concluded that classroom observation should be done by a combination of observers from within and outside a school building.

Gates suggested that teacher evaluation systems that weigh observation at 50 percent or more and value-added at less than one-third are "counterproductive" because such systems lower "the correlation with state achievement gains." Instead, it advocated an evaluation system that weighed classroom observation, student surveys, and value-added equally, at one-third each, writing that it would better predict a teacher's future success in raising students' state standardized test scores. The size of the correlation between such a system and student growth, however, was tiny. As Jay P. Greene noted after examining MET technical documents, "[A] standard deviation improvement in classroom observation or student survey results is associated with less than a .1 standard deviation increase in test score gains."[31]

Challenges in Researching Teaching

MET echoed previous research in suggesting that it is very difficult to randomize the assignment of students to teachers. In three of the districts— New York, Denver, and Memphis—compliance rates were below 50 percent, and in the city with the highest compliance rate, Dallas, only 66 percent of students remained with their randomly assigned teacher.

The dialogue around MET did not end in 2013. The 2014 MET book that Pianta co-edited with Kane and Kerri Kerr, *Designing Teacher Evaluation Systems*, includes chapters on several elements of MET that Gates largely bypassed in its previous documents, such as the positive correlations between teacher working conditions, teacher content knowledge, and student outcomes; the limits of overly control-oriented teaching strategies; and the shortcomings of the current generation of state achievement tests.[32] "The end result where we got to with MET was a much more nuanced approach" than initially suggested by the Gates Foundation's interest in human resources policies, Pianta said.[33]

FUTURE RESEARCH QUESTIONS AND THE GATES
FOUNDATION'S ROLE

The Gates Foundation continues to support research based on the MET data set, which it has released to qualified scholars. Several forthcoming projects will use the videotaped lessons to consider the relationship between specific classroom teaching strategies and student achievement. Cantrell said such scholarship could lead to the creation of new classroom observation rubrics that are more sensitive predictors of student achievement gains on state standardized tests than the current generation of rubrics.[34]

One of the most exciting pieces of upcoming research funded by the Gates Foundation addresses a key shortcoming of MET: that it was conducted in a low-stakes environment and thus did not test how teacher evaluation tied to human resources decision-making affects student achievement in environments where there is real pressure on both adults and kids to raise test scores. AIR and RAND will use Gates Foundation grants to study how human resources reforms the foundation funded at "Intensive Partnership Sites" will affect student outcomes.[35] It is so far unclear to what extent the partners—Hillsborough County Public Schools in Florida, Shelby County Schools in Tennessee, Pittsburgh Public Schools, and several charter management organizations in California—will use teacher evaluation systems to terminate employment. But if any do so, it may provide a real-world test of the policy that Kane first advocated for in his 2006 Brookings paper and pushed for again in his contribution to the 2014 MET book: laying off the bottom-performing 25 percent of first-year teachers annually.[36] Since Kane, Staiger, and Gordon first floated this idea in 2006, a developing body of research has suggested that teacher turnover itself harms student achievement, even if overall teacher quality in a school remains constant. Thus, it is fair to ask whether mass layoffs would impact school climate in a way that would depress, not enhance, student outcomes.[37]

The Gates Foundation is also funding MDRC to research teacher professional development systems in several districts, and whether they actually help teachers improve. A grant to the National Center for Research on Evaluation, Standards, and Student Testing at UCLA will support research on an effort to help teachers create more rigorous lessons aligned with the Common Core. And together with the Kenneth and Anne Griffin Foundation, the Gates Foundation is funding a small randomized controlled trial by Kane on whether in-person or videotaped classroom observations are more helpful in improving teacher effectiveness.[38]

Cantrell says he is unsure whether enough preliminary evidence exists in fields such as teacher professional development to justify Gates investing in another large-scale randomized controlled trial. Yet several of MET's investigators believe the foundation could make an important contribution by doing so. Kane suggests a study of how educational software—long a funding priority for the Gates Foundation—affects student outcomes: "What's the most effective way to use this software? Are there certain kinds of students that actually could be hurt by too much" learning via computer? He would also like to see a large-scale study of teacher preparation, comparing programs like the Relay Graduate School of Education to one-year teacher residencies such as Boston's Match Teacher Residency program and to traditional teachers' colleges. Kane wonders if "you could show that there is a program that makes first-year teachers look like third-year teachers" in terms of their impact on student achievement.[39]

Pianta, too, would like to see Gates or another foundation invest in more rigorous research on teacher preparation, and he has a particular study design in mind:

> Imagine where you might enroll a national sample of ten thousand or twenty thousand people who declare an interest in becoming a teacher. What are their initial attributes? What skills and dispositions do they bring? Then track them through experiences where they train. Observe their teaching . . . We know enough to do this. You could start immediately, asking questions like, How much do cognitive abilities matter relative to performance in the classroom? In middle school math versus kindergarten? What sort of social skills do they demonstrate early on? All these things we think are indicators. Does the amount of hours of student teaching matter? When should that be dosed? You would start getting some traction on these questions that right now are all subject to great debate. People are passionate about their stances on these issues, and yet those stances are mostly informed by folk wisdom.[40]

CRITIQUES OF MET AND FOUNDATION-FUNDED RESEARCH

There are two major critiques of MET: first, that the study's data does not support the Gates Foundation's strong preference for value-added measurement as the "privileged" tool in evaluating teachers, and second, that the very questions the Gates Foundation sought to answer limit policy makers' conceptions of how to improve student achievement.

The most prominent critique of MET was written by Jesse Rothstein and William J. Mathis, managing director of the National Education Policy Center (NEPC) at the University of Colorado-Boulder. NEPC, which published the critique, has a history of poking holes in foundation-funded research. NEPC also receives philanthropic funding from sources including the Ford Foundation, the Atlantic Philanthropies, and the two national teachers' unions.[41] Rothstein and Mathis acknowledged that MET was "a monumental undertaking" whose six-city randomized controlled design "generated an enormous amount of valuable data." Yet they highlighted several important limitations to the study. Students of teachers who participated had higher baseline math and English test scores than other students at their schools and were less likely to have special-education designations or to be English-language learners. MET was therefore limited in what it could tell practitioners about evaluating teachers with the most challenging assignments. Rothstein and Mathis demonstrated that, although MET trumpeted that high value-added scores on state tests were correlated with student growth on more rigorous exams, the correlation, at less than 0.5, was weak—as were the correlations between student surveys, classroom observations, and those more difficult tests. The modest correlations called into question the Gates Foundation's assertion that there is one single skill set, measured by test scores, associated with effective teaching. The authors wrote:

> [The] MET study makes clear . . . that different ways of evaluating teachers will yield very different rankings, that none are clearly better than the others, and that there are potentially important dimensions of effectiveness that are not captured by any of the available evaluation measures. Distinctions based on any particular measure will generally—with a great deal of measurement error—identify teachers who excel on that measure, but these teachers will often be unexceptional along other dimensions.[42]

Finally, Rothstein and Mathis pointed out that MET took place in a low-stakes environment, and thus it tells us little about how using student test scores to evaluate teachers actually changes instruction, student achievement, or children's experience of school.

Harris agrees that the Gates Foundation could have been more forthcoming in its shorter research briefs and statements to the press about the limitations of MET's methodology, particularly the way in which it is unsurprising that past value-added scores ended up being a better predictor of future value-added scores than classroom observation. "The best predictor of anything in the future is that same thing in the past. Here we're talking about teachers, but you could say that about weather. Or anything . . . They were not sufficiently cautious in explaining that major caveat. At the same time, they didn't have much of an alternative"—in that Kane and the research team needed one common yardstick by which to measure all the various teacher evaluation tools—and thus chose student growth on state standardized test scores.[43]

A simplistic critique of MET would discount the study's conclusions because the Gates Foundation plays an advocacy role on teacher evaluation. Such a critique would not be fair. "The main way bias gets reflected in think tanks and foundations is through the questions they ask, not so much through the answers," Harris continues. "If you ask the question, 'Is value-added a valid measure?' and you have the right researchers, you're going to get the same answer no matter who funds the work. But that is a particular question. Another foundation may ask a different question."[44] Indeed, an analysis of recent Spencer Foundation grants for K–12 education research demonstrates that a foundation without an advocacy agenda funds a broader range of research than do Walton, Gates, and other venture philanthropies. In 2012, Spencer funded inquiries on school discipline, the impact of arts education on high school graduation rates, how children learn biology, and the history and philosophy of education—in addition to several projects on teacher effectiveness, the current focus on the national education reform movement.[45]

Douglas Reed is an associate professor of government at Georgetown University whose research focuses on the challenges of school improvement in a decentralized, federalist political system. He believes that the convergence between foundation-funded research like MET, venture philanthropy advocacy, and the federal teacher evaluation agenda has "narrowed the public conversation" around school improvement.[46] Beyond the reach of that conversation, academics are asking a much broader range of questions about education, such as Dan Willingham or Andrew Butler's work on the cognitive science of how children learn or a new study from C. Kirabo Jackson, Rucker C. Johnson, and Claudia Persico showing that more equitable school financing produces lifelong higher incomes for students.[47]

The media, too, is largely unaware of this broader landscape of education research. When New York City schools chancellor Carmen Fariña announced in October 2014 a new set of policies meant to enhance "trust" between policy makers, administrators, teachers, students, and families, the shift was interpreted by many as a retreat from evidence-backed policies designed to improve student achievement outcomes—even though a body of research from Anthony Bryk and Barbara Schneider shows that "relational trust" is an essential component of improving student test scores.[48]

In this environment, research that does not use student testing data as a measurement tool is even less likely to get support or attention. In their paper "The Hub and the Spokes," Janelle Scott and Huriya Jabbar of the University of California, Berkeley, report on a number of research ideas that have encountered trouble winning funding from venture philanthropies, such as an effort by Teach For America to study its corps members' impact using data other than test scores.[49]

The limited premise of MET within the diverse landscape of education research is perhaps best reflected in the introduction to *Designing Teacher Evaluation Systems*, the 2014 book published to help policy makers and administrators put the study's findings into practice. It reads, "The habits of inquiry modeled by the MET project are meant to support the best use of measurement to promote effective teaching. Measures will evolve, as does our understanding of student learning needs, but the commitment to quality measurement must endure."[50]

All three major tools tested through MET—student surveys, VAM, and classroom observation rubrics—rely on giving teachers numerical ratings for their work. A larger question, which MET could not answer because of its low stakes and relatively short-term design, is whether making the measurement of teaching practice more sensitive actually improves instruction for children. History suggests reasons to be skeptical. Attempts to reform how teaching is measured date back to the early twentieth century. New York City superintendent William Maxwell was frustrated that 99.5 percent of his teachers were rated "good" on the city's good/fair/poor evaluation system. He created a new system that rated teachers from A to D based on principal observations. Principals quickly became overwhelmed by the paperwork and time the observation system required. They rushed through the motions and gave almost every teacher a B+. In 1919, the *New York Times* declared the system "a joke."[51]

Given that the typical American principal or assistant principal is untrained in complex teacher evaluation methods and supervises as many as forty teachers, new evaluation systems have often suffered the same fate. In 2012, 98 percent of Michigan and Tennessee teachers, 95 percent of Florida teachers, and 94 percent of Georgia teachers were rated effective or better using methods meant to be far more discerning.[52]

Have the state lawmakers, superintendents, and principals who create and implement these new teacher evaluation systems been swayed by the MET project's key recommendation to weigh VAM, student surveys, and classroom observation equally? No such survey of policymaker and practitioner reactions to MET exists. Yet other scholarship suggests that granular recommendations drawn from research do not tend to reach this audience, in part because practitioners feel unequipped to interpret complex and contradictory research evidence. Rather, the influence of foundations over practitioners lies primarily in foundations' access to the policy makers who create programs like Race to the Top, as well as in foundation funding for conferences and consultant positions that allow researchers to advise school districts on practice.[53]

As the history of value-added measurement since the 1990s demonstrates, foundations like Gates also create change by funding think tanks such as EdTrust, the Center for American Progress, and The New Teacher Project to "translate" complex research findings into policy language accessible to the media and to local and national lawmakers and their staffs.[54] In a study of the interplay between research, policymaking, and practice in New Orleans, state superintendent John White reported on the limited landscape of education research he is exposed to, which is mostly filtered through the venture philanthropies' focus on teacher accountability and VAM:

> I'll call Kati Haycock [of Education Trust] a lot and ask her what's the best study on this. Tim Daly [of The New Teacher Project], Anne Weisberg [of the Families and Work Institute], Andy Rotherham [of Eduwonk and Bellwether Education Partners], Tom Kane [of Harvard University and the Gates Foundation]. Those are people I call a lot and ask for particular studies, and they tend to be able to point me toward the right stop.[55]

White's comment reflects what Jeffrey Henig has called the search for a single "killer" study on any given question in education policy, from charter schools to merit pay.[56] Undoubtedly, the Gates Foundation hoped that MET would play that role for teacher evaluation. It is too soon to evaluate the project's ultimate impact, yet its complexity, small effect sizes, and its more disappointing findings—such as the suggestion that teachers of poor students receive lower ratings regardless of their own performance—suggest that its impact may never be what the foundation initially hoped for in terms of an unmitigated validation of a reform agenda built around supposedly objective measures of teacher performance.

CONCLUSION

The Gates Foundation does not conceal the fact that its research agenda is driven by its advocacy. Yet it refutes the argument that it is looking to fund safe research sure to bolster its policy investments in teacher accountability systems. Steven Cantrell says:

> There is a big difference between funding research within areas most important to your strategy and funding research where you already know the answer. The latter is a waste of time. The former is necessary if you are committed to adjusting your strategy in light of new evidence. We don't invest in research where we already know the answer. Naturally, we're hoping that the research shows positive impacts from our work. When it doesn't, we are obligated to adjust what we are doing. Either way, we're better off knowing than not.[57]

Gates's previous investment in small high schools provides an interesting test case. It largely pulled its funding from that effort after initial foundation-funded research showed disappointing impacts on student test scores. Yet, in October 2014, MDRC announced that longer-range outcomes at some of those small schools were positive. Low-income students of color who attended Gates-funded small high schools in New York City were 9 percent more likely to graduate and 8 percent more likely to enroll in college than demographically similar peers at traditional high schools.[58] Even so, the foundation continues to see school "structure" as an "insufficient" change agent, says Cantrell, adding, "I don't foresee a repeat of our past small schools investments."[59]

What will happen if the coming research on the Intensive Partnership Sites shows that the measurements of teaching practice, and accountability tied to those measures, are also insufficient levers on their own to pull to raise student test scores? Will the Gates Foundation turn away from teacher evaluation as a major interest? Could it rethink the use of student test scores as the primary measure of success? Could it develop a deeper interest in school climate and student discipline, teacher working conditions, neighborhood socioeconomic segregation, or parent-school relationships—all factors that other research, including some of the less-heralded results of the MET project, shows do have an impact on student achievement?

Those questions might seem far afield from the Gates Foundation's interests over the past decade. And yet, few could have predicted in 2000 that a foundation committed to connecting public libraries to the web would become a leader in reforming teacher work laws and school district human resources practices across the country and would fund the largest-ever randomized controlled trial in education. However, it is easier for a philanthropic organization to shift course than it is for federal or even state governments to do so. And in a highly polarized political climate, it may be many years before we again see the bipartisan consensus that led to the standards-and-accountability school reform policies of the Bush and Obama eras.

If history is any guide, complex or disappointing research findings on teacher evaluation will not lead to a quick reset of the federally and privately funded teacher accountability reforms of recent years. Rather, disappointing research results or barriers to implementation not imagined by funders and policy makers may result in those reforms simply withering on the vine—remaining official policy, but implemented cynically by frustrated principals and teachers, without a commitment to continuous improvement. Yet, if one were to check back a decade later, no-longer-trendy reforms might show unexpected promise—like what happened with the small high schools model. To avoid the hype-disillusionment cycle that can occur when philanthropy, government, and the research community focus disproportionate attention on one narrow set of reform ideas, foundations could invest in researching a broader set of potential policies for improving education—drawing from fields such as organizational sociology, cognitive psychology, and political science, in addition to economics—and could commit to evaluating change and engaging with local practitioners over longer periods of time, say, ten to fifteen years instead of one to five. Such efforts could help ensure policy coherence and maturation while engaging with a broader range of potentially transformative education scholarship.

6

The Backlash Against "Reform" Philanthropy

Michael Q. McShane and Jenn Hatfield

I ndividuals rising to great wealth and then giving that money away to improve children's education is about as American as mom and apple pie. Many of our nation's greatest industrialists and businesspeople, from Andrew Carnegie to Cornelius Vanderbilt to Thomas Jefferson to Henry Ford, have donated some or all of their fortunes to try to improve the American education system. By and large, these philanthropic efforts are remembered fondly.

Today, philanthropy in education is under attack, seemingly from across the political spectrum. A few minutes on Google turns up dozens of articles, even entire webpages, criticizing what are sometimes called the "big four" education reform foundations: the Bill & Melinda Gates Foundation, the Walton Family Foundation, The Eli and Edythe Broad Foundation, and the Laura and John Arnold Foundation. The conservative *RedState* blog blasts the headline, "Bill Gates' Reckless Meddling with US Education Through Common Core."[1] *The Daily Kos*, a liberal blog, lets its readers know "What Bill Gates Really Thinks of the Common Core State Standards."[2] The Moyers & Company website asks, "Why Are Walmart Billionaires Bankrolling Phony School 'Reform' in LA?"[3]

Where is this animosity coming from? Is this a new phenomenon? Is this the ranting of a vocal minority, or have these beliefs trickled into the mainstream? These are the questions we hope to answer in this chapter.

To do so, we will first take a historical look at criticism of philanthropic efforts in education and then attempt to quantify media coverage (and particularly the negative media coverage) of prominent education reform-promoting foundations. Next, we will try to parse the political origins of the criticism: Is criticism bipartisan? Does it exist only at the poles of the political spectrum? Finally, we will allow critics to tell their story. Why do they oppose these philanthropies?

To give away the ending, while criticism of philanthropies is clearly not new, it has been increasing, both in absolute terms and in terms of the proportion of media coverage devoted to philanthropy in education. Given the vim and vigor of opponents, it doesn't seem to be going away any time soon. But before we get there, let's look at some history.

IS THIS NEW?

Philanthropic efforts in education have been criticized for many years. When the Rosenwald Fund built thousands of schools for African Americans across the South in the 1920s and 1930s, individual white communities tried, and largely failed, to stop them. In Warren County, Mississippi, for example, the Ku Klux Klan unsuccessfully sought a court injunction to block construction of new schools.[4] In 1968, the Ford Foundation's involvement in an experiment in local control fanned racial tensions in the Ocean Hill-Brownsville community of New York City. When the predominately African American board moved to fire a white, Jewish, unionized teacher, racial tensions boiled over and triggered a teachers' strike that lasted for several months.[5] When the Annenberg Challenge was launched in 1995 to give $500 million to a set of urban public school districts, critics like Jeanne Allen of the Center for Education Reform and Checker Finn, then of Vanderbilt and the Hudson Institute, voiced concerns that the effort was pouring money into an ineffective system.[6]

But many of these criticisms were ad hoc and fleeting. Rick Hess demonstrated this phenomenon in a 2005 article in *Philanthropy* magazine.[7] Hess and a team of researchers used Lexis-Nexis to find every mention of five major education-related philanthropies of that time (the Annenberg Challenge, The Broad Foundation, the Gates Foundation, the Milken Family Foundation, and the Walton Family Foundation) in major national media from 1995 to 2005. They coded the first forty-six articles, sorted by relevance, about the Annenberg Challenge and the first twenty-five articles about the rest of the foundations based on whether they were primarily positive, primarily negative, balanced, or primarily factual. Of the 146 articles they coded, only five (a little more than 3 percent) were critical. Sixty-five were positive, meaning that for every negative account of a philanthropy's actions, there were thirteen positive ones.

We wanted to bring Hess's analysis to the present and add our own twist to it. As a quick measure, we first used Lexis-Nexis to search all American news outlets for the names of the "big four" education reform foundations (Gates, Walton, Broad, and Arnold) paired with the term "education" from 2000 through 2013. Although this search excludes blogs and some online outlets, it is an accurate look into the types of publications that most Americans use to get their news. Since 2000, there has been a substantial increase in the amount of coverage of philanthropies engaged in education reform, as shown in figure 6.1.

In 2000, there were 368 mentions in total of the "big four" education reform foundations. These mentions were dominated almost entirely by the Gates Foundation, with 342, while the Walton Foundation had 6 and The Broad Foundation had 19. By 2013, the total number of mentions had risen to 3,146. While Gates was still far and away the most covered foundation, with 2,625 mentions, the Walton Foundation had ticked up to 235 mentions, the Broad Foundation had risen to 218 mentions, and the Arnold Foundation (which got no coverage in 2000 because it didn't exist yet) got 68 mentions, more than Walton and Broad combined in 2000.

Criticism has also seen an uptick. For a rough estimate, we decided to pair our first search terms with words that would clearly indicate extreme criticism: "plot," "scheme," "destroy," "subvert," and "undermine." The results, displayed as a proportion of total mentions, are shown in figure 6.2.

Starting from a base of 3.5 percent of all articles in 2000, the percentage of articles with clearly negative keywords almost doubled, to 6.2 percent in

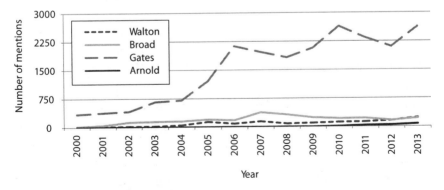

FIGURE 6.1 All mentions of "big four" foundations paired with "education," American print news outlets, 2000–2013

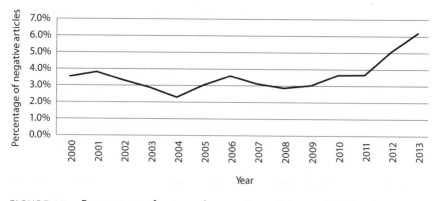

FIGURE 6.2   Percentage of extremely negative articles on "big four" foundations, 2000–2013

2013. But, as figure 6.1 shows, because there were substantially more articles written about these four foundations in 2013, in real terms this represents fifteen times more negative articles than were written in the year 2000.

To dig deeper into the degree to which opposition has seeped into the public consciousness, we again used Lexis-Nexis to search for all articles on the "big four" and "education," but this time we read a sample of articles to determine their tone—positive, neutral, or negative. We sampled 1 percent of the articles on the Gates Foundation and education (214 articles), 2 percent of the articles on the Broad and Walton Foundations and education (52 and 26 articles, respectively), and 10 percent of the articles on the Arnold Foundation and education (17 articles). We did a Power Search for "foundation name" and "education" from 2000 to 2013 and sorted the results by relevance.

After reading each article, we coded its tone on a 1–5 scale, on which 1 was overwhelmingly negative, 2 was negative, 3 was neutral, 4 was positive, and 5 was overwhelmingly positive. By way of example, "The Broad Foundation Infiltrates the Worcester Public Schools" from the March 2011 *Worcester Magazine* received a score of 1. It accuses The Broad Foundation of "pushing a Trojan horse" in the form of a superintendent trained in the Broad Superintendents Academy.[8] An example of an article rated 2 would be *Education Week*'s May 2013 article "Rifts Deepen over Direction of Ed Policy in US," which mentions the Walton Family Foundation and Gates Foundation. The article lists numerous complaints against both foundations, but other pro-reform voices are given space to respond.[9] Articles rated 3, like the *Houston Business Journal's* June 2012 article "Laura and John Arnold Foundation Launch Education Database," simply list the facts about the activities of a particular foundation without offering any judgment one way or the other.[10] "Gates Grants Aim to Help Low-Income Students Finish College" from the *New York Times* in December 2008 is an example of an article rated as a 4. It uncritically touts the benefits of a particular proposal—in this case, the Gates Foundation's funding of an array of nonprofits geared towards college persistence.[11] When it comes to overwhelmingly positive, the *Seattle Times'* October 2000 article "$2 Million Goes to Seattle Schools" is a prime example. It includes the following quotation from Rodney Wheeler of the Alliance for Education: "The impact of [Gates's] giving is incredible. It's always a big gulp. It's like Mount Rainier. It overwhelms you with its beauty and its immenseness."[12]

On average, articles trended slightly positive. The average score for all 309 articles was 3.28. As figure 6.3 shows, while the modal article coding value was 3, indicating a neutral article, the next-highest was 4, meaning that the foundation was discussed positively.

Although this coding strategy uncovered more positive than negative articles, it also identified a higher proportion of negative articles than our previous Lexis-Nexis search. We coded 41 of 309 articles as a 1 or 2, for a total of 13.2 percent of all articles. This increase is not surprising, given that our previous Lexis-Nexis search was designed to capture only the most extreme terms.

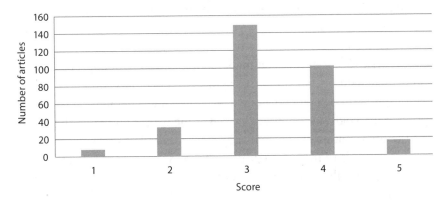

FIGURE 6.3   Frequency distribution of article coding

WHERE IS CRITICISM COMING FROM?

A cursory Google search (like the one we conducted to write the second paragraph of this chapter) shows criticism from across the political spectrum. Liberals appear to take issue with the Walton Family Foundation's support of school choice, the Arnold Foundation's support of pension reform, and The Broad Foundation's preparation of new school leaders who embrace data-driven decision making, among other issues. It is hard to overstate conservatives' visceral reaction against the Gates Foundation's support of the Common Core. In the middle, there appears to be a group of critics who generally fear an erosion of democracy by moneyed interests and are less than enthused when they feel that a small number of wealthy philanthropists are dictating policy for their children's schools. A second group of moderate critics feels that schools are generally doing fine and don't see why philanthropists should be involved in their children's education at all. It looks like philanthropists are being attacked from all sides.

But these are just perceptions, impressions we formed as we observed and participated in education reform debates. We also sought to try and quantify these criticisms to see if our gut reactions were accurate.

To ascertain political leanings, we dug deeper into the forty-one negative articles in our sample. Was criticism really across the board, or was it concentrated in particular parts of the political spectrum? To answer this question, we coded the political leanings of the articles and analyzed the results.

Though we admit this is an inherently subjective process, we tried our best to be fair in how articles were coded. To arrive at a determination, we used a two-step process. First, we evaluated whether the article appeared to have an ideological leaning by the way it argued against the foundation or enterprise. If, for example, it made arguments about inappropriate federal involvement or state and local rights, we coded it as conservative. If it made arguments referencing equity, we coded it as liberal. If there was no apparent ideological leaning, we looked at the people quoted in the article and the organizations for which they worked. If all of those quoted were on the same side of the ideological spectrum, we concluded that the criticism was primarily from that side. Otherwise, we concluded that the article was neutral.

We identified a leftward slant in three of the articles, a rightward slant in eighteen, and a neutral presentation of criticism in twenty. Figure 6.4 has the

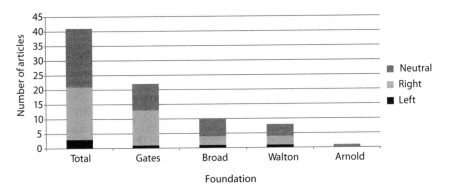

FIGURE 6.4   Criticism by political leaning

total breakdown, as well as the findings disaggregated by foundation. Criticism of the Gates Foundation overwhelmingly came from the right side of the political spectrum, with twelve articles from the conservative perspective compared with only one from the liberal and nine from the neutral perspective. For the other three foundations, criticism was more likely to be from neutral commentators, though both the Walton and Broad Foundations saw three criticisms from the conservative perspective.

FROM THE HORSE'S MOUTH

To round out our findings, we thought it would be helpful to identify some key voices from different points on the political spectrum and interview them about their thoughts on educational philanthropy. To this end, we interviewed six prominent critics. From the political left, we spoke with Diane Ravitch, prominent blogger, NYU professor, and former assistant secretary of education; Leonie Haimson, founder of Class Size Matters and Parents Across America; and Mark Naison, a professor at Fordham University and cofounder of the Badass Teachers Association. Although voices from the middle of the political spectrum proved slightly harder to find (by their very nature, they are less likely to write the attention-grabbing articles that inject their personality into the public consciousness), we were able to speak with teacher and writer Michael Mazenko, who self-identifies as a "Colorado moderate." Finally, we spoke with two prominent conservative commentators, Joy Pullmann of *The Federalist* and the Heartland Institute and Emmett McGroarty of the American Principles Project.

To draw together their at-times disparate opinions, we have organized their responses by the classic journalists' questions. Critics oppose education philanthropy because of *what* philanthropists are pushing, *who* is pushing it, *why* they are pushing it, and *how* they are pushing it.

The *What*

The most obvious and straightforward explanation for the pushback against philanthropy in education is that it often supports policies that various constituencies oppose. Critics of particular policies then move readily and opportunistically to criticize the philanthropic organization that supports those policies. If that criticism can undercut the financial or political backing of the program, it can be a fruitful strategy for the opposition.

Our interviews confirmed that this is a strong explanation for much of the current pushback against philanthropy. Criticism of the *what* of philanthropy generally stemmed either from the belief that research did not support a particular intervention or from a personal philosophy of education that contradicted a particular reform strategy.

It is helpful to look at each policy in turn.

School Choice and "Privatization." Our interviewees see all four major foundations as advocates for some form of school choice, primarily charter schools. In particular, the Walton Family Foundation has been associated with promoting private school choice—that is, voucher and tuition tax credit scholarship programs that allow tax dollars to flow into private schools. Several opponents of philanthropy decried this "privatization" of public schooling.

In general, opposition to the school choice policy agenda was voiced by our interviewees on the political left. In contrast, those on the political right generally supported school choice and did not have a problem with any of the foundations that advocate for more charter schools, provide financial assistance to charter or private schools, or are seen as promoting private school choice.

Mark Naison criticizes Walton's support of charter schools and Teach for America's model because he considers them both "highly problematic in their long-term effects on inner-city communities." More specifically, Naison argues, given the high rates of mobility within the low-income population, students need established, stable schools and trained teachers.

Leonie Haimson also objects to Walton and other foundations' support of charter schools because she believes that charter schools are often created against parents' wishes (despite public officials' claims to the contrary). She calls the "Walton-supported law" in New York that provides free space for charter schools at the city's expense "probably the most egregious charter law in the entire nation . . . It has to do with power and [powerful people] getting their way, not good governance, political philosophy, ethics, or education reform."

Diane Ravitch criticizes school choice because she sees it as a corporate intrusion into public schooling. The Walton Foundation is one of her biggest targets because of its sustained efforts to promote charter schooling in Dallas and elsewhere, but she argues that nearly every single foundation (including each of the four major ones) wholeheartedly supports school choice. According to Ravitch, foundations' failure to question whether there might be negative effects of charters could result in a fully privatized education system in the near future—an outcome she would consider tragic. Ravitch decries this as "not the America I grew up in, and this is not the America I want. I'm on the side of Main Street, not Wall Street."

"Anti-Teacher" Policies. Among the four foundations, the Laura and John Arnold Foundation is most strongly associated with supporting reform to public-sector pensions. Like school choice, this tended to be something that our interviewees from the political left vocally opposed. By and large, they saw it as a benefit cut for teachers during a time when our nation should do everything it can to attract the best and brightest into education and remunerate them at a level that respects their contributions to society. Similarly, the political left often sees teacher evaluation as a misguided policy that threatens teachers' livelihoods by holding them responsible for student test scores without accounting for other factors affecting those scores—including poverty. Leonie Haimson argues that philanthropists "colluding with President Obama and [Secretary of Education] Arne Duncan" created a teacher evaluation system where the weight given to test scores is "a number they drew out of a hat" but will cost many teachers their jobs. Haimson sees the Department of Education's moratorium on using test scores to evaluate teachers as a hypocritical about-face—and as further evidence that teacher evaluation, as currently construed, has serious problems and should not be used to determine whether teachers should keep their jobs.

Standardized Testing. All of our respondents had some form of concern about standardized testing. Interestingly, their criticisms struck a common chord. They believed that tests were not an accurate measurement of every-thing they want children to know, and that the more reliant accountability systems are on tests, the more homogenized education will become. Those on the political right would prefer to have parents dictate the content of their children's education with direct school choice, while those on the left would prefer to entrust teachers and local school boards to safeguard the values of their community.

Mark Naison's opposition to test-based school and teacher accountabil-ity, and the foundations that support its development, began when schools around Fordham in which he had been volunteering pushed out his com-munity history lessons to maximize the time available to prepare for read-ing and math standardized tests. He argues that his classes offered the type of enrichment activities available to the children of the elites who make education policy. Shouldn't low-income students have access to them as well? Instead, what those students are getting is "teachers being so terrified of their schools closing that all they do is test prep. Kids are being made to hate school, and the teachers leave as fast as they can. I think we've done something very destructive."

The Common Core. As with standardized testing, every one of our respon-dents expressed criticism of the Common Core State Standards. In fact, it was really the Common Core that brought the right flank of journalists and activists into the fight against education philanthropy and helped the pushback swell to its current levels. Mark Naison, himself a liberal, credited protests by conservative parents for bringing Common Core opposition to the mainstream (the "'big bang' moment") and getting people to listen to concerns from those on both sides of the aisle.

Speaking about the Common Core, Emmett McGroarty says, "What we have is a product of demonstrably low quality. I mean, it's appallingly low quality. And parents understand that it's low quality . . . I think the lesson for these funders is that they can no longer decide on their own what should be taught. There really has to be true debate and true notice about these products." Naison agrees, arguing that teachers are angry because they feel "forced to implement policies that they [think are] professional malpractice."

Leonie Haimson, a liberal, has concerns similar to those of the conser-vative McGroarty. She contends that the Gates Foundation, assuming that software can be a "magic bullet" solution to fix education, "wants one bunch of stuff for kids to learn and one bunch of tests." But, she said, "I think that this whole thing [the Common Core and its associated tests] is going to crumble because the policies are wrong."

The *Who*

Another strand of pushback against education philanthropy concerns the individuals at the helm. On both sides of the political spectrum, Leonie Haimson claims, there is opposition to a centralized philanthropic entity that pushes for a single, rigid, potentially harmful type of education and manages to overpower the public voice by virtue of its wealth. Critics argue that the founders, from Bill Gates to John Arnold to Eli Broad to the Walton family, either do not know what is best for America's children or push policies that they would never accept for their own children.

Michael Mazenko, a moderate, told us that the composition of the groups pushing reforms excludes the very people who would know most about what schools need to improve—teachers and school leaders: "There is just this bubble of people [business leaders and entrepreneurs] who talk about education as if they are the deciding factor." According to Mazenko, these people erroneously believe that they are reform experts simply by virtue of having gone to school themselves or having kids in the school system. He was appalled that, in a recent article he read, a superintendent said he was "happy to be invited" to a meeting of education reformers; in his view, superintendents, because of their direct experience and expertise, should expect to be invited to such affairs and that it is the others who should be thankful to be asked. (Mark Naison has a similar viewpoint. He contends that foundations "have no respect for teachers, no real confidence that their voice should matter.")

The result, according to Mazenko, is that the reform movement fundamentally misunderstands the issues of contemporary school systems, to the point that "[it] begs the question of whether public education is, in fact, failing." He thinks that the answer to that question is no. The school where he teaches is doing great. Families are satisfied. Students are going on to top colleges. Although the reform agenda might fit a small number of urban, low-performing schools, he argues, the nationwide alarmist rhetoric obscures a generally well-functioning school system. As a result, "many of these philanthropic efforts are based on the myth that schools are failing" and thus push solutions that are often unhelpful or even actively harmful.

Critics also argue that reformers are pushing solutions that are "good for thee but not for me." Leonie Haimson's qualms about the Gates Foundation were sparked by its push for small schools in New York City, because in her estimation the small schools movement also ramped up class sizes. She sees hypocrisy: people of means, including those who who have created these prominent foundations, look for schools with small classes for their own children but push reforms that eliminate small classes for thousands of other students, often those without means.

Haimson also sees hypocrisy in a raft of other policies. Schools attended by the children of elites don't use formulaic teacher evaluation systems based on standardized test scores. They don't try to replace teachers with computers. They don't generally hire teachers with only a few weeks or months of training, as is the case with Teach for America. Elites want their kids attending excellent neighborhood schools, not "unproven charter schools." In short, she argued, foundations are all too comfortable "experimenting" with the education of poor children, but they would never allow it with their own children.

Diane Ravitch makes a similar case against the John and Laura Arnold Foundation's push for public-sector pension reform: "John Arnold is a billionaire. He is never going to have to try and live on a teacher's pension." With the Gates Foundation, the push for test-based accountability has created a situation where "real, living people are being hurt," but the foundation is not reconsidering its position—and Bill Gates doesn't feel the repercussions personally.

The *Why*

None of the interviewees suspected the foundations of malign motives. Instead, critics on both the right and left saw the philanthropies as being fundamentally wrongheaded in their assessment of the problems that need to be solved, and, as a result, in their assessment of what interventions will succeed. Good intentions, according to the critics, don't make wrongheadedness any less damaging. Our interviewees believed that both the arguments underpinning the push for education reform and the arguments for particular reforms—the *why* of education philanthropy—are problematic.

Joy Pullmann sees the Common Core as a solution in search of a problem. By misapprehending the causes of underperformance in the American education system (one of which, she contends, is too much centralization), the Gates Foundation advocated for a solution that she believes is ultimately harmful to the American education system. Mark Naison sees urban communities as suffering from instability driven by poverty, so advocating for charter schools or Teach for America—which, he argues, will only promote greater organizational or personal turnover—is exactly the wrong solution. "Equity and global competitiveness is what mom and apple pie were fifty years ago," he told us. They are the feel-good pieces of rhetoric that philanthropists and the US Department of Education use to curry public favor for new policies.

But, beyond simple misapprehension, several of our interviewees argued that philanthropies are actively attempting to remake America in harmful ways. Not out of malice, it should be noted, but the result is harmful nonetheless. Diane Ravitch argues that the Walton Family Foundation's reform agenda is "built on what Walmart does. Low-wage workers, billionaire owners. When they come to town, Main Street dies." Haimson sees the Gates Foundation's foray into the InBloom data warehouse and its advocacy for computer-based instruction as pushing for an impersonal system that "plugs kids in" and "gets rid of teachers." McGroarty commented that, although it's too broad to say that everyone involved in the Common Core was acting maliciously, anyone who pushed for the Common Core to be "shoved in . . . before people really realized what was happening" was, "at the very least, reckless . . . I think it was a really arrogant decision by philanthropies."

It is also important to note that, across the board, our interviewees did not suspect conspiracies. While some corners of the blogosphere cast aspersions about the possible profit motives of Microsoft or Walmart, our interviewees said, on multiple occasions and regarding multiple foundation leaders, that they "mean well." They just think they're wrong.

The *How*

One common thread in almost all of our interviews was a belief that large philanthropies subvert the democratic process. In our estimation, although the *what* of the reforms the foundations advocate for is the strongest driver of pushback, *how* foundations—particularly the Gates Foundation—advance their agendas might be number two.

Emmett McGroarty outlined how policy should be made: "Laws are authored by the legislature and implemented by the executive in a public process." Although McGroarty is a conservative, we don't imagine any of our liberal interviewees would disagree with this formulation. But, McGroarty argues, this is not the way the Common Core came about; instead, it was created through "private entities and a private process" in which legislators did not receive necessary notice, feedback was limited to a nonrepresentative sample of individuals, and meetings were conducted outside the scope of Freedom of Information Act requests. This caused the Common Core to lose the "guarantors of quality" that both democracy and the free market create, as both open participation and open competition can serve to weed out bad ideas and advance better ones. Mark Naison went so far as to call the $200 million he estimated the Gates Foundation fed into organizations like the National Governors Association, teachers' unions, and the National PTA an "unprecedented" effort, a "subversion of the democratic process," a "fait accompli," and a "coup d'état."

Respondents from both the left and right took a populist tone, decrying what they see as the back-scratching relationships foundations have created with political and business leaders. Leonie Haimson declared it a conflict of interest for public officials, and therefore a threat to the democratic process. Joy Pullmann particularly took issue with the hand-in-glove relationship between the Gates Foundation, the Common Core effort, and testing organizations like the College Board and ACT, who are, in her mind, creating a testing monopoly. Another big concern for Pullmann was the mixing of the public and private spheres that occurs when philanthropists use private funds to carry out public functions: "It's big business and big philanthropy colluding behind closed doors. They are circumventing my voice with their money. I have no problem with them advocating in the public sphere, but they're doing more than that. They're literally writing policy." In a sentiment echoed by many from the political left, she argues, "Just because you have money doesn't mean you should have more power."

Naison goes further, arguing that philanthropists have no business being in the political arena. He argues that "[t]here's supposed to be a kind of disinterested, apolitical dimension to philanthropy," which makes the actions of the four major foundations more insidious than other wealthy people who have sought political influence in the past (e.g., through professional organizations like the National Association of Manufacturers or the Chamber of Commerce). But, according to Naison, Gates and others eventually figured out that they could make the biggest impact in the shortest amount of time through targeted giving, and "[w]hen you discover you have power, there's a great temptation to use it."

Several interviewees also lamented what they thought was a pernicious effect of foundations on research. Diane Ravitch mentioned a "chilling" effect from the Gates Foundation. She believes that researchers are worried about losing funding, so they do not want to say anything that contradicts the Gates Foundation's company line. And, she argues, the company line is no longer established through rigorous research. In the past, philanthropies created pilot programs like Head Start, then either reevaluated their hypotheses or sought federal funding depending on the outcome of the pilot. But now, according to Ravitch, the major foundations know exactly what they want to be done, have the money (and thus the power) to impose their wishes on others, and make those things happen without much questioning or pushback from those around them. Instead of soliciting ideas, like the Annenberg Challenge did, these foundations tell organizations or districts what to do with the money they propose to hand out—and if they cannot get a recipient to carry out their wishes, they often create new organizations to do it. "We've gone from a varied menu of options for spending philanthropic contributions to a fixed set of courses," Ravitch said. "If you don't eat the food available, you don't eat anything."

MAKING SENSE OF IT ALL

To answer a question posed early in this chapter, it appears that criticism of philanthropy in education is not merely the ranting of a vocal minority. Criticism has trickled into the mainstream national consciousness, and it only appears to be increasing. Though far from dominating discussion of philanthropy (we classified between 6 and 13 percent of news stories about these organizations as critical), it is certainly a notable presence.

Why is this happening? After reviewing articles written about philanthropy in education reform as well as talking to critics themselves, we think we're seeing more and different reactions to education philanthropy because the nature of education philanthropy itself is changing. Generally speaking, even "controversial" efforts in the past were aimed at simply providing a good (like a school) to an underserved community (though the Ford Foundation's foray into promoting local control would be a notable exception to this). Although some folks might have taken issue with Andrew Carnegie, the founder of the Carnegie Corporation of New York, funding a library on a particular street corner, we can find no evidence that there was widespread belief that he should not have spent his considerable fortune building libraries.

Philanthropy today is about changing policy and influencing politics. Rather than trying to create schools that teach to the Common Core State Standards, the Gates Foundation funded a series of nonprofit organizations across the country to promote statewide adoption of the standards for exist-ing schools. The decision was not made at the school or community level. It was generally made by state boards of education that few people in those states actively monitor. All told, forty-five states and the District of Columbia, which educate more than forty million children in total, chose to adopt the standards (though several states have since chosen to abandon the effort).

This means that philanthropists, rather than trying to simply add new dollars into a system, are trying to use their money to redirect the flow of tax dollars. Interestingly, this appears to be directly out of the playbook pro-posed by fellow contributor to this volume Jay P. Greene, who wrote in his chapter "Buckets into the Sea" in 2005's *With the Best of Intentions* that if philanthropic organizations wanted to meaningfully effect change and not simply tinker around the edges, they would need to redirect public dollars, not just add their own on top of existing programs.[13] While perhaps mak-ing philanthropies more effective at reaching their policy goals, redirection means that dollars that previously went to a certain set of schools and pro-grams, and to the individuals who worked in those schools and programs, are now headed to a different set of schools and programs and a different set of workers. That is going to ruffle some feathers.

At the same time philanthropy is changing, the landscape of politics and society is changing as well. With groups like Occupy Wall Street decrying the space between the 99 percent and the 1 percent, philanthropists, who are firmly ensconced in the top 0.01 percent of American wealth, are seen less as bighearted do-gooders and more like corporate raiders trying to save their image or, at worst, plutocrats trying to subvert American democracy. There is much grist for opponents' mill.

CONCLUSION

Educational philanthropy is not going away, nor should it. From Carnegie's libraries to the Rosenwald Schools to the thousands of charter schools that were able to open in traditionally underserved areas with start-up grants from the Gates or Walton Foundations, philanthropy has played a role in expanding educational opportunity in America for a very long time. With some recentering, and with some understanding of the concerns of its crit-ics, it can orient itself toward even greater success.

Education reform is a long game. Opponents of reform appear to under-stand this. As Mark Naison put it, "This is the most uphill battle that I've been in since the Vietnam War. My position is that school reform is the most bipartisan, damaging policy since the Vietnam War, and it's going to take as long as the Vietnam War to turn it around. So twelve years. Ten, twelve, fifteen years." If opponents are ready for fifteen years of opposition, foundations should prepare themselves for at least fifteen years of advocacy. The US education system is enormous and has become the way that it is over a very long period of time, so any effort to change it will occur in fits and starts over a long period of time. The sooner philanthropists internalize this, the better.

The billionaires at the helm of these major foundations made their money by being aggressive businesspeople. Eli Broad's autobiography is called *The Art of Being Unreasonable* for a reason. He, like Bill Gates and John Arnold, was a risk taker, deal maker, and relentless workhorse. Those are great skills to have if you want to make yourself a boatload of money. But the skill set that can give you the financial resources to become a major philanthropist is not necessarily the same as the one that makes you a successful philanthropist.

Political science would define the issue of the modern educational philanthropist as a classic principal-agent problem. The principal (the philanthropist) has something that he wants school teachers and school leaders (the agents) to do. However, the philanthropist actually has very little leverage over the people on the ground working to implement his vision. As the leader of a company, he can hire managers to directly control what those at the ground level do. If one of the agents doesn't buy into the program, he can fire him. This is not so with schools. Teachers do not answer to Bill Gates or Eli Broad. At best, philanthropists can incentivize, cajole, or convince teachers and school leaders to do what they want them to do. But control is weak.

As a result, a philanthropist has to spend a considerable amount of time and energy convincing teachers and school leaders, as well as parents and community members, that the policies the philanthropist wants are in their best interest. This goes deeper than "grasstops" political advocacy, and it goes deeper than laying out the plan in a boardroom meeting and hoping that people come around to the idea. As Emmett McGroarty put it, "Hopefully, [the backlash against the Common Core] will be a lesson learned on the charitable giving side . . . Hopefully, they'll learn that they really have to respect the people, they really have to try not to shove things into the states and schools so quickly that all guarantees of quality are lost, and that it's not shoved in so quickly that people don't have the opportunity to debate them." This means deep, long-term engagement with the people who will feel the effects of education reform, in a way that is fundamentally different from how philanthropists have recently gone about their business.

What's so confounding about this approach is that philanthropists don't have to be impatient. When they were CEOs, they were in trouble if they didn't post profits quarter after quarter. But it's their money now—they can go at whatever speed they want. They should see this as an opportunity to do the deep engagement work necessary to promote their agenda and to have the open and transparent process they need to have for their work to be successful.

Through transparency, respect for democracy, and serious, long-term engagement with the communities they are trying to help, philanthropists can be more successful in reaching their goals. If they can get communities and the agents of change to buy into the program, the likelihood of it actually doing good for students increases dramatically. It will take patience, humility, and strategy. But it appears possible, and for philanthropists' sake, worth it.

7

A Critique of Contemporary Edu-Giving

Larry Cuban

Historians have richly documented both the praise and criticism that philanthropists have received since the establishment of the Russell Sage Foundation, the Carnegie Corporation, and the Rockefeller Foundation in the late nineteenth and early twentieth centuries. Although praise was far more common than criticism, critics have raised several issues with philanthropy over many decades.[1]

Here is US Senator Frank Walsh in 1915:

> [I] challenge the wisdom of giving public sanction and approval to the spending of a huge fortune thru [sic] . . . philanthropies . . . The huge philanthropic trusts, known as foundations, appear to be a menace to the welfare of society.[2]

In 1973, conservative scholar Jeffrey Hart said:

> [T]ax-free foundations represent a conspicuous form of irresponsible power.[3]

And historian of education Diane Ravitch wrote in 2010:

> [T]he Gates, Walton, and Broad Foundations . . . set the policy agenda not only for school districts, but also for states and even the US Department of Education . . . There is something fundamentally antidemocratic about relinquishing control of the public education policy agenda to private foundations run by society's wealthiest people.[4]

In the past decade, however, that disapproval has reached a deafening decibel range. The pervasiveness and loudness of the dissatisfaction invites an analysis of these criticisms while calling attention to one question missing from faulting donors engaged in reforming public schools.

In this chapter, I will analyze three current criticisms: first, that philanthropists and business and civic leaders seek the privatization of public schools; next, that donors have muffled public and professional voices; and finally, that philanthropists are not held responsible for their mistakes. After a brief analysis of these criticisms, I will ask a question that has too often gone unasked by either critics or self-aware donors: *Why have major donors such as Broad, Walton, and Gates given (and continue to give) large sums of money to programs to improve academic performance in the face of mediocre results in altering classroom teaching practices and student learning?* The rest of the chapter will answer this neglected question.

THREE PREVAILING CRITICISMS OF TODAY'S EDUCATIONAL PHILANTHROPY

Philanthropists and Business and Civic Leaders Seek the Privatization of Public Schools

Since the 1983 report *A Nation at Risk*, the logic of reform spurred by business and civic leaders and endorsed by major donors is that failing public schools have substantially weakened the United States economically. The report energized civic, business, donor, and educational leaders to press public schools to fundamentally change their graduation requirements, curriculum standards, testing, and other structures.

Over the past three decades, these policy and donor leaders cobbled together reform portfolios of innovations such as vouchers, charter schools, high academic standards, testing, and rule-driven accountability. Critics of this strategy have argued that such ventures—tossed together helter-skelter and supported by sketchy evidence—sought to privatize public schools through expanded parental choice of public schools and instilling market competition in a quasi-monopolistic institution. They cite the growth of for-profit companies taking over low-performing public schools (for example, K12 Inc., Edison Learning, Inc.), nonprofit charter organizations (for example, KIPP, Aspire, Green Dot) expanding their reach, and No Child Left Behind requiring districts with persistently low-performing schools to outsource educational services to private companies.[5]

Critics have called those shaping these changes *corporate reformers*. From the center and left of the political spectrum, denunciations have poured over them for destroying public schools.[6]

I have tried to avoid using *corporate reformers* and other such terms because, in my opinion, they imply absolute certainty about reformers' motives, smell of conspiratorial decision making, ignore historical patterns of private-public collaboration, and, most compellingly, overlook the embrace of market-driven capitalism and business practices that have swept across all US institutions in recent decades. Moreover, much of the back-and-forth about who is and who is not a corporate reformer takes the form of venomous personal attacks. I am allergic to these implications and ad hominem language because they neglect an obvious historical pattern: close linkages between public schooling and commerce have informed American society for decades because they have both been (and are) deeply anchored in democratic capitalism.[7]

For one thing, while the current generation of civic and business leaders, donors, and elected federal officials—policy elites—believes in the crucial importance of schooling spurring economic growth and market forces advancing equal opportunity and democracy, similarities in beliefs hardly equal a concerted effort to privatize public schools. Contemporary critics have converted business involvement in schools, a tradition stretching back well over a century, into a motive to privatize as many public schools as possible.[8]

The charge that a profit motive drives current efforts to privatize schools (for example, testing and test-writing organizations, technology companies, for-profit charter schools) also rings hollow, given that much transacted business is made public and foundation officials and CEOs are shy of negative publicity. Furthermore, current critics have forgotten a history of failures of for-profit companies running public schools. Few of them remember the collapse of contracting-for-performance in Texarkana, Arkansas, in the 1960s, the belly flop that Education Alternatives Inc. (EAI) took in the Baltimore public schools in the 1990s, or the way Edison Inc. fled the Philadelphia schools a decade ago.[9]

Finally, critics paint the current "corporate" reform agenda as privatizing the entire nation's public schools—almost 14,000 school districts with nearly 100,000 schools and over 3 million teachers housing about 50 million students in 2012. Yet the constant refrain that US schools in general have failed and need to be transformed trips over the obvious fact that nearly all parental choice reforms focus not on suburban, exurban, or rural districts, but on urban schools with low-income minority students, a fraction of the US student population.[10]

For these reasons, I have concluded that the common charge leveled by critics about a closely tied coalition of corporate reformers—CEOs, hedge fund managers, philanthropists, civic leaders, and similarly situated wealthy people—seeking to convert public schools into private ones is hyperbolic.[11]

Donors Have Muffled Public and Professional Voices

Critics point to a two-pronged approach that Gates, Walton, Broad, and other foundations have used to push their market-friendly reform agenda forward: making substantial grants to programs, and creating advocacy organizations to shape policies consistent with their reform agenda, such as centralizing educational authority. Donors, for example, have endorsed mayoral control in cities, state laws that expanded school choice, and parent trigger laws that, in effect, stripped local school boards of their authority to make decisions, thereby shrinking public participation in educational affairs and diminishing teacher and principal professional judgment.[12]

Consider donor support for mayoral control of urban public schools. Installing charter schools, new curricular standards, and changes in teacher evaluation becomes easier when school authority resides in the mayor's appointed superintendent rather than an independent school board. Instead of boards squabbling over members' questions and trying to control raucous community hearings, decisions can be reached efficiently in a school chief's office.

I do not suggest that educational philanthropists caused centralized policymaking or eroded faith in professional educators' judgment. Both these trends had begun in the mid-1960s with the Elementary and Secondary Education Act underwriting federal and state actions. I do suggest, however, that "muscular philanthropy" has further consolidated policy authority at local, state, and federal levels, eroding citizen participation in governing schools and practitioner involvement in instructional-based policies even further.[13]

Donors have also helped state and district officials compete for federal Race to the Top (RTTT) funds by bankrolling organizations aiding administrators in applying for funds and filling posts in the US Department of Education with former foundation officials. Furthermore, state legislation complying with RTTT regulations allowed more charter schools, called for evaluating teachers on the basis of student test scores, and adopted Common Core State Standards, leaving little room for local school boards to act on or hear practitioner voices.[14]

Centralized governing of schools over the past three decades has been done not only in the name of increased efficiency, but also in the name of egalitarian outcomes. Many foundation and corporate executives share a deep concern for those who are educationally disadvantaged; they have pushed for expanded parental choice of schools, curriculum and testing mandates, and accountability rules.

The sum total of these public and private ventures has meant that big donors have not only set the reform agenda, but also championed laws that have diminished public participation and professionals' judgment in significant decisions.[15]

I doubt that foundation leaders intended to centralize school decision making and deprive local policy makers, professionals, and citizens of their voices. Nonetheless, these unintended consequences unfolded over the past thirty years, so I do agree with the second criticism.

Philanthropists Are Not Held Responsible for Their Mistakes

Consolidating school governance has led to increased federal and state accountability rules. But no such rules apply for donors. Under the law, donors have no accountability for mistakes. They are beyond the reach of being fired or voted out of office. They have no responsibility to districts, individual schools, teachers, students, or parents for hopes raised and dashed.

For venture philanthropists and their supporters, this nonaccountability provides valuable flexibility in acting for the public good and is in the best tradition of a democracy.[16] As some have argued, "such virtual immunity represents foundations' greatest strength: the freedom to take chances, to think big, to innovate, to be, in the words of the late Paul Ylvisaker of the Ford Foundation, 'society's passing gear.'"[17]

But this argument assumes that funders and their retinue of experts can identify educational problems, sort out symptoms from fundamental causes, and adopt solutions that target those causes. And that assumption is not necessarily valid. As one observer noted: "Just because you were great at making software or shorting stocks doesn't mean that you will be good at . . . ensuring that kids can read by the third grade. If you're worth billions, though, nobody may tell you that."[18]

And importantly, this nonaccountability means that if their grants fail to achieve the desired objectives, philanthropists can just shrug and walk away.[19] There are many examples of major donors stumbling and then walking away unscathed. Recall the Ford Foundation sponsoring community control in New York City in the late 1960s. And the Annenberg Challenge spreading nearly a billion dollars among selected urban school districts in the early 1990s, but producing little lasting change in student outcomes. And, of course, the Bill & Melinda Gates Foundation advocating for small high schools in the early 2000s, only to retreat hastily a few years later.[20]

This lack of responsibility for policy errors to improve schooling has been a constant criticism, past and present, and one that I find warranted.

Missing from these familiar criticisms, however, is an analysis of the theory driving donors' reform agenda and its outcomes, particularly the obvious gap between donor-approved policies aimed at school improvement and what happens in classrooms. Venture philanthropy may or may not be "society's passing gear," but it is too often a "slipping gear." That is, it neglects the crucial policy-to-practice journey from donors' offices to classrooms.[21]

THE POLICY-TO-PRACTICE JOURNEY

Background: Assumptions Driving Current School Reform

Before tracing the journey itself, it will be useful to look at the background of the giving, especially at the ideas and assumptions major donors held when they pressed for market-based school reforms and at what was to occur after grants left donor suites and policymaker offices and traveled to schools and classrooms.

Two basic ideas have anchored (and continue to anchor) policymaker and donor assumptions:

- Schools are like businesses, and failures in schooling can be fixed by applying efficient and effective business practices.
- Current philanthropists have created successful business organizations; they are smart and resourceful and know how to fix school problems using their intuition, research, and engineering skills.

Civic, business, and philanthropic leaders have assumed that US schools have failed because educational leaders were more concerned about protecting the status quo than about improving student outcomes. Leaders assumed that effective teachers and administrators were either trapped in a bureaucratic system that blocked their daily efforts to succeed or surrounded by inept colleagues (or both). To achieve success, then, they assumed that schools, not students, had to be overhauled. Because they assumed that students' low performance was located in classrooms, not families or neighborhoods, they ascribed students' poor performance on international tests to low curriculum standards, inefficient and rule-governed schools, and a lack of competition. Moreover, they believed that teachers' unions resisted changes in salary, seniority, and evaluation rules. Policy elites (including donors) argued that unless there were changes in who taught, what was taught, parental choice of schools, accountability for results, and union rules, US students would continue to fail in acquiring essential skills for working in a global economy.[22]

Armed with these assumptions about what the basic problems were and what had to be done to solve them, donors granted billions of dollars to states, districts, and newly created advocacy organizations. In return, foundations have received a decade-long barrage of criticism of their ideology, intent, and favored "solutions." Yet, amid those salvos, one issue has largely escaped notice.

Beyond swaying decision makers to adopt market-driven solutions is an overlooked fact that adopted policies were seldom put into classroom practice.[23] Large foundations, for example, have invested heavily in broadening parental choice, getting better school leaders, toughening curriculum, and enhancing instruction through new technologies. Donors have worked closely with, advocated for, and depended on policy makers to convert their reform ideas into school practices.

Why do donors rely on policy makers? The simple answer is that policy makers have legal authority to make decisions, provide incentives to act, and provide public funds, while donors do not. To get what they want, foundation officials directly fund programs (for example, the Gates Foundation funded the conversion of large high schools into small ones) and give monies to organizations that support their interests and create advocacy groups (for example, the Walton Foundation funded pro-charter organizations). Even though donors rely on policy makers' legal authority to adopt reforms, both lack the expert savvy to put policies into actual school and classroom practice. That is the job of district officials, principals, and, yes, classroom teachers.[24]

Current entrepreneurial donors share a similar ideology and school reform agenda with business and civic leaders. Accordingly, these donors have funded programs that widened the pool of teachers and principals (for example, Teach for America, New Leaders for New Schools). They promoted policies that shifted public funding (for example, vouchers and charter schools), altered structures such as school size (for example, small high schools), modified time spent in school (for example, extended school day and year), fortified curriculum (for example, Common Core State Standards), improved instruction (for example, more computers in schools), and toughened accountability for teachers and students (for example, test-driven evaluations of practitioners, graduation tests). Major donors also funded organizations that challenged union protections in compensation, seniority, and teacher evaluations (for example, the *Vergara* decision).[25]

Policy makers and funders assumed that such top-down policies would change classroom practices, which would in turn improve students' academic achievement, increase college entry, and secure jobs in an information-driven economy. This theory of change, however, has been no better than whistling in the dark when it comes to converting policies into teaching practices and student outcomes.

The Uncertain Road

The path from donor-endorsed policies aimed at improving student outcomes and what happens in millions of classrooms is twisted and filled with sinkholes. Note that since the Elementary and Secondary Education Act (1965) and its reauthorization as No Child Left Behind (2001), many reform-driven policies now travel from the US Secretary of Education to state officials to district school boards to superintendents' offices, and then pass over district administrators' desks into schools, where principals are expected to ensure that the new policies enter their schools, from kindergartens to advanced placement classrooms.

Then, and only then, do teachers actually determine whether and to what extent they are ready to put federal, state, or district policies (for example, new technology, Common Core) into practice with their students. In effect, teachers have always been gatekeepers to their classrooms; they shape policy as it is handed to them by deciding what and how to teach.[26]

In some instances, that journey ends up altering how teachers teach in unintended ways. For example, the No Child Left Behind Act required states to set curricular standards and test all students in reading and math. Variations in state standards and test results were both evident and serious. Nonetheless, if students performed poorly on tests year after year, stiff federally mandated penalties fell on districts, schools, teachers, and students.[27]

Over the past decade, out of fear of penalties (or of being shamed), schools with large minority and poor enrollments narrowed what teachers taught, revised daily schedules to spend more time on reading and math, and coached teachers and students to raise test scores. In effect, NCLB strengthened traditional approaches to student learning. There is ample evidence that this policy strongly influenced classroom practice, but hardly in the ways that policy makers intended. Whether such changes led to increases in academic achievement and reduced the test score gap between whites and minorities remains in doubt.[28]

The spread of charter schools and charter management organizations, handsomely supported by the Walton Foundation and other donors, offers another example of the slip between policy and practice. The growth of charters illustrates a signal success of focused grant giving in altering state and local funding for public schools. The policy sought to generate innovations in school organization, curriculum, and instruction that would spur regular public schools to improve. Stellar examples of gains in student achievement show up in scattered individual charter schools and charter management organizations such as YES Prep, KIPP, Green Dot, and Aspire. And occasional competition between charters and regular schools has occurred within a few districts.[29]

But those high-achieving schools and fruitful competitions are a drop in the bucket of the six thousand charter schools nationwide, some of which have become academically and fiscally bankrupt. The variation in academic performance across the spectrum of charters is similar to the variation in non-charter schools.[30]

A similarly mixed pattern of occasional victories amid frequent failures to improve student outcomes characterizes donor efforts over the past three decades in spreading new technologies, getting urban superintendents to improve student performance, and promoting adoption of the Common Core State Standards.

Consider the use of new technologies in schools. The hype surrounding the introduction of computers into public schools in the early 1980s promised to transform students' academic achievement, alter how teachers taught, and multiply high school graduates' job opportunities in an increasingly changing economy. Helped by the Bill & Melinda Gates Foundation and other donors, states and districts deployed new desktop and eventually laptop computers in schools and classrooms. The ratio of computers to students dropped from over one for every 125 students in 1983 to one for just over every three students in 2008. By the late 1990s, Internet connections had spread to most schools and in the next few years, wireless became standard.[31] By 2010, laptops and a cornucopia of software were ubiquitous. And within a few years, tablets, interactive whiteboards, and smartphones were in many classrooms.

But did academic achievement improve as a consequence? Did teaching and learning change? Did the use of devices in schools lead to better jobs?

The answers to these questions are "no," "no," and "don't know." Test scores, the current gold standard policy makers use to determine academic achievement, show little evidence that using new hardware and software has improved student performance on tests.[32]

The evidence of transforming traditional teaching practices is equally underwhelming. Nearly all teachers now use these devices. *How* they use them, however, varies from unimaginative to creative, from daily to non-use.[33]

Laptops, desktops, tablets, and interactive whiteboards have yet to alter traditional ways of teaching that have marked classrooms for years. The devices are used as tools to support the dominant teacher-centered approach to instruction rather than promoting the hoped-for student-centered approach. Teachers have expanded their repertoire to incorporate new software and hardware to do what they have been doing all along—no surprise there, since teachers have mixed old and new practices in their lessons for decades. New technologies have found a niche in most classrooms, but their impact is much smaller than what was initially sought. In effect, new hardware and software have strengthened, not altered, prevailing teaching approaches.[34]

Finally, there is the question whether using soon-to-be-obsolete hardware and software helps students gain entry-level jobs in a knowledge-based labor market. There, the answer is just a "don't know."[35]

For another instance of negotiating the pot-holed road from policy to practice, turn to The Eli and Edythe Broad Foundation's Broad Superintendents Academy (BSA). Eli Broad made it clear that he knew how to run successful businesses. He wanted customer-driven knowledge to be applied to urban public schools. At one conference, he said, "We don't know anything about how to teach or reading curriculum or any of that, but what we do know about is management and governance." What Broad did not acknowledge was that managing and governing are not the same as converting key policies into classroom lessons.[36]

The BSA was created to prepare a new breed of market-aware district leaders to raise student academic achievement and reduce the test score gap between minorities and whites. BSA, however, has quietly struggled with the trip from policy to practice. It is an eighteen-month program of extended weekends and internships for educators and noneducators (for example, ex-military officers, business leaders, and government officials). But determining how many graduates have become urban superintendents and how long they have served is difficult because of fragmentary and biased data salted liberally with conflicting accounts from Broad and its critics.[37]

In attracting fresh recruits from the military, businesses, and government to enter urban education posts, the Academy has, to a small degree, altered the administrative workforce in urban settings. But whether Broad graduates stay longer or perform better as school chiefs than those trained in traditional university administration programs, I do not know. That's because since 2002, when BSA began, none of its nearly two hundred graduates have stayed in a district superintendency for over seven years—a term that some observers believe is sufficient to show signs of student success. Broad officials say five years is sufficient for such evaluation, but I could still only find two BSA graduates who served that long: superintendents Abelardo Saavedra in Houston, Texas, and Mark Roosevelt in Pittsburgh, Pennsylvania.[38] Lacking data on longevity and performance of urban school chiefs has persuaded independent observers (including myself) that the Broad pipeline into top leadership posts has not led to better test scores or significantly altered existing school structures.[39]

The difficulty of moving from adopted policy to classroom lessons is also evident in the widespread embrace of the Common Core State Standards since 2010 and philanthropists' strong advocacy for this reform-driven policy. In less than four years, forty-three states and the District of Columbia have adopted these ambitious standards in reading and math and started district pilot projects implementing the standards and testing students.[40]

The mantra voiced by Common Core designers and champions has been that the standards are not a curriculum and that teachers make the decisions on what and how to teach. Both statements are, of course, accurate. States and districts come up with the curricular guides, instructional materials, and commercial products aligned to the standards that are supposed to be taught. All that dancing around whether or not the Common Core is actually a national curriculum obscures the fact that teachers continue to be gatekeepers of what enters their classrooms. Except for one thing: state tests will determine whether students have reached those standards.[41]

Ah, the tests. All states adopting the Common Core will administer new tests, to be taken online. In the past, such tests have carried stiff consequences for students (for example, results are used to promote or retain students), teachers (nearly forty states have passed laws that require test scores to be used to judge teacher performance, and schools (for example, continued low performance could lead to restructuring or closure). Thus, Common Core standards and the accompanying state tests have created great angst among practitioners, parents, and donors. Teachers have doubled down on traditional practices to get students to pass tests.[42]

Parents and teachers angry with the number of tests have fought against implementing Common Core tests in the 2014–2015 school year. And those donors who backed Common Core are worried that the entire standards structure might be in jeopardy as a result.[43]

In 2014, Vicki Phillips, director of Gates Foundation's College-Ready program, wrote in a widely published letter:

> [N]o evaluation system will work unless teachers believe it is fair and reliable, and it's very hard to be fair in a time of transition. The standards need time to work. Teachers need time to develop lessons, receive more training, get used to the new tests, and offer their feedback. Applying assessment scores to evaluations before these pieces are developed would be like measuring the speed of a runner based on her time—without knowing how far she ran, what obstacles were in the way, or whether the stopwatch worked!
>
> [A]ssessment results should not be taken into account in high-stakes decisions on teacher evaluation or student promotion for the next two years, during this transition.[44]

The call for the moratorium on testing has gained widespread support from those who back the Common Core and, of course, from those who have fought against the proliferation of standardized testing across the country. Here is another instance of how policy makers and donors have missed all-important signals and struggled as desired policies wend their way down the policy-to-practice path.[45]

SO WHY DO THEY GIVE?

All of these examples of negotiating the sinkhole-strewn road from policy to practice—NCLB, charter schools, new technologies, Broad Superintendents Academy, and Common Core standards—return to that unasked question: *Why have major donors such as Broad, Walton, and Gates given (and continue to give) large sums of money to programs to improve academic performance in the face of mediocre results in altering classroom teaching practices and student learning?*

I offer a two-part answer. First, policy elites, including philanthropists, live in a very different world than school practitioners. The beliefs, values, incentives to do well, and basic questions being asked differ. Second, because of these differences between these two worlds, current decision makers, including donors, generally favor structural solutions to problems (for example, funding, governance, curriculum, organization). Teachers do not.

Different Worlds

A familiar story illustrates what I mean by policy elites living in a different world than practitioners:

> A man in a hot-air balloon realized he was lost. He reduced altitude and spotted a woman below. He came lower and shouted, "Excuse me, can you help? I promised a friend I would meet him an hour ago, but I don't know where I am." The woman below replied, "You're in a hot-air balloon hovering approximately thirty feet above the ground. You're between 40 and 41 degrees north latitude and between 59 and 60 degrees west longitude."
>
> "You must be a teacher," said the balloonist.
>
> "I am," replied the woman, "How did you know?"
>
> "Well," answered the balloonist, "everything you told me is technically correct, but I've no idea what to make of your information, and the fact is I'm still lost. Frankly, you've not been much help at all. If anything, you've delayed my trip."
>
> The woman below responded, "You must be a policymaker."
>
> "I am," said the balloonist, "But how did you know?"
>
> "Well," said the woman, "you don't know where you are or where you are going. You have no map and no compass. You have risen to where you are due to a large quantity of hot air. You made a promise, which you've no idea how to keep, and you expect people beneath you to solve your problems.

The fact is you are in exactly the same position you were in before we met, but now, somehow, it's my fault."[46]

Funny or not, the distinctions between what policy makers do and think and what teachers do and think are indeed worlds apart.

Consider that local and state school boards, superintendents, governors, mayors, and legislators, including federal education officials, do not lead schools or teach lessons. They all concentrate on making policy and use mandates, incentives, and resources to get policies put into practice. Like donors, they neither focus on nor dictate how teachers should teach or principals should run their schools. They see the "big picture" of the system. They look for effective solutions to problems they have identified that can be scaled up to touch thousands rather than dozens of schools.

Here is how Frederick Hess describes the policymaker world:

Policy is a blunt tool . . . [Policy makers] can require schools or systems to comply with punch lists—hire a parent liaison or set aside forty minutes a day for literacy instruction—but they can't require them to do any of those things well . . .

In the end, policy makers only have three crude levers at their disposal. They can *give away money* for particular purposes, tell you *what you must do*, and tell you *what you can't do* [original italics]. That's about it. Yet, with just these three blunt instruments, policy makers are under immense pressure to make the world a better place.[47]

And teachers? Here's how historian of education David Labaree puts the differences between teachers and reformers, be they donors, policy makers, or researchers:

Teachers focus on what is particular within their own classrooms; reformers focus on what is universal across many classrooms. Teachers operate in a setting dominated by personal relations; reformers operate in a setting dominated by abstract political and social aims. Teachers draw on clinical experiences; reformers draw on social scientific theory. Teachers embrace the ambiguity of classroom process and practice; reformers pursue the clarity of tables and graphs. Teachers put a premium on professional adaptability; reformers put a premium on uniformity of practices and outcomes.[48]

Key players in the game of schooling do indeed inhabit different worlds. As a result, inhabitants of each world ask dissimilar questions.

Favoring Structures

Policy makers and donors ask a bottom-line question: what causes students' low academic performance, especially in big cities? One answer they give is that parents have limited choices of schools. Providing more choices for parents (for example, through vouchers, charters, or magnets) by restructuring funding is one solution. Schools can then compete for students and, from that competition, innovations will emerge that improve student and school performance.

Another answer is that teachers have few incentives to improve their teaching because prevailing rules of evaluating, paying, and retaining teachers reward time served rather than teacher effectiveness in raising student test scores. The solution, key donors believe, is to restructure the system to use outcomes as the determinants of reward and retention in order to spur teachers to teach more, faster, and better than they currently do.

And still another answer to the question is introducing Common Core standards and tests. Advocates among both donors and policy makers believe that higher standards and harder tests combined with new curricular materials will prod teachers to teach differently and students to learn far more than they had before.

Those answers to the problem of low academic performance dominate the current generation of muscular philanthropists. In considering these policy solutions, policy makers ask the following questions:

- Will the new policy cost more, less, or equally effective as the existing policy?
- Will the new policy be more, less, or the same in achieving instructional and curricular objectives as the current policy?
- What incentives and sanctions are there to reward and penalize principals and teachers charged with implementing new policies?
- How can what works in some schools scale up to encompass more schools across states and the nation?

Teachers ask different questions.[49] If the teacher is the most important in-school factor influencing learning, as researchers have established and policy makers and donors acknowledge, should not teachers' ideas, beliefs, values, and questions get respectful attention and action from grant givers and decision makers? The answer is obviously yes, but in most instances, practitioners fail to receive that basic consideration. Philanthropists rarely do more than occasionally consult teachers, give teachers token representation on advisory groups, or conduct drive-by visits to schools. No dark motive rests behind philanthropists largely ignoring the differences between their world and that of teachers. I believe that donors and policy makers acquire a blind spot (or perhaps myopia) from the insulated world they inhabit and that it becomes a major hazard along the road from policy to practice.[50] Questions that teachers ask, then, about policies aimed at what and how they teach seldom get noticed, much less considered.

To illustrate, here are questions many teachers ask after finding out that school officials have purchased and deployed new hardware and software into their classrooms:

- How much time and energy will have to be invested to learn the new devices and accompanying software?
- Will the time spent learning to use the new technology yield a comparable return in student learning?
- What evidence is there that the new technology will help students meet district standards and score better on tests than without these devices and software?
- When glitches in integrating hardware and software occur—and they will occur—will on-site professional and technical help be immediately available?[51]

These questions come from the world of classroom teachers, a world that policy makers and donors largely ignore or tiptoe around. Because these questions go unanswered, the policy-to-practice journey often stops at the classroom door, where teachers, as gatekeepers, ultimately decide what gets put into lessons and what gets put in the closet.

FINAL THOUGHTS

Tax-subsidized philanthropy in a democracy will not disappear. Criticism of donors pushing a market-influenced reform agenda is part of a long history of dialogue around educational reform extending back to Senator Frank Walsh in 1915. Yet attempts to square that circle will persist. Critics and supporters of venture philanthropists will wrestle with the conflicting values inherent to wealth being used for the public good long after this chapter has been published.

In analyzing how policies do (or do not) get into classroom lessons, I have sorted through varied criticisms of donors and assessed each one's merit. On the charge of privatization attributed to large donors, I found that critics overstated the case, even slipping into hyperbole. I did find merit, however, in the charge that, in centralizing school governance, donors and policy makers have stifled public participation in school decisions and deepened distrust in teachers' professional judgment.

I also found merit in the criticism that donors shirk responsibility for errors in grantmaking. Donors have created intermediaries that come close to or even cross the line into lobbying—which is banned by law—for particular policies. Yet that advocacy evaporates when projects fail or entrepreneurial donors walk away untouched by their errors, leaving the odor of unfairness in the air.

Finally, I added to the list of contemporary criticisms by identifying a common blind spot for venture philanthropists: converting policy into effective practice. Like most educational policy makers, donors have largely lived in their own world where *idées fixes* about school problems—better schooling strengthens the economy, schools are like businesses, and successful business practices can fix any problems schools have—dominate their thinking. These shared ideas have spurred grants for reforming structures, allocating ample resources, and scaling up successful ventures. But the world that practitioners live in—a world of different *idées fixes* and behaviors—is crucial for policies to turn into classroom practices, and donors have largely ignored it.

Now I have reached the point in this chapter where I am expected to propose solutions that would help donors make wise decisions and remedy mistakes in achieving their reforms. But I have no list of recommendations beyond the obvious one: that donors become far more aware of the practitioner world and act on that knowledge in advocating particular public policies and making grants. Beyond this self-evident suggestion, I have no other. Why is that?

I have learned from my past writings and others that a section on recommendations is usually the weakest part of a chapter or book because the necessary conditions for proposals to succeed are usually absent. Moreover, recommendations tend to reflect the author's pet solutions. So, in reflecting on my work as a practitioner and researcher for over five decades, rather than present disposable advice, I offer a few educated guesses about what might happen in the next decade as a result of the current muscular philanthropy in school reform.

Continuing Vestiges of Reform Efforts

Every reform movement leaves a residue in public schools. Consider the progressive education movement over a century ago. *Administrative progressives*—mostly policy makers and academics—championed "scientific management" and "efficiency engineers" tying public schools to the early twentieth-century economy, while *pedagogical progressives* glowed over the "whole child," "learning by doing," and tying curriculum to the "real world." Bits and pieces of those two wings of the progressive education movement settled into public schools by the 1940s with standardized testing, measures of school efficiency, small group work, project-based learning, and individualized instruction.[52]

And so it will be after the current reforms—in play since the early 1980s—become footnotes for future scholars. Vestiges of existing market-driven school reforms will be quietly incorporated into public schools. Look for charter schools, reduced standardized testing, a scaled-back national curriculum, routine use of technologies in classrooms, noneducators entering schools, downsized accountability regulations, and a continuing high regard for student outcomes.

Also, the *idée fixe* of current schooling—that is, concentrating on producing human capital first and civic engagement second—will persist but slowly lose its potency as popular pushback against too much standardized testing and a national curriculum grows in momentum.[53]

Other existing reforms, such as evaluating teachers on the basis of student test scores, ending tenure and seniority, calling principals CEOs, and teaching children to code, will be like tissue-paper reforms of the past (for example, zero-based budgeting, right- and left-brain teaching) that have been crumpled up and tossed away.[54]

Contemporary policy makers and philanthropists who invested much time, energy, and monies into these reforms will not break out the champagne for leftover debris. They will join their reform-minded predecessors in being disappointed and blaming school boards, administrators, and teachers for being resistant to change.

Unintended Consequences

If vestiges of older reforms remaining is one lesson from earlier reforms, so is the idea that unintended outcomes inevitably haunt reform movements. Every school reform I have researched, from improving curriculum to changing instruction to redesigning organizations, has had unanticipated results.

Even the smartest policy makers discovered, to their surprise and chagrin, unforeseen consequences. Recall how contemporary donors inadvertently helped shrink public involvement in school decisions through support for mayoral control, state laws expanding charter schools, and parent trigger laws. Some unintended outcomes, depending on where one stands, are positive, others are negative, and a few are even perverse.[55]

My educated guess is that donors may see that the crisis rhetoric they have used in past decades, extensive media exposure, and their market-based reform agenda have had perverse outcomes in that they end up not privatizing public schools, but actually preserving the status quo they fought against.[56] Let me unpack this observation.

The notion of institutions adopting certain reforms in order to maintain stability—sometimes called *dynamic conservatism*—captures how US public schools, especially in big cities, have embraced new policies (for example, charter schools, Common Core State Standards, technologies) to signal to stakeholders that schools are indeed changing. Yet those districts and schools leave untouched fundamental structures that have made US urban, suburban, and exurban schools the way they are (and have been). Few, if any, donors, for example, seek changes in using property taxes to support schools or abolishing local school boards, age-graded schools, and high-stakes tests.[57]

In keeping their hands off these basic structures, reform-minded donors have unwittingly reinforced the stability of the very organizations they want to transform. In the face of occasional dumb policies and strong external pressures to alter traditional structures, cultures, and practices, school districts have learned over time to adapt and preserve overall stability as a natural response, not Machiavellian or even necessarily planned.

One example of grant-giving strengthening the status quo occurred in the early twentieth century when Northern white philanthropists gave money to improve what was then called "colored" or "Negro" education in the South. John D. Rockefeller, Julius Rosenwald, and other donors sent money to improve black education in the South by building schools, helping teachers gain more knowledge and learn new pedagogies, and raising salaries. However, these donors gave the money directly to white school boards, which then dispersed funds sparingly to black principals, teachers, and communities. In effect, these grants maintained the Jim Crow system of separate schooling for blacks and whites. Positive, negative, and perverse outcomes were rolled into one.[58]

Fast-forward to the early twenty-first century, and a similar phenomenon of high-profile reforms breaking against a frozen status quo is evident. For example, donor-supported reforms in urban districts, such as opening new charter schools, closing "dropout factory" high schools, distributing vouchers, and deploying new technologies, have proliferated. These changes rescued small numbers of motivated parents and students who were stuck in under-resourced and inequitably staffed schools within highly bureaucratic urban systems. Those parents and students benefited. That was an intended and positive outcome.

However, for the vast majority of parents outside of a Harlem's Children Zone or those passed over in charter school lotteries, their children continue to attend low-achieving schools, drop out of high school, and face dead-end jobs. Age-graded schools persist, as do segregated poor and minority schools. Inequalities in who teaches in middle-class and poor schools linger. In other words, the status quo in low-performing schools remains. And the primary reason is that these donor-pushed reforms concentrated on schools rather than the economic and social structures outside of schools that freeze institutional inequalities in place.[59]

In making these educated guesses about untoward effects, I see that donors have erred in framing the problem of failed schools as a national phenomenon rather than an urban one and as a problem located solely in schools rather than in multiple institutions and structures inside and outside schools. Battling low academic performance requires crossing institutional boundaries. Many researchers, parents, and practitioners know this in their bones. But venture philanthropists who shape school reform agendas do not.

Because of their can-do and business-oriented ideology, donors have largely devoted their grantmaking to fund changes aimed at existing school structures in governance, organization, curriculum, and instruction. In doing so, they have unwisely reinforced the myth that schooling alone, not in concert with other institutions, produces miracles that will end economic and social inequalities.

And for that error, I believe, donors will receive a full measure of criticism in the next decade for failing to budge the status quo.

8

Seven Lessons on Education Giving from Funders and Grantees

Alexander Russo

During the last decade or so, education foundations have embarked on a number of dramatic-sounding new endeavors, including common standards, teacher effectiveness, charter school growth, teacher and parent voice, journalism/mass media, big data, extended learning, universal preschool, charter expansion, and improved teacher preparation. It's not just *what* they fund that's evolved. To various extents, they've also embraced a new set of strategies for *how* they give out money—new approaches and tools that they hope will improve the chances of the money they give out making a difference.

Some observers see a much-changed approach to grantmaking in recent years—more urgent and focused and savvy—that's been much more effective at generating improvements in the $700-billion-a-year K–12 education world than it was in the past. Extended school days and years, changes to teacher evaluation, and Race to the Top and the Common Core might be among the foundation-supported changes that they'd list. Others, noting setbacks such as the decision to shutter the Gates small schools initiative, the demise of inBloom and ED in '08, and declining recruitment numbers for Teach for America, among other developments, see the current era of foundation grants to education as deep pockets trying hard but generally failing to accomplish anything particularly notable (or worthy).

Of course, not all education foundations operate the same way or approach education grantmaking with the same model of change (see chapter 2 for a comparison of different funders). The last decade has seen a mix of new and old approaches. Education grantmakers are an extremely diverse group of funders, and in most cases they have evolved rather than done any sort of about-face in how they give out money and what they fund.

But what about those who operate inside the funding community? What have foundations learned over the last decade? As education grantmaking has noticeably shifted, what successes and failures do they think they've experienced, and how have they responded so far? These questions are what this chapter examines.

To this end, I interviewed a number of notable foundation insiders, whose names appear in these pages.[1] Other key figures agreed to be interviewed only on the condition of not being named or having their views attributed to them in print. Ranging from relative newcomers to philanthropy to veterans with decades of experience behind them, they come at education from diverse perspectives and ideological viewpoints. Not surprisingly, there's no real consensus among them about what's worked, although they readily admit that there's no definitive answer to whether the new philanthropy is any more effective than its predecessors.

As you'd expect, long-time foundation veterans like the Chicago Community Trust's Terry Mazany, the Ford Foundation's Fred Frelow, and Harvard professor emeritus Robert Schwartz (a former foundation officer) are generally more critical of the "new" approach to education grantmaking and some of its goals and funded activities. And those most involved in the "new" approach—Marc Sternberg and Jim Blew (current and former Walton staffers, respectively) and the Doris and Donald Fisher Fund's Christopher Nelson—are generally most optimistic about its successes and future prospects.

But, as I will show, there are some lessons and concerns that come up repeatedly across ideological lines—for instance, concerns shared by Tom Vander Ark (former Gates Foundation program officer), Stacey Childress (Gates alumna and current head of the NewSchools Venture Fund), and Mazany. And some of the most pointed criticism of the new philanthropy comes from those who are themselves a part of it, either on the giving or receiving sides (in particular, Jim Blew and StudentsFirst founder and former head Michelle Rhee).

SEVEN LESSONS

These insiders identify seven main lessons whose common theme is the need to maintain or restore a balance around grantmaking priorities and strategies, which can become exaggerated in their importance or too rigidly applied:

- *Lesson 1: Policy and advocacy are great tools—to a point.* The move toward funding policy and advocacy has obvious strengths over funding programs and direct services; however, there are also downsides and concerns about overreliance on short-term changes.
- *Lesson 2: Newly created organizations bring focus and fidelity but can lack credibility and engagement.* A new nonprofit created specifically to meet a need doesn't have to change its spots to take on new efforts, but it may struggle to ramp up and become effective.
- *Lesson 3: "Strategic" philanthropy is a powerful way to narrow priorities—unless it's applied too rigidly.* Focusing grantmaking on a few key areas makes sense, compared with spreading grants willy-nilly, but too narrow a scope can exclude new ideas or approaches that might emerge.
- *Lesson 4: Setting clear metrics helps—but advocacy is particularly hard to measure.* As difficult as evaluating the impact of programs and services can be, evaluating the impact of diffuse policy and advocacy efforts can be even harder.
- *Lesson 5: Fail fast—but don't overreact to bad news, either.* Recognizing when an investment or strategy isn't going to pan out is especially important when pursuing a tight set of priorities, but overreacting to preliminary results can be just as damaging in the long run.
- *Lesson 6: Don't underplay "the grind."* There are lots of things— capacity building, implementation, leadership development, research—that are essential to long-term improvements that aren't particularly sexy or transformative.
- *Lesson 7: A little more coordination, please (but not too much!).* When funders operate in isolation from each other—and allow or encourage their grantees to do the same—the results can be frustrating and ineffective.

The overarching lesson those inside the education foundation world seem to have gleaned is that although many of the changes in grantmaking in recent years have been constructive overall, they have downsides and drawbacks. Maximizing the strengths and potential effectiveness of some of the new approaches and areas—without overdoing it—is perhaps the real lesson from philanthropy's last decade.

POLICY AND ADVOCACY ARE GREAT TOOLS—TO A POINT

Much has been written about the shift in funding toward advocacy and policy in recent years. Indeed, this new focus may be the defining feature of the new education philanthropy. Most of the experts interviewed for this chapter seemed to view policy and advocacy as effective and important activities for foundations to fund—but not without accompanying challenges and downsides. "One of the things that philanthropists learned was that, if you spend most of your funding on direct investments in traditional schools or districts, you'll find that the education system is able to absorb hundreds of millions without anything really changing," observes Joanne Weiss, former NewSchools Venture Fund executive (and former head of the Obama administration's Race to the Top program). "So you've got to think about different ways to spend the funding to have impact."[2]

One of the foundations that has moved into advocacy during the past decade is the Fisher Fund. The foundation helped start the National Alliance for Public Charter Schools and funds the California Charter Schools Association. "Just starting great schools isn't enough," says managing director Chris Nelson. "They need environmental support."

Advocacy efforts aren't something everyone in the funding community has been comfortable with, however. Influencing the policy agenda shapes the use of public dollars and creates concerns that the foundation may be undermining the democratic process and "becoming just one more influence peddler," said former Grantmakers for Education head Chris Tebben in a 2012 interview. "Foundation boards are very risk-averse." She further noted that they are often concerned about legal and reputational considerations. Foundation boards and program officers with a more traditional background may not necessarily have their hearts in aggressive policy positions or hard-charging advocacy. They often don't want to take a side.[3]

Insiders acknowledge that the focus on advocacy and policy can go too far, eclipsing other key activities like capacity building, engagement, and research. Overfocusing on policy and advocacy can sometimes even create problems for future refinements that may be needed, notes NewSchools's Childress. She describes situations when policy "gets out ahead" of practice and codifies rules that may turn out not to be well designed or flexible enough to adapt to inevitable changes. Short-term policy wins at the state or district level can unintentionally limit innovation or improvement. She adds, "I worry sometimes that we move too early to regulate—to put things specifically into policy—rather than continuing to support innovation and improvement."

The advocacy approach, which is generally more public than other forms of grant-funded activities, can also generate resentment, resistance, and the perception—real or imagined—that foundations have become overly influential in pushing publicly funded initiatives like Race to the Top and the Common Core State Standards. (The *Washington Post*'s Lyndsey Layton has written somewhat simplistically about the Gates Foundation's full-throated effort to persuade government agencies to adopt and implement the Common Core State Standards.[4])

There are other long-term downsides to an overreliance on policy and advocacy, according to Childress. "I think having competing priorities in government and civil society is a very healthy tension," she says. On the Common Core, for example, foundation involvement "just overcomplicated what was already off to a pretty good start" at the state level.[5] The involvement by outside funders at the national level might have turned robust and constructive debate into an adversarial issue.

Given the conflicts and opposition that advocacy can generate, it might be better to stay away from this arena entirely, says the Chicago Community Trust's Mazany. "Education is deeply infused with political and ideological positions. There's essentially no neutral ground, and a funder, either intentionally or unintentionally, will end up being aligned with a point of view." From his perspective, it would be better to stick closer to research and local needs. Grantmakers should step back and let policy bubble up from research and local successes, taking a following rather than a leadership role.

But for all its challenges and potential drawbacks, the shift toward advocacy and policy work doesn't seem likely to slow. According to Jim Ferris, professor in the University of Southern California's School of Policy, Planning, and Development, that's a good thing: "It's clear that, to have impact, you need to change policy and systems."

NEWLY CREATED GRANTEE ORGANIZATIONS BRING FOCUS AND FIDELITY BUT CAN LACK CREDIBILITY AND ENGAGEMENT

Changes in funders, strategy, and approach have had notable effects on which organizations get funded, and again, these shifts have had drawbacks as well as advantages.

Whereas the traditional approach to grantmaking had been to find existing nonprofits and talented individuals to support, based on the idea that they represented community needs and the best of educational practice, the newer approach adopted by some funders has been to conduct an internal review and assessment process (sometimes with the help of outside consultants), determine priorities, and then help create new nonprofits and find talented individuals who will implement funders' ideas.

Some examples of newly created grantees include advocacy groups like 50CAN (the 50-State Campaign for Achievement Now), teacher voice efforts like Educators 4 Excellence, and parent engagement efforts like Families for Excellent Schools. Think of them as pop-up shops for education philanthropy.

In a few cases, such as New York City's New Visions nonprofit and Washington, DC's Education Trust, existing grantees have been able to evolve along with funder priorities. But, in many others, new organizations and new leaders seem to be required. The national network of district-based foundations, the Public Education Network (PEN), closed up shop not too long ago, though the weekly newsletter continues as part of the Los Angeles Education Partnership. District-based grantees like Chicago's Public Education Fund may continue to receive funding but are no longer at the forefront of education improvement efforts as they were during the Annenberg Challenge in the 1990s or the more recent Gates small schools initiative.

In at least some cases, funders announce that they aren't even accepting unsolicited proposals, much less funding older nonprofits. "It's a kind of decision that sends a signal that basically says, 'We've got the ideas in house, we'll find you out there,'" says Harvard's Bob Schwartz. Some foundations have even decided to do the work on their own, in-house, rather than finding or creating outside groups to meet their goals.

The result of this trend has generally been that grantees' work is much more aligned with funders' priorities—an improvement in the short term. An organization created to fulfill a funder's priorities is much more likely to focus on and execute that agenda than an established organization with its own history and competing priorities.

But the downsides are significant, according to some. "I worry that the dominant model is increasingly, 'We'll design it ourselves,'" says Schwartz. "Perhaps it's just false nostalgia, but I don't think that's ultimately really good for the field . . . You really have to support people and teams committed to doing something. You can't as a philanthropist have your own idea and go shopping for someone to implement it. Or rather, you can, but it's not nearly as effective an approach." He describes the new approach as resembling contracting more than grantmaking.

Funding the creation of new organizations with a clear preestablished focus can also undercut community and public trust in that organization's efforts. Schwartz continues, "One of the consequences of this trend . . . is, I think, to exacerbate the tensions and outright hostility between the field (people who work in education, teachers in particular) and the funding world."

Schwartz isn't the only one to raise this concern. "The line between grant-making and contracting has really gotten blurred," according to Jim Blew, who half-jokingly describes the process: "We sit in our offices in Seattle or Indianapolis and cook up the ideas and then we go and find good people to implement our ideas." The obvious advantages are fidelity to the foundation's ideas, he notes. But: "Surprise, surprise—what you get is much more of a compliance relationship."

Some grant recipients seem to agree. "If you really want people to be having a strong sense of ownership over what they're working for, they can't feel like they're carrying out someone else's mission," says 50CAN founder Marc Porter-Magee. "No one washes a rented car."

Those who have embraced this new approach aren't entirely convinced, however, noting the failures of previous eras of grantmaking, when resources were absorbed by preexisting nonprofits whose leadership was more interested in the funding than the mission. The halfhearted and disjointed efforts of Annenberg Challenge grantees are an obvious example of how relying on existing organizations to propose and implement the work can lead to little change.[6]

And even newly created nonprofits can in theory balance independence and fidelity, with some attention and effort. "There have definitely been some times when we've felt like things were getting distorted," says Porter-Magee.

But 50CAN, launched in 2010, has generally managed to be careful about "what does and doesn't go into a grant application," he says. For example, grant agreements don't say what specific policies are going to be pursued.

"STRATEGIC" PHILANTHROPY IS A POWERFUL WAY TO NARROW PRIORITIES—UNLESS IT'S APPLIED TOO RIGIDLY

It's not just what kinds of activities and what kinds of nonprofits get funded that have changed. Funders' underlying strategies have also shifted dramatically during this 2005–2015 period. Many have become more strategic, seeking to closely align their investments and often narrowing priorities down to just one or two main items.

This approach is sometimes called *strategic* or *impact* philanthropy, and it's become common in recent years—especially among newer funders. "I would say that the theme has been a narrowing of focus and greater imposition of discipline," says the Fisher Fund's Chris Nelson. Fisher used to fund some non-charter efforts, like GreatSchools and The New Teacher Project (now TNTP), that seemed promising, but it no longer does so. "Over time," she notes, "we've narrowed our core strategic focus down to one main thing: high-quality charters and the policies and conditions to help them thrive."

"There are lots of interesting and effective ways that a foundation could approach [the education] challenge," says Nelson. "But for us, it has really helped our impact by staying focused on high-quality charters as our core focus and to stay with that over time." Largely through this logic, foundations like Walton, Fisher, Wallace, and even Ford have developed a clear set of priorities and stuck to them fairly strictly.

According to many of the insiders interviewed for this chapter, the trend toward impact philanthropy has been a positive one overall. More traditional, nonreform foundations have continued to invest in curriculum, traditional programs, and K–12 "adjacencies" such as preschool, after-school, and summer programs, according to Jim Blew. He says this is "all good stuff, but not systemic solutions to the problems"—and, even more importantly, it's not always tightly coordinated.

However, some of those inside the grantmaking community view this new strategic approach as narrowly technocratic, ignoring underlying issues and dynamics such as poverty and culture and other realities on the ground. "The shift to strategic philanthropy over the last decade has, by design, made foundations less random and more selective," according to former Gates grantmaker Tom Vander Ark. But in the process, he observes, foundations have become too prescriptive and rigid to see new opportunities that might make a real difference: "In many foundations, very smart people have very little authority."[7]

Grantmakers from a more traditional background are more even critical. "Wait a minute, we're smart too!" is the rationale behind strategic grantmaking, according to Ford Foundation alumna Jeannie Oakes. "We can figure out what some solutions are to problems and then use our resources to buy and build capacity to solve those particular problems in the way we think they should be solved."

According to Oakes, there's actually nothing inherently wrong about the strategic approach (and she sees no real lack of wiggle room for grantees within a strategic model). And yet, maybe being so focused "is not the best way to go." Policy changes in areas such as teacher evaluation that have been promoted through strategic philanthropy haven't resulted in measurable improvements, she notes. Another reason to reconsider the approach is more philosophical: "It's anti-democratic."

SETTING CLEAR EVALUATION METRICS HELPS—BUT IT'S PARTICULARLY HARD TO MEASURE ADVOCACY

Another big evolution in grantmaking has been the focus on measurable results. In Childress's words, foundations are "more interested in specific outcomes than in the past, and increasingly think of outcomes as defined by student learning gains," rather than focusing on procedural accomplishments or outcomes that seem good or make sense but aren't specifically intended to change students' academic lives.

For many funders, good intentions and vague promises aren't enough anymore. "When I got into this business, there was a feeling that nonprofits were doing God's work," recalls Robin Hood's Emary Aronson. "They were good people doing good things." Now, says Aronson, that's not nearly enough: "God also wants financial statements." Robin Hood is well known for its sophisticated metrics and its focus on business practices and outcomes. Grants are given for a single year at a time. The organization uses roughly 170 algorithms to measure grantee performance and now has a six-person data team.

The infusion of metrics has been a mixed blessing, according to Fred Frelow, who worked at Rockefeller and the Woodrow Wilson Institute before joining Ford. Reformers aren't the only ones to focus on metrics; civil rights cases and school finance lawsuits often involve detailed measures of progress on impact and equity. And, in some cases, the additional rigor has added value. But, he says, "I don't think that social problems are so neatly understood or explained" in that way of thinking about things. Deeper, longer-term objectives may require broader, less concrete requirements from funders. Otherwise, everyone ends up focusing on what's easily measured but may be superficial or manipulable at the expense of deeper change.

Frelow isn't alone in expressing concerns about overuses and misuses of metrics. Program officers sometimes fall into making investments that can satisfy available metrics, according to Jim Blew, rather than those that might push the agenda forward. At times, the use of metrics can even hinder grantees' efforts and create a bureaucracy between funders and grantees that has an unsettling resemblance to the efforts and agencies that they are trying to replace.[8] In some cases, funders are so focused on wanting to see a concrete return on their investment that "they overstructure everything," said Michelle Rhee about her experiences raising funds. The focus on data can also slow things down and make the funder-grantee relationship bureaucratic. "They want to disparage the bureaucracy of traditional public schools. But the bureaucracy that exists in some of these foundations is insane," says Rhee, describing multiple iterations and more than a year of negotiations over a grant before it's awarded. "You can't complain about somebody else's bureaucracy when yours is just as bad."

But it is possible to find the right balance between metrics and flexibility, according to Rhee and others. Rhee says that the grant that funded the DC teachers' contract is an example of appropriate balance of monitoring and flexibility: "They didn't know it was going to work, but we put on the table what we thought we could do and, despite a very long process of establishing metrics and dashboards, they weren't overly prescriptive. They got the big picture of it. They overcame the desire to set up a thousand different metrics."

The Gates Foundation's Small Schools Initiative also had a good mix of structure and flexibility, recalls former NYC Department of Education staffer Marc Sternberg, who worked on the project and described it as "the best philanthropy I've ever been a part of." The Foundation and the district worked together well, established clear criteria, and then went to work, says Sternberg, who is now at the Walton Family Foundation. "The process was precisely where it needed to be in terms of having the right amount of structure and flexibility."[9]

Flexibility is key, says Fisher's Nelson. "We've tried to strike a balance between focus on metrics and confidence in leaders we have chosen to support," he says. The metrics that are the most useful are "the ones that we have worked on collaboratively with our grantees." It's also important to be flexible with grantees who may, for example, miss a growth target in order to address a quality issue. "We would reward that, not punish it," says Nelson.

Measurement issues are all the more challenging when it comes to advocacy and policy efforts that don't involve concrete services or products and may unfold messily over time. The scientific model is inappropriate, and other attempts to generate specific, quantifiable measures could lead funders astray. "People are still trying to figure out what an advocacy grant should look like," says 50CAN's Marc Porter-Magee. "What do we track? What do we care about?"

Indeed, many who study advocacy note its challenges for those implementing and evaluating it. "Effective advocacy is difficult, and evaluating whether various approaches are working is even harder," write Johns Hopkins University political scientist Steven Teles and Roosevelt Institute senior fellow Mark Schmitt. "The political process is chaotic and often takes years to unfold, making it difficult to use traditional measures to evaluate the effectiveness of advocacy organizations."[10]

Joanne Weiss asks, "If foundation-funded advocacy and direct charter school funders hadn't so dramatically raised the visibility on 'charters,' would the charter movement have been stopped—or slowed—in its tracks? . . . I could make an argument either way."

One widely noted concern is that the measures of success established at the start of an advocacy cycle (usually two to three years) may or may not be appropriate to an effort that's more likely to unfold over three to five years or even longer. The data may be abundant, but it's not always particularly useful or illustrative of what a grantee has accomplished. "Be wary of measuring accomplishments based on what people promised to do" at the outset of a grant, warns Schwartz. Those metrics may be particularly unhelpful.[11]

FAIL FAST—BUT DON'T OVERREACT TO BAD NEWS, EITHER

"Failing fast"—and talking about it publicly—is all the rage in Silicon Valley, where start-ups launch and close up shop all the time. The culture is generally the opposite in the world of education grantmaking. Yet the need to admit failure and make improvements—or move on—is all the more important in an environment in which foundations may have preselected a small set of priorities before looking at any grant applications and are planning on sticking with one or two main objectives for a while. "You'd better have an appetite for iteration," says Childress, describing the need to make "constant adjustments, phase out things that aren't proving effective, and double down on those that are."

But it's not so common that foundations take that approach. Although some funders attempt to imitate the impatient, aggressive, and unsentimental strategies of Silicon Valley, by and large, they seem to have held onto the long-standing notion that failures should be rare—and rarely noted. A recent NSVF Summit panel on failure was an unusual public discussion of approaches and efforts that didn't work. As a result, some foundations are "taking less risk when they should be taking more risk," according to Vander Ark.

Obstacles to failing fast in foundations include concerns about experimenting on public schools and students and political and reputational considerations, says Childress. "I think it's really hard. I wish I saw more of it."

Even when funders do actually consider their failures and successes, they often do so with too broad a brush, according to Blew. "Philanthropy could learn lessons from all of their grants, if only they would take the time to honestly assess how each grant was successful and how each one was a failure." Too often, foundations want to put grants in one bucket or the other and learn only positive lessons from "good" investments and only negative lessons from "bad" investments.

Sometimes funders get it wrong or go too far in making changes. The Gates small schools initiative is one obvious example. Recent research suggests that small schools weren't as much of a failure as the Gates Foundation seems to have thought when it abandoned the strategy. "I'm not sure we have the patience as a country to wait and see whether something works before we change course again—given the long time frames that it takes to see, or to admit that, actually, maybe it worked," notes Joanne Weiss.

Nevertheless, Ford alumna Oakes credits grantmakers like Gates for changing course when the evidence demanded it. And she notes that the problem may be a lack of time and energy that limits responsiveness more than stubborn resistance to seeing what's working and what isn't: "Program officers don't have much time to read anything besides proposals or write anything down except strategic plans."

DON'T FORGET "THE GRIND"

The focus on policy and advocacy—as well as the goal to scale up effective programs in large numbers as quickly as possible—has sometimes obscured other necessary aspects of the education improvement process, according to many of those interviewed. Some of the most important aspects of effective grantmaking that may have been left behind or underplayed during recent years include capacity building, implementation/follow-through, and attention to research.

Even within the scope of advocacy and policy, some believe that there hasn't been enough attention or funding for implementation of efforts. "This new breed of advocacy folks thinks they are 'the bomb' if they write a lot and get quoted," said one longtime insider. "Advocacy has somehow been defined as the ability to blog, write, and Tweet, not that you actually got a policy changed."

Some of philanthropy's strongest critics are among those who generally agree on the need for urgent change. Reformers "think they've done their job when they get a law passed, an evaluation system created, a new program launched, then sit back on their haunches, give short shrift to implementation, but defy anyone who might suggest that their proud accomplishment isn't actually working," writes the Fordham Institute's Checker Finn.[12]

However, implementation, capacity building, and research are still tough sells, according to several insiders. "Funding 'the grind' [of legislative work, for example] is not exciting" to program officers or impatient board members, says Rhee. But the big, sexy new things distract from the reality that many changes require efforts that won't show results any time soon. "This is hard work. I underestimated how hard," she says. "Funders don't have an understanding of how it's the long game."

"What I find in most of those conference conversations that the majority of people are enamored by the bright shiny object," says Chicago's Mazany. Ideas get marketed as new or transformative. "Less experienced foundation leaders will grab onto the flavor of the month or a silver bullet solution and just run with that."

Reform-oriented funders need to operate more like unions, says Marquette University professor and Institute for the Transformation of Learning director Howard Fuller, meaning that they need to become part of the community they're trying to help. That might mean contributing $5,000 to a fundraising dinner, attending other organizations' events, socializing, and joining protests. "It's important to show a level of support for a community," he says. "It's those other types of activities that help you build stronger community support."

However, there are dangers of funders becoming over-involved in implementation, too. Complaints about micromanagement of operational and strategy development were common from staff charged with running the Gates- and Broad-funded "ED in '08" advocacy campaign. And, as I detailed in a recent *Education Next* piece, funders such as Gates and the Helmsley Charitable Trust are deeply involved in Common Core implementation work, a role that can reinforce the notion that an effort is too much the product of private giving and not truly a public effort. "You have to be careful [about getting involved in implementation]," says USC's Ferris. "You can't *not* play with the people who are in the middle of making the change, but to some it's a slippery slope."

A LITTLE MORE COORDINATION, PLEASE (BUT NOT TOO MUCH!)

One common concern from critics outside the foundation world is that funders and grantees are all working closely together, tightly coordinating efforts to achieve maximum effect. In chapter 3, Reckhow and Tompkins-Stange note that Gates- and Broad-funded advocacy grants have often gotten grantees (not to speak of public agencies) singing from the same policy handbook.

But, in many other cases, foundations still don't seem able or willing to convince their grantees to work together other than in an ad hoc kind of way—or to coordinate effectively with each other. Foundations often seek some sort of distinctive identity, which precludes their ability to co-fund projects. They sometimes pit current and potential grantees against each other, relying on competition between grantees and encouraging them to work in isolation rather than together.

"There's a lot of interest [in coordinating more frequently], but it's hard to do," says Walton's Sternberg. "We each have our own history of deliverables and plans. There are obvious points of intersection, but coordinating takes work and time and patience and compromise, and I would argue that we need to do a lot more of it."

As a result, much of the work being done by like-minded organizations has been highly fragmented and uncoordinated. "I've told funders multiple times that this space is not going to be successful until we get our act together," says Rhee, talking in particular about advocacy work. She says funders have "created a dynamic where advocacy groups feel like they can't or shouldn't collaborate or coordinate. This creates an incentive for groups to trash each other's work, says Rhee (who has herself been accused of doing the same thing). "We can't even get to the battle line with the other side because we're too busy fighting amongst ourselves."

Of course, this kind of cooperation among like-minded funders and grantees would strike some observers and opponents as frighteningly anti-democratic. And it's not going to happen any time soon, given the high degree of polarization in education and the differences among even the most like-minded funders.

WHAT'S NEXT?

Here are some of the responses and adjustments that insiders see coming down the line:

Returning to Focus on Race and Inequality

Social justice activists and teachers' union heads often point out that reform-minded foundations and advocates downplayed structural race and inequality issues in their push for quick changes in schools and student outcomes.

Reform funders in particular were mistaken to think that their efforts could match the effects of what Terry Mazany identifies as the "macro forces, shifts in educational funding, and the concentration of poverty in urban schools." But they weren't the only ones, points out Jeannie Oakes. "There was a real shift away from looking at issues of race in the US," she says, noting that it was fueled in large part by the assessment that these issues were so intractable. "We'd tried so many things in education [to lessen segregation and racial bias] that the thinking was that maybe it would be more productive to focus on making places that were segregated better." Ford was one of these funders, and it's something Oakes regrets. She predicts that Ford and other outfits retooling their agendas for 2015 and beyond may return to focus on race and class.

Parent Organizing—Not Just Mobilization

Parent-focused efforts are one issue that several insiders raised as a new and growing area for education grantmaking. Overall, funders have been slow to recognize the importance of parent engagement, sometimes misidentifying parents as obstacles rather than allies. "Too few of us pushing to improve education in America are working hand-in-hand with the people most likely to be passionate about the cause and help us win: parents," wrote Suzanne Tacheny Kubach, head of the Policy Innovators in Education (PIE) Network, in a recent newsletter. But it's not enough to engage or mobilize parents, says grantee Howard Fuller. "Mobilization is very important in the short term, but long term, there's got to be some understanding about the necessity of organizing."

Bigger/Smarter Advocacy

Foundations and grantees need "to embrace the importance of being formidable advocates," says one program officer at a reform-oriented foundation. "We need to embrace that work. It's not a tertiary consideration for us. It's a core competency. We have to be as good at [building and mobilizing a constituency] as our very worthy adversaries are." And, like teachers' unions and others who oppose these efforts, reform foundations and grantees need to "know how to win."

Agenda setting by foundations has both pluses and minuses, according to Teachers College professor Priscilla Wohlstetter. Government agencies can't bring education changes to the top of the political agenda on their own, she notes. That's where foundations can help. And the fear that foundations involved in advocacy become overly powerful isn't warranted, despite the Gates Foundation's full-bore support for the Common Core. Wohlstetter says, "We can still identify several groups with some stature who are against it." But there isn't always enough openness to new ideas or accountability when the efforts of insider policies don't pan out.

More Coordination Between Grantees and Funders

The lack of coordination I mentioned above may have been lessening in recent years. For example, the foundation-funded PIE Network brings grantees together and helps them remain in contact with each other even as they pursue funding from the same sources. In 2014, Walton, Broad, and Bloomberg combined to fund the nonpartisan communications organization Education Post.

Some funders already work together on issues of common interest, but there is great variation in funders and approaches, according to Ana Tilton, executive director of Grantmakers for Education, who observes, "This community is extremely diversified." Collaboration between grantmakers is increasingly one of funders' big conversations, however. "They're looking to leverage their investments," says Tilton about her members. "They're realizing that there is an ecosystem that enables success, and that there's a context for which that is going to be successful," no matter what they're funding.

"We need more strategic alignment and more funders who see themselves as part of an ecosystem and act in that context, rather than a lone hero acting independently," says former Grantmakers in Education head Chris Tebben.

Modifying—but Not Abandoning—Strategic Grantmaking

Criticism of strategic philanthropy may be on the rise, but it isn't entirely warranted, according to Jodi Nelson, director of strategy, measurement, and evaluation at the Bill & Melinda Gates Foundation. "[Critics'] assumption that the existing tools of strategic philanthropy have failed to be effective" is simplistic and premature, she commented last summer. The same holds for the notion "that we need new tools, especially to address complex problems."

The best way to go might be to make decisions on a more situational basis, rather than applying the same approach to every circumstance, says Ford's Frelow. "Sometimes making change is finding the best people and giving them core support, even if they're actors who don't necessarily all agree," he says. And other times it's better to go with a more strategic "engineered" approach like Gates and other foundations have taken in recent years.[13]

Diversity

Diversification is a goal that funders need to prioritize within the education movement as well, according to Marc Sternberg and others. "We need to diversify the movement and the leadership of the movement has to reflect the community it intends to serve," says the Walton staffer. This includes diversity of school choices, reform strategies, leadership development routes, and reform leaders. Existing talent development routes have been great, but there need to be "different additional supplemental local channels of talent," he says. "The lack of that additional pipeline is the biggest inhibitor for additional growth."

In the end, the "new" philanthropy may not be as new or different as it may seem, warns Jim Blew. "One of the curses of philanthropy is that the investors aren't eager to learn from each other or from their own past investments," he says, attributing the lack of internal or public self-reflection to funders who want to show that their work is uniquely powerful and brand their efforts as well as to sentimental thinking by program officers. "People imagine, 'My predecessors couldn't execute as well as I will,' or 'My grantees are better,'" says Blew. Or they imagine that previous situations weren't analogous to the current scenario. "It's easy to dismiss the history."

Conclusion

Philanthropies on a Shifting Landscape of Policy and Practice

Jeffrey R. Henig and Frederick M. Hess

I s there a new education philanthropy, intentionally and aggressively working to change the landscape of education policy and practice? Or are
donors just applying long-standing tactics to drive change (albeit perhaps
in more visible and aggressive ways)?

Are foundations and other donors serving as critical linchpins in the
creation of new coalitions—creating new battle lines in the struggle to set
priorities and shape approaches to school improvement? Or have critics on
the left and right overstated the influence of funders and the uniformity of
their efforts?

Do the evidence and arguments presented in this volume tell a tale of a
new era or a familiar story?

While the events are fluid, the research base still nascent, and even basic
facts more than a little hazy, our preliminary answers are yes, yes, yes,
yes . . . and yes.

In this final chapter, we summarize some of the themes and takeaways
that have emerged to this point and offer some insights and suggestions.
The contributors to this volume bring different views about philanthropy,
employ different analytic approaches, and hold varied assumptions about
education policy and politics. Not surprisingly, not all of the findings and
interpretations point in a single direction.

There are also methodological limitations when it comes to making sense
of all this. One important limitation is that our emphasis in this volume on
the largest and most active foundations means we should be very cautious
about characterizing the sector as a whole. A second is that a heavy reliance on Federal 990 reporting forms and on the Foundation Center database, while unavoidable, provides a rich comparative analysis fueled by

underutilized tools—but also means that there are real limitations when it comes to the precision of the findings. A third is a deliberate focus on the first decade and a half of this century, which has been an era marked by a particular alignment of ideas and political dynamics. It's too soon to say whether this era represents the dawn of a new age or an idiosyncratic and ephemeral stage. Nonetheless, even with these caveats in mind, we think the findings offer some telling points of convergence and commonality, informing our sense of what has transpired and providing grist for understanding the road ahead.

WHERE IS THE "NEW" IN THE NEW EDUCATION PHILANTHROPY?

The involvement of philanthropy in American education in itself is nothing new. When it comes to some of the ways that philanthropy goes about this project, it's a different story. For much of the twentieth century, foundations like Ford, Carnegie, Rockefeller, Bradley, and Olin were engaged in programs and research intended to influence educational policies and practice, and they sometimes waded into advocacy and public policy. Remembering this legacy is important; tensions between democratic processes, bureaucratic tendencies, and the role of foundations as agents of change are not new, and proactive involvement by foundations is not limited to the particular school reform agenda that has recently been ascendant. The *extent, intensity, coordination,* and *directness* are markedly different, but today's activity is not unprecedented.

This is easy to forget, because policy discourse in the United States can be disconcertingly ahistorical. Lightly refurbished ideas get greeted as radical innovations. Old tensions, such as between those who see certain philanthropy as catalyzing much-needed societal reform and those who see it as little more than an expression of elite biases, are "discovered" anew and thought to be unprecedented. Hard-won lessons from earlier experiences can be lost. This recurring amnesia may be a broad cultural phenomenon rather than something more specific to education. Regardless, the tendency to view contemporary questions as if they are newly discovered can come at the expense of healthful perspective.

While muscular education philanthropy is not new, it is striking how prevalent it has become among major donors. Nearly every chapter in this volume identifies ways in which the role of foundations has become, in recent years, more strategic, policy-oriented, and self-consciously political. When Jay P. Greene, in 2005, called for foundations to become more strategic in using their resources to leverage policy change, he may have thought he was speaking to an indifferent audience, but a number of major foundations were already shifting their efforts in just this direction, as he now observes.[1]

Sarah Reckhow and Megan Tompkins-Stange, looking specifically at the Gates and Broad Foundations, note the marked shift from giving to local nonprofit providers to giving to advocacy. Although both foundations still provide some support to school districts and charter schools, their funding is increasingly aimed at national groups with reputations for access and influence in Washington, DC. Although Alexander Russo's interviews with insiders show some ambivalence about whether these changes have gone too far, there seems to be little question that strategic philanthropy has become the default lodestar for major donors.

There are signs that this shift may be more reflective of generational rather than systemic changes. While the new giving might be attributable to systemic changes in the education policy landscape, such as the increasing concentration of authority in state capitals and Washington, DC, the burgeoning number of nontraditional providers, or the attenuated power of the teachers' unions, Jeffrey W. Snyder's comparison of newer and older foundations offers reason to think that the behavior of the newer donors really *is* distinctive.

If the newer foundations are different, it matters *why*. One possibility is that their approach to educational improvement reflects the fact that they *are* new: that their style reflects the presence of living donors whose hands-on control and intense desire to see an impact create a sense of focus and urgency. Things are different in older, more mature foundations, where a single donor's vision is replaced by that of a board, generations of professional staff have come and gone, and bureaucratic routine takes hold.

It may also be that the stylistic differences are coded into the genetic core of these foundations and have to do with the differences in the nature and style of the business sectors that produced the initial wealth—the entrepreneurial and venture capital culture of Silicon Valley, for instance, as compared with the steel, railroad, and petroleum fortunes that birthed the foundations of the industrial age. Today's major new donors made their fortunes in the world of high technology or by putting new tools and technologies to work in the worlds of retail or finance, and that background may inform their thinking of how best to tackle the nation's educational challenges. If that's the case, the changes might be tightly intertwined in the DNA of the newer foundations. The key question is whether these new-generation foundations will continue to behave as they have in the past decade, or whether they'll begin to look and act more like the Carnegies, Fords, and Rockefellers when their founders reduce their involvement or eventually pass from the scene. To make sense of all this will require both additional inquiry and the simple passage of time.

IMPORTANT ACTORS IN A MULTI-ACTOR GAME

Given the visibility of today's education philanthropists, it may be natural to imbue them with great influence—whether or not that's truly the case. Michael Q. McShane and Jenn Hatfield find evidence of a small but growing body of analysis that portrays foundations as sinister conspirators scheming to "destroy," "subvert," and "undermine" American education. Some of that criticism comes from the political left and portrays the threat as a plot to dismantle democracy and privatize American education. More criticism—most of it focused on the Common Core—comes from the political right and decries an attempt by liberal elites in foundations and in Washington to impose a national, secular, antiliberty, antireligion, anticapitalist, and even anti-American agenda. The volume of that criticism is nearly double what it was a decade ago, but is still awfully rare—with less than 10 percent of the media accounts of education philanthropy adopting a negative tone.

McShane and Hatfield's interviews with some of the leading critics present more nuanced criticisms and concerns. That may reflect the nature of the public debate or the specific individuals they interviewed. In seeking out responsible and articulate critics, McShane and Hatfield may have been less likely to speak with those who hold a more black-and-white understanding of foundation influence. It's equally possible, however, that their media analysis exaggerates the harshness of the criticism. After all, writers may adopt shocking language in reaching for impact in a noisy, multimedia world.

Critics on both right and left express distress at what they see as growing, unaccountable influence by deep-pocketed donors. These concerns are valid, though it's also true that these donors are only a few of the actors (albeit unusually influential ones) in a complex, multi-actor game. The contributors to this volume paint a picture of philanthropy less as a Godzilla overpowering opponents and more as loosely jointed coalitions of convenience working with a variety of groups that share some (but not all) common interests, goals, and perspectives. This coalition includes New Democrats, moderate pro-choice Republicans, a swath of equity-conscious progressives, and the business community and excludes groups like the teachers' unions and the more energetic proponents of local control and school vouchers.

To the extent that the major foundations share common views on charter schooling, test-based accountability, teacher evaluation, or the Common Core, they face substantial opposition. Those on the other side of contemporary school reform are—like the reformers—a loosely knit coalition. It has frequently included the teachers' unions, but also some strange political bedfellows (e.g., the anti–Common Core coalition includes Tea Party libertarians, antitesting lefties, school voucher advocates, and parents concerned about narrowed curriculum and stressed-out kids). The influence of the pro- and anti-"reform" coalitions is not fixed, but varies by issue and by the level and branch of government addressing that issue.

Amid these pluralistic struggles, foundations often play the role of political brokers and policy entrepreneurs: their resources help them attract and equip allies. The ability of foundations to do this is enhanced by the fact that the battle lines in education reform tend to be more unpredictable and obscure than the sharp partisan cleavages that characterize much of American politics today. Foundations are generally loath to be seen as falling too squarely on one side or another of those partisan divides. The blurry lines we see in education provide leeway to be more active. The fluidity of the debates, and the fact that they don't map neatly onto established partisan machinery, also provides funders more opportunity to serve as political brokers and policy entrepreneurs. At the same time, there are plenty of other political entrepreneurs playing similar roles. Thus, the leading eduphilanthropies can play an outsized role in the public debate, but they are not driving policy on their own—or in a vacuum.

LEARNING AND ADAPTING

At times, it seems pretty clear that certain foundations can come to view education reform as a political battle. When they do, rightly or wrongly, they may be tempted to hunker down in their positions, speak openly only with trusted allies, and use research more as a weapon than as a learning opportunity.[2] By the same token, though, there are plenty of times when foundations are not in that mode. And, if analysts regard foundations as just one more interest group narrowly pursuing a predetermined agenda, they may miss the extent to which foundation officials are learning, adapting, and adjusting. Several of the contributions in this volume remind us that the foundations that embody the new education philanthropy often make concerted efforts to think deeply about what they are doing, reassess priorities in response to empirical evidence and feedback, and shift strategies for asserting influence based on experience.

The contributors' accounts suggest that research as a knowledge-generating activity—as distinct from advocacy and the dissemination of research—does not appear to be a priority for foundations today. Jay P. Greene estimates that research accounts for only about 5.9 percent of total spending. Greene chalks this up to a sense that research just isn't that useful, opining: "For the most part, foundations . . . appear confident that they know what is good and just want to do it." In higher education, Andrew P. Kelly and Kevin J. James flag Gates and Lumina as exceptional in their research investment, but estimate that most funders of higher education devoted only about 2 percent of their funding to research organizations. Some current and former funders note a reluctance to invest in research. Alexander Russo quotes Jim Blew, formerly head of education giving at the Walton Foundation, as observing, "One of the curses of philanthropy is that the investors aren't eager to learn from each other or from their own past investments."

Yet Dana Goldstein's look at the Gates Foundation's massive Measures of Effective Teaching (MET) project also suggests that foundations sometimes take research quite seriously. Gates, as Goldstein notes, famously pivoted on the small schools issue after research suggested that the results were disappointing (though a spate of research in 2013 and 2014 has reopened the question of whether Gates may have pulled the plug a decade too early). While the MET project can be seen, in part, as a strategic use of research to support an effort to reshape teacher hiring, evaluation, tenure, and pay, Goldstein makes clear that such a reading is far too facile an account.

The foundation's initial commitment was likely motivated by the desire to find promising ways to integrate value-added measurement of student achievement into teacher accountability. Given the political and policy climate when MET was launched, a reasonable defense of value-added measurement's properties and an exploration of complementary tools appeared to be an immensely practical way to help states and districts shift to teacher accountability models more attuned to teacher effectiveness—especially with the push provided by the Obama administration's Race to the Top program. In this context, value-added measurement held a particular appeal, as it had the virtue of being relatively inexpensive, less subject to manipulation than existing methods, more reliable than judgment by imperfect principals, and likely to improve over time as the methodology was honed and data improved. Yet it is worth noting that MET may have served some other purposes for the foundation as well. Before MET, Gates was subject to relentless criticism for being indifferent to questions about pedagogy and the inner workings of classrooms and for focusing overmuch on incentive structures, organizational structure, and system design. MET drew Gates into the domain of teaching and learning in a way that helped Gates start speaking much more directly to practitioners.

In a notable development, Gates committed to making the data from MET broadly available. By making the MET Longitudinal Database, which includes video and quantitative data collected by the project, available to researchers by way of the Inter-university Consortium for Political and Social Research, the foundation gave up its role as the arbiter of which researchers would have access to the data and what research questions would be pursued. This is a meaningful and admirable step to supporting learning, and one hopes the foundation did this thinking that it might aid its own learning process.

Foundations' willingness to facilitate research they do not control, with findings they cannot anticipate, could be enormously helpful, especially when it helps foundations understand the impact of their actions and the unexpected consequences of their giving. Larry Cuban charges that the new education philanthropy generally fails to deliver on its aims because donors have been inattentive to the core aspects of teaching and how schools work. In particular, Cuban faults the emphasis on policy, politics, and structure for missing the fact that it's ultimately the teacher who is the "gatekeeper" to classroom change.

Political scientists frequently talk about the power of *path dependence*, or the way that decisions made at one time limit and influence those that come after. Even as foundations may recognize missteps or misjudgments— for instance, an overly optimistic estimate of the extent to which charters as a whole would dramatically outperform traditional district schools; an underestimate of how teachers, schools, and even districts might behave perversely to game high-stakes accountability systems; or a misreading of the potential backlash against Common Core standards, especially if the effort was pursued too rapidly or with federal encouragement—the best response they may be able to muster is adding some new elements to commitments and strategies that they are unlikely to abandon.

GOVERNMENT, MARKETS, AND PHILANTHROPY

While our focus here has been on foundations as actors in pursuit of particular social and educational visions, relevant throughout this volume has been the way that foundation efforts reinforce or conflict with governmental activity on the one hand and the actions of corporations and markets on the other. One can imagine a textbook picture of how these sectors coexist—a form of parallel play, if you will. Yet, in reality, it's a more complicated arrangement, one in which the sectors often find themselves in the same sandbox, sometimes reinforcing one another, sometimes at cross-purposes, sometimes attempting to bully the others, sometimes learning from one another.[3]

Recent decades have seen key new foundations champion concepts more typically associated with the private sector—like competition, disruptive innovation, human capital, and data dashboards. At the same time, foundations are also borrowing strategies from political interest groups in self-conscious attempts to mobilize advocacy and influence government policies in order to have greater impact. While this convergence of the philanthropic and the political has the potential to leverage greater change, it has also fueled concerns that those with money and influence may be narrowing the range of voices and visions involved in the decision-making process. Reckhow and Tompkins-Stange describe elements of just such a phenomenon, and even some foundation heavyweights seem to concede to Russo that they've wondered about this. Further complicating the tale is Greene's contention that philanthropy is ill suited to advocacy because all it can do is hire mercenaries whose numbers and effectiveness will inevitably be dwarfed by the array of other political actors with deeper roots and more established followings. Are Reckhow and Tompkins-Stange correct to worry that foundations' efforts at advocacy will circumscribe national policy debates, or is Greene right to argue that, in the final analysis, foundations aren't good at advocacy? We see these as open questions: important, still unanswered, and deserving of more extensive exploration.

Determining how the philanthropic sector should relate to government has important parallels to the debates about how to apportion federal, state, and local authority in our federal system. Throughout American history, analysts of all stripes—including jurists, politicians, and academics—have argued that different levels of government function best when they embrace the distinctive roles for which they are best suited.[4] This notion of federalism as a neatly sectioned "layer cake" has been contrasted with the notion of federalism as a "marble cake" in which responsibilities overlap—with the various levels of governments sometimes working together and sometimes at cross-purposes but only rarely working in isolation.[5] The consensus is that the marble cake metaphor best captures the real world, although debate continues about whether that is to the good or a problem to be remedied.

But the argument that foundations should embrace their own sphere of action and their own ways of getting things done has much of the flavor of the layer cake ideal. The notion is typically articulated something like this: compared with government, foundations are better able to innovate and experiment. Foundations can act more quickly and freely, don't have to negotiate all the veto points of the public system, and have the luxury of being able to attempt things that may fail without having to worry about the public glare. Foundations can also serve as a kind of counterweight to the dominant political state of affairs, nurturing liberal ideas during conservative eras and sponsoring conservative thought in eras of liberal dominion. Unlike private market actors, foundations don't have the same pressure to maximize profits—giving them the freedom to march out of step with market demand and to pioneer things that may not be popular or self-sustaining (at least in the short term).

In practice, of course, the new philanthropy has been characterized by its rejection of the idea that donors should "stick to their sphere." It has been informed by the notion that inside the box philanthropy is self-defeating, as its good works are impeded or undone by political resistance, status quo policies, and a lack of advocates supporting their successes. The logic is sensible enough. The problem is that when major philanthropies align themselves closely with government, especially with the federal government—and especially when their agenda is the dominant agenda of the moment—they can make it difficult for constructive critics to speak up or to be heard. When foundations see themselves as political actors, try to shape policy directly, mingle funds with government to support the same initiatives, and/or open a revolving door with the executive branch, it poses grounds for concern.

When influential foundations and the federal government link arms, critiquing the reigning administration's policies is tantamount to attacking that foundation's agenda—and the foundation's agenda, however subtly, gets politicized. It's no fun for superintendents to square off against the US Department of Education or for state chiefs to be out of favor with the White House. Indeed, it's when presidential initiatives like No Child Left Behind or Race to the Top dominate the landscape and political pressures encourage leading thinkers to close ranks that the availability of diverse funders with distinctive views and priorities can be especially valuable in fostering independence and honest appraisals. When foundations stand shoulder to shoulder with the executive branch or feel pressure to be "team players," it erodes some of the last redoubts for officials who otherwise might be inclined to carefully weigh and speak honestly about the merits of either federal or foundation efforts.

The tale told by many of the contributors is of increasingly blurry lines between government, foundations, and the market. Prime examples include the Innovations in Investing (i3) grants, which quite deliberately fostered partnerships between districts, nonprofits, and foundations; the "revolving door" that has seen prominent individuals move back and forth between foundations and the federal government; and the growing place of advocacy in foundation grantmaking. Indeed, some of the policy initiatives that have received the most support—charter schools, portfolio districts, accountability systems—are themselves best understood as blended hybrids with roots growing out of democratic oversight, public bureaucratic implementation, philanthropic infusions, and market principles. On an optimistic note, to the extent that the educational challenges we face are those of capacity—the resources, will, know-how, and tools for getting things done—this kind of sectoral convergence may hold the promise of making collective endeavors less disjointed and feeble, reducing duplication and friction and lending coherence and focus.

Yet it may not be that capacity is our biggest challenge. Getting the various sectors working hand in hand may be desirable if there is a clear, wise, and broadly shared set of animating values and priorities. In reality, it seems to us that American education is beset by competing visions and values. Americans are not of one mind about a range of big questions, including how to judge school quality, the proper extent of parental choice, what good teachers do, whether schooling is a private concern or a collective one, whether schools should be a tool of racial integration in communities, or whether we should prioritize creating global citizens or transmitting traditional values. If the challenges are about selecting priorities and aims, and not simply about execution, then philanthropy-government partnership comes at the expense of democratic pluralism.

In fact, the ideal and the reality may point to a third course: the "creative tension" scenario, in which the sectors simultaneously overlap and compete, sometimes tugging against one another and sometimes pulling in the same direction. This is the vision that may be most likely and ultimately most desirable.

THE CHALLENGE OF CHANGING PRACTICE

Almost two decades ago, one of us wrote a book decrying the tendency of school reform efforts to engage in "spinning wheels."[6] The metaphor referred to the reliance of school systems on shallow and superficial change at the expense of the patience and focus that might deliver real improvement in schools and classrooms. Larry Cuban's contribution to this volume makes a complementary point about the new education philanthropy and its "slipping gears" on the policy-to-practice journey. Taken together, the chapters in this book make it clear that there has been a frenzy of activity in what was once regarded as a rigidly recalcitrant sector. And, while not the prime mover, philanthropy has been very much involved in that change. But is this all much ado about nothing?

As social scientists, we were trained to resist hasty conclusions, and in truth it is still too early to know the full range of consequences of the present battles over school reform. It will matter, we think, whether advocacy for accountability, charter schooling, the Common Core, "closing" of achievement gaps, teacher quality, and much else is informed by hard lessons and smart criticism—or whether it seems to be the work of true believers mostly focused on notching policy wins in a Manichean morality play.

All this aside, the reform movement and the new education philanthropy have been hugely consequential simply because they show that the American system of public education is more flexible, resilient, and responsive than many had come to believe. Beginning at least as early as the mid-1960s, critics from across the ideological spectrum had come to see the system—particularly large urban school districts—as rigid, bureaucratic, interest group–infested bulwarks against any and all change. School districts in which half of students attend charter schools, value-added teacher evaluation, the Common Core: for better or worse, none of these seemed likely even a decade ago. While things are still very much up in the air, it seems likely that each of these more recent developments will leave a permanent mark. These changes, moreover, have altered public education but have certainly not "destroyed" it. For much of the past few decades, the proponents and opponents of contemporary reform have frequently portrayed themselves as engaged in an existential battle to remake the familiar system of American education, for good or for ill. What we have seen instead is that, at least to this point, most of the real change has unfolded within the recognizable public sector. And while there are important debates about whether the impetus for this change reflects the will of the majority, it seems clear that the impetus came from outside the public education system—from a smaller alliance of advocates, entrepreneurs, and funders—and that the system has responded in generally healthy ways.

Establishing that the system is flexible, resilient, and responsive is an important remedy to fatalism and indifference and a reminder that the battles over public priorities matter. Foundations, and philanthropy more broadly, are enmeshed in these contests, and we think that's as it should be. But it matters whether they use their influence wisely and in pursuit of the right goals, and we think the research and conversation about that needs to be more open and thoughtful.

Further Reading

This volume doesn't seek to provide an exhaustive treatment of education philanthropy. Given that, we'll take a moment to point readers to some additional works that may be useful. In particular, there are two books of recent vintage that interested readers may find especially on point.

One is Sarah Reckhow's *Follow The Money: How Foundation Dollars Change Public School Politics* (2012). Reckhow offers a sophisticated analysis of case studies of New York and Los Angeles, exploring how foundations have collaborated and how their efforts have impacted reform in those two cities. Bringing a strong political science bent to the topic, Reckhow explores how much mayoral power matters and how local agendas are shaped. It's a good and useful book, with much insight to offer about how education philanthropy plays out in urban centers.

Another volume published that same year, Olivier Zunz's *Philanthropy in America: A History*, presents a historical overview of philanthropy and its relationship to government, arguing that philanthropists have become more like investors as their power has grown and their ideas have been valued more highly.

For readers who are directly involved in philanthropy, there is a shelf of contemporary work focused on advising donors. A few of the more notable works include Paul Brest and Hal Harvey's *Money Well Spent: A Strategic Plan for Smart Philanthropy* (2010); Bill Damon and Susan Verducci's *Taking Philanthropy Seriously: Beyond Noble Intentions to Responsible Giving* (2006); and Thomas Tierney and Joel Fleischman's *Give Smart: Philanthropy That Gets Results* (2011).

Amid the heated debates over contemporary school reform, it's no surprise that there is also something of a cottage industry of books decrying the "new philanthropy." Readers interested in reading more on this score can turn to Kenneth Saltman's *The Gift of Education: Public Education and*

Venture Philanthropy (2010) or Diane Ravitch's influential works *The Death and Life of the Great American School System: How Testing and Choice Are Undermining Education* (2010) and *Reign of Error: The Hoax of the Privatization Movement and the Danger to America's Public Schools* (2013).

Finally, given our broad focus in this volume on K–12 schooling, readers with a special interest in how "venture philanthropy" is playing out in higher education may want to avail themselves of a number of recent volumes, including Noah Drezner's *Philanthropy and Fundraising in American Higher Education* (2011); Vida Avery's *Philanthropy in Black Higher Education: A Fateful Hour Creating the Atlanta University System* (2013); Andrea Walton and Marybeth Gasman's *Philanthropy, Volunteerism and Fundraising in Higher Education* (2012); and Alison Bernstein's *Funding the Future: Philanthropy's Influence on American Higher Education* (2013).

Notes

Introduction

1. The Annenberg Foundation and the Annenberg Institute for School Reform, "The Annenberg Challenge: Lessons and Reflections on Public School Reform," June 12, 2002, http://annenberginstitute.org/Challenge/pubs/Lessons/Lessons_Report.pdf.
2. Frederick M. Hess, ed., *With the Best of Intentions: How Philanthropy Is Reshaping K–12 Education* (Cambridge, MA: Harvard Education Press, 2005).
3. Jim Abernathy, "Foundation Staff Turnover Creates Problems for Grantseekers," The Grantsmanship Center, April 2012, http://www.tgci.com/foundation-staff-turnover-creates-problems-grantseekers.
4. Michael Lipsky, *Street Level Bureaucracy* (New York: Russell Sage Foundation, 1983).
5. Diane Ravitch, "How Philanthropic Giving Has Changed in the Past Decade," *Diane Ravitch's Blog* (blog), July 22, 2014, http://dianeravitch.net/2014/07/22/how-philanthropic-giving-has-changed-in-past-decade/.
6. Jay P. Greene, "Buckets into the Sea: Why Philanthropy Isn't Changing Schools, and How It Could," in Hess, *With the Best of Intentions*, 49–76.
7. National Alliance for Public Charter Schools, "A Growing Movement: America's Largest Charter School Communities," December 2014, http://www.publiccharters.org/wp-content/uploads/2014/12/2014_Enrollment_Share_FINAL.pdf.

Chapter 1

1. I want to thank Cari Bogulski and Deborah Greene for their valuable research assistance on this project.
2. See US Department of Education, Institute of Education Sciences, National Center for Education Statistics, "Table 236.10. Summary of Expenditures for Public Elementary and Secondary Education and Other Related Programs, by Purpose: Selected Years, 1919–20 Through 2010–11," http://nces.ed.gov/programs/digest/d13/tables/dt13_236.10.asp.
3. See Jay P. Greene, "Buckets into the Sea: Why Philanthropy Isn't Changing Schools, and How It Could," in *With the Best of Intentions: How Philanthropy Is Reshaping K–12 Education*, ed. Frederick M. Hess (Cambridge, MA: Harvard Education Press, 2005), 49–76; Sarah Reckhow and Jeffrey W. Snyder, "The Expanding Role of Philanthropy in Education Politics," *Educational Researcher* 43, no. 4 (2014): 186–195.
4. See US Department of Education, "Table 236.10."
5. Stuart Buck and Jay P. Greene, "Blocked, Diluted, and Co-opted: Interest Groups Wage War Against Merit Pay," *Education Next* 11, no. 2 (2011): 26–31.
6. Greene, "Buckets into the Sea."
7. Reckhow and Snyder, "The Expanding Role of Philanthropy."

8. Rosalind S. Helderman, "Uber Pressures Regulators by Mobilizing Riders and Hiring Vast Lobbying Network," *Washington Post*, December 13, 2014, http://www.washingtonpost. com/politics/uber-pressures-regulators-by-mobilizing-riders-and-hiring-vast-lobbying-network/2014/12/13/3f4395c6-7f2a-11e4-9f38-95a187e4c1f7_story.html.

9. See Bob Fredericks and Antonio Antenucci, "Charter School Supporters Rally in Albany to Fight De Blasio Cuts," *New York Post*, March 4, 2014, http://nypost.com/2014/03/04/ charter-school-supporters-rally-in-albany-to-fight-de-blasio-cuts/; "Thousand Brave Cold In Albany To Take Sides In Charter School Vs. Pre-K Debate," *CBS New York*, March 4, 2014, http://newyork.cbslocal.com/2014/03/04/de-blasio-heads-to-albany-to-push-for-pre-k-plan-amid-protest-by-charter-school-advocates/.

10. Javier C. Hernández and Susanne Craig, "Cuomo Played Pivotal Role in Charter School Push," *New York Times*, April 3, 2014, http://www.nytimes.com/2014/04/03/nyregion/ cuomo-put-his-weight-behind-charter-school-protections.html?_r=0.

11. Noreen Ahmed-Ullah, "Chicago Teachers Vote to End Strike," *Los Angeles Times*, September 19, 2012, http://articles.latimes.com/2012/sep/19/nation/ la-na-chicago-teachers-strike-20120919.

12. Buck and Greene, "Blocked, Diluted, and Co-opted."

13. See Stuart Buck, *Acting White* (New Haven, CT: Yale University Press, 2010) and "Rosenwald School," http://en.wikipedia.org/wiki/Rosenwald_School.

14. Reckhow and Snyder, "The Expanding Role of Philanthropy."

15. Bill & Melinda Gates Foundation, "Green Dot Public Schools," http://www.gatesfoundation .org/How-We-Work/Quick-Links/Grants-Database/Grants/2013/11/OPP1096252.

16. Bill & Melinda Gates Foundation, "School District of Philadelphia," http://www.gates-foundation.org/How-We-Work/Quick-Links/Grants-Database/Grants/2013/11/ OPP1100296.

17. Bill & Melinda Gates Foundation, "Center for Education Reform," http://www.gatesfoun-dation.org/How-We-Work/Quick-Links/Grants-Database/Grants/2013/10/OPP1099267.

18. Bill & Melinda Gates Foundation, "Pennsylvania Partnerships for Children," http://www. gatesfoundation.org/How-We-Work/Quick-Links/Grants-Database/Grants/2013/04/ OPP1082178.

19. See Ron Chernow, *Titan: The Life of John D. Rockefeller, Sr.* (New York: Random House, 1998).

Chapter 2

1. "How Many Billionaires Does It Take to Fix a School System?" *The New York Times Magazine*, March 9, 2008.

2. Conservative-leaning foundations have a history of targeting their grants to achieve change in the education sector. See Rick Cohen, *Strategic Grantmaking: Foundations and the School Privatization Movement* (Washington, DC: National Committee for Responsive Philanthropy, 2007).

3. Although Annenberg was founded in 1989, its grantmaking style aligns with older foundations. Walton was founded in 1987, but the style and expansion of its K–12 granting aligns with new foundations. Wallace is a consolidation of multiple foundations established in the 1950s and '60s and most aligns its style with other older foundations.

4. I do not use the term *old* pejoratively or *new* positively. These terms are used for brevity only and to indicate an established presence in education philanthropy versus more recent ascendency in K–12 granting.

5. Raymond Domanico, "Introduction: An Unprecedented Challenge," in *Can Philanthropy Fix Our Schools? Appraising Walter Annenberg's $500 Million Gift to Public Education*, ed. Raymond Domanico (Washington, DC: Thomas B. Fordham Foundation, 2000), 1. For other critiques, see Frederick M. Hess, ed., *With the Best of Intentions: How Philanthropy Is Reshaping K–12 Education* (Cambridge, MA: Harvard Education Press, 2005).

6. For example, see Vartan Gregorian's response to characterizations of the Annenberg Challenge as failure in Vartan Gregorian et al., "Rethinking America's Schools: Four Major Funders Respond to Frederick Hess's Critique of the New Education Philanthropy," *Philanthropy*, March/April 2005, http://www.philanthropyroundtable.org/magazine/march_april_2005.

7. Carnegie Corporation of New York, *Annual Report 2000*, 19–20.

8. Diane Ravitch, *Reign of Error: The Hoax of the Privatization Movement and the Danger to America's Public Schools* (New York: Alfred A. Knopf, 2013).

9. This is not meant as a negative statement. On the contrary, many questions explored necessarily limit scope to newer foundations. For example, see Janelle Scott, "The Politics of Venture Philanthropy in Charter School Policy and Advocacy," *Educational Policy* 23, no. 1 (2009): 106–136.

10. Sarah Reckhow and Jeffrey W. Snyder, "The Expanding Role of Philanthropy in Education Politics," *Educational Researcher* 43, no. 4 (2014): 186–195.

11. Author's calculations based on foundation granting data used in this chapter and the Foundation's Center's 2010 grant total for elementary and secondary education, http://data.foundationcenter.org/#/fc1000/subject:education/all/total/list/2010.

12. Paul J. DiMaggio and Walter W. Powell, "The Iron Cage Revisited: Institutional Isomorphism and Collective Rationality in Organizational Fields," *American Sociological Review* 48, no. 2 (1983): 147–160.

13. Jeremy Levine and William Julius Wilson, "Poverty, Politics, and a 'Circle of Promise': Holistic Education Policy in Boston and the Challenge of Institutional Entrenchment," *Journal of Urban Affairs* 35, no. 1 (2013): 7–24.

14. For example, Sarah Reckhow, *Follow the Money: How Foundation Dollars Change Public School Politics* (New York: Oxford University Press, 2013); and Reckhow and Snyder, "The Expanding Role of Philanthropy in Education Politics." These pieces show that the set of largest givers in K–12 education increasingly gave to a subset of grantees sharing common funders.

15. Foundation Stats can be found on the Foundation Center's website, http://foundation-center.org/findfunders/foundation-stats.html.

16. Any and all mentions of "Carnegie" refer to the Carnegie Corporation of New York, not the Carnegie Foundation for the Advancement of Teaching.

17. Not all foundations share the same fiscal year. For example, while the Gates Foundation aligns its tax reporting with calendar years, the Kellogg Foundation's fiscal year runs September–August. In cases where fiscal and calendar years are different, I use the tax filing for whichever fiscal year covers the calendar year's majority (or first half, if fiscal year is split evenly over different calendar years).

18. While some data were culled for this chapter alone, past projects by Sarah Reckhow and myself employed this same coding scheme. The most recent example is Reckhow and Snyder, "The Expanding Role of Philanthropy in Education Politics."

19. S. P. Borgatti, M. G. Everett, and L. C. Freeman, *UCINET for Windows: Software for Social Network Analysis* (Harvard, MA: Analytic Technologies, 2002).

20. Libby Quaid and Donna Blankinship, "The Influence Game: Bill Gates Pushes Education Reform," *Associated Press*, October 29, 2009.

21. Wallace Foundation, IRS Form 990-PF, 2005.

22. See Reckhow, "Follow the Money," and Reckhow and Snyder, "The Expanding Role of Philanthropy in Education Politics."

23. Richard Lee Colvin, "A New Generation of Philanthropists and Their Great Ambitions," in Hess, *With the Best of Intentions*, 21–48.

24. Gregorian et al., "Rethinking America's Schools."

25. For example, Jay P. Greene, "Buckets into the Sea: Why Philanthropy Isn't Changing Schools, and How It Could," in Hess, *With the Best of Intentions*, 49–76; and Jay P. Greene, "Buckets into Another Sea," in this volume.

26. For example, see Atila Abdulkadiroğlu, Weiwei Hu, and Parag A. Pathak, "Small High Schools and Student Achievement: Lottery-Based Evidence from New York City," NBER Working Paper No. 19576, National Bureau of Economic Research, October 2013.

Chapter 3

1. We would like to acknowledge the excellent research assistance provided by Laura Holden and Jacob Crouch in preparing this manuscript.

2. Sarah Reckhow and Jeffrey Snyder, "The Expanding Role of Philanthropy in Education Politics," *Educational Researcher* 43, no. 4 (2014): 186–195.

3. Janelle Scott and Huriya Jabbar, "The Hub and the Spokes: Foundations, Intermediary Organizations, Incentivist Reforms, and the Politics of Research Evidence," *Educational Policy* 28, no. 2 (2014): 157–233. Scott and Jabbar describe this pattern of foundation investment in numerous organizations to promote a shared advocacy agenda as the "hub and spoke" relationship.

4. Center for Education Policy, "Trends in Teacher Evaluation: At a Glance," http://www.centerforpubliceducation.org/teacherevalreview.

5. Janelle Scott, "The Politics of Venture Philanthropy in Charter School Policy and Advocacy," *Educational Policy* 23, no. 1 (2009): 106–136; Reckhow and Snyder, "The Expanding Role of Philanthropy in Education Politics"; Rand Quinn, Megan Tompkins-Stange, and Debra Meyerson, "Beyond Grantmaking: Philanthropic Foundations as Agents of Change and Institutional Entrepreneurs," *Nonprofit and Voluntary Sector Quarterly* 43, no. 6 (2014): 950–968.

6. Issue priority was determined based on the grantee alone if the grantee was specifically associated with a single issue area (e.g., The New Teacher Project and teacher quality). Otherwise, we evaluated the purpose based on the description of the grant. It was not possible to assign an issue area to every grant, because some grants were made for general purposes. These grants were not coded with a specific issue area. Issue categories included: charter schools/school choice; teacher quality; standards; high school reform; urban education; and principal leadership.

7. Bill & Melinda Gates Foundation Form 990-PF (Washington, DC: US Department of the Treasury, Internal Revenue Service, 2005).

8. Eli & Edythe Broad Foundation Form 990-PF (Washington, DC: US Department of the Treasury, Internal Revenue Service, 2010).

9. Bill & Melinda Gates Foundation Form 990-PF (Washington, DC: US Department of the Treasury, Internal Revenue Service. 2010).

10. Alexander Russo, *The Successful Failure of ED in '08* (Washington, DC: American Enterprise Institute, 2012).

11. Strong American Schools, "ED in '08: Strong American Schools," http://mikefalick.blogs. com/my_blog/files/sas.Toolkit.Complete%20021208.pdf.

12. Paul Burstein, *American Public Opinion, Advocacy, and Policy in Congress: What the Public Wants and What It Gets* (New York: Cambridge University Press, 2014); Matthew Grossmann, *The Not-So-Special Interests: Interest Groups, Public Representation, and American Governance* (Stanford, CA: Stanford University Press, 2012); Paul Burstein and Elizabeth C. Hirsh, "Interest Organizations, Information, and Policy Innovation in the U.S. Congress," *Sociological Forum* 22, no. 2 (2007): 174–199; Frank Baumgartner and Bryan Jones, *Agendas and Instability in American Politics* (Chicago: University of Chicago Press, 1993).

13. Witnesses representing states, school districts, individual schools, and universities are excluded because they are less clearly associated with representing a constituency, advocacy position, or organizational interest.

14. The New Teacher Project, *The Widget Effect: Our National Failure to Acknowledge and Act On Differences in Teacher Effectiveness*, http://tntp.org/assets/documents/ TheWidgetEffect_2nd_ed.pdf.

15. *ESEA Reauthorization: Teachers and Leaders: Hearing before the Committee on Health, Education, Labor, and Pensions, United States Senate*, 111th Cong. (2010) (testimony of Randi Weingarten).

16. *ESEA Reauthorization: Teachers and Leaders: Hearing before the Committee on Health, Education, Labor, and Pensions, United States Senate*, 111th Cong. (2010) (testimony of Tim Daly).

17. *ESEA Reauthorization: Teachers and Leaders: Hearing before the Committee on Health, Education, Labor, and Pensions, United States Senate*, 111th Cong. (2010) (testimony of Thomas Kane).

18. Our data begins in 2003, due to limitations on data availability for Broad grants prior to 2003.

19. *Education Reforms: Exploring Teacher Quality Initiatives: Hearing before the Committee on Education and the Workforce, United State House of Representatives*, 112th Cong. (2011).

20. Steven G. Rivkin, Eric A. Hanushek, and John F. Kain, "Teachers, Schools, and Academic Achievement." *Econometrica* 73, no. 2 (2005): 417–458.

21. *Importance of Highly Qualified Teachers in Raising Academic Achievement: Hearing before the Committee on Education and the Workforce, United States House of Representatives*, 108th Cong. (2004) (testimony of Ross Weiner).

22. *NCLB Reauthorization: Strategies for Attracting, Supporting and Retaining High Quality Educators: Hearing before the Committee on Health, Education, and Pensions, United States Senate*, 110th Cong. (2007) (testimony of Amy Wilkins).

23. *ESEA Reauthorization: Boosting Quality in the Teaching Profession: Hearing before the Committee on Education and Labor, United States House of Representatives*, 110th Cong. (2007) (testimony of John Podesta).

24. Daly, 2010.

25. Robert Gordon, Thomas Kane, and Douglas Staiger, *Identifying Effective Teachers Using Performance on the Job* (Washington, DC: Brookings Institution, 2006).

26. The New Teacher Project, "*The Widget Effect.*

27. Linda Darling-Hammond, "A Marshall Plan for Teaching," *Education Week*, January 10, 2007.

28. Anthony S. Bryk et al., *Organizing Schools for Improvement: Lessons from Chicago* (Chicago: University of Chicago Press, 2010).

29. Scott and Jabbar, "The Hub and the Spokes."

30. Quinn, Tompkins-Stange, and Meyerson, "Beyond Grantmaking."

31. Sarah Reckhow, *Follow the Money: How Foundation Dollars Change Public School Politics* (New York: Oxford University Press, 2012).

32. Lyndsey Layton, "How Bill Gates Pulled off the Swift Common Core Revolution," *Washington Post*, June 7, 2014.

33. Barry Karl, "Philanthropy, Policy Planning, and the Bureaucratization of the Democratic Ideal," *Daedalus* 105, no. 4 (1976): 129–149.

34. Reckhow, *Follow the Money*.

Chapter 4

1. Tom Loveless, "The Structure of Public Confidence in Higher Education," *American Journal of Education* 105, no. 2 (February 1997), 127–159.

2. As Senator Lamar Alexander, now the chairman of the Senate Committee on Health, Education, Labor, and Pensions, told National Public Radio in November 2014, "We have a marketplace of colleges and universities. It has produced the best system of higher education in the world. We don't need the federal government overregulating it." See Lamar Alexander, interview by Claudio Sanchez, *nprED*, National Public Radio, November 11, 2014, http://www.npr.org/blogs/ed/2014/11/11/363055451/q-a-lamar-alexander-on-education-in-the-new-congress.

3. The lead author would like to acknowledge up front that he has received grants from both the Bill & Melinda Gates Foundation and the Lumina Foundation to conduct higher education research.

4. Organisation for Economic Co-operation and Development, *Education at a Glance 2010* (Paris, 2010), http://www.oecd.org/dataoecd/45/39/45926093.pdf.

5. National Center for Education Statistics, *Graduation Rate from First Institution Attended for First-Time, Full-Time Bachelor's Degree-Seeking Students at 4-Year Postsecondary Institutions, by Race/Ethnicity, Time to Completion, Sex, Control of Institution, and Acceptance Rate: Selected Cohort Entry Years, 1996 Through 2007*, http://nces.ed.gov/programs/digest/d14/tables/dt14_326.10.asp?current=yes; National Center for Education Statistics, *Graduation Rate from First Institution Attended Within 150 Percent of Normal Time for First-Time, Full-Time Degree/Certificate-Seeking Students at 2-Year Postsecondary Institutions, by Race/Ethnicity, Sex, and Control of Institution: Selected Cohort Entry Years, 2000 Through 2010*, http://nces.ed.gov/programs/digest/d14/tables/dt14_326.20.asp?current=yes.

6. Rohit Chopra, "Student Debt Swells, Federal Loans Now Top a Trillion," Consumer Financial Protection Bureau, July 17, 2013, http://www.consumerfinance.gov/newsroom/student-debt-swells-federal-loans-now-top-a-trillion/; Jaison R. Abel, Richard Deitz, and Yaqin Su, *Current Issues in Economics and Finance: Are Recent College Graduates Finding Good Jobs?* (New York: Federal Reserve Bank of New York, January 2014), http://www.newyorkfed.org/research/current_issues/ci20-1.pdf.

7. US Department of Education, *A Test of Leadership: Charting the Future of American Higher Education* (Washington, DC, September 2006), http://www2.ed.gov/about/bdscomm/list/hiedfuture/reports/pre-pub-report.pdf.

8. Barack Obama, "Remarks of President Barack Obama—As Prepared for Delivery Address to Joint Session of Congress" (speech, State of the Union Address, Washington, DC, February 24, 2009), http://www.whitehouse.gov/the_press_office/Remarks-President-Barack-Obama-Address-to-Joint-Session-of-Congress/.

9. Libby A. Nelson, "'Gainful' Comes to the Nonprofits," *Inside Higher Education*, January 30, 2012, http://www.insidehighered.com/news/2012/01/30/obama-higher-education-plan-signals-policy-shift.

10. Barack Obama, "Remarks by the President on College Affordability— Buffalo, NY" (speech, College Affordability Bus Tour, Buffalo, NY, August 22, 2013), http://www.whitehouse.gov/the-press-office/2013/08/22/remarks-president-college-affordability-buffalo-ny.

11. Bill & Melinda Gates Foundation, *New Initiative to Double the Number of Low-Income Students in the U.S. Who Earn a Postsecondary Degree*, December 2008, http://www.gatesfoundation.org/Media-Center/Press-Releases/2008/12/New-Initiative-to-Double-the-Number-of-LowIncome-Students-in-the-US-Who-Earn-a-Postsecondary-Degree; Lumina Foundation, "Goal 2025," http://www.luminafoundation.org/goal_2025/.

12. Cassie Hall and Scott L. Thomas, "'Advocacy Philanthropy' and the Public Policy Agenda: The Role of Modern Foundations in American Higher Education" (working paper, American Educational Research Association, April 2012), http://chronicle.com/items/biz/pdf/Hall%20&%20Thomas%20AERA%202012.pdf.

13. Hall and Thomas, "Advocacy Philanthropy," 17.

14. Times Higher Education, "World University Rankings 2014–2015," www.timeshighereducation.co.uk/world-university-rankings/2014-15/world-ranking; Academic Ranking of World Universities, "Academic Ranking of World Universities 2014," http://www.shanghairanking.com/.

15. Associated Press and Stanford University, "AP-Stanford University Education Poll, 2010," October 1, 2010, http://surveys.ap.org/data%5CSRBI%5CAP-National%20Education%20Poll%20Topline%20100110.pdf.

16. William J. Bushaw and Valerie J. Calderon, *The 46th Annual PDK/Gallup Poll of the Public's Attitudes Toward the Public Schools* (Arlington, VA: Phi Delta Kappa International, 2014), http://pdkintl.org/noindex/PDK_Poll46_2014.pdf.

17. Andrew P. Kelly and Kevin James, *Untapped Potential: Making the Higher Education Market Work for Students and Taxpayers* (Washington, DC: American Enterprise Institute, 2014), http://www.aei.org/wp-content/uploads/2014/10/Untapped-Potential-corr.pdf.

18. Institute for Higher Education Policy, *Private Scholarships Count: Access to Higher Education and the Critical Role of the Private Sector* (Washington, DC, May 2005), https://scholarshipproviders.org/Documents/PrivateScholCount.pdf.

19. See Robert Martin, "Incentives, Information, and the Public Interest: Higher Education Governance as a Barrier to Cost Containment," in *Stretching the Higher Education Dollar: How Innovation Can Improve Access, Equity, and Affordability*, ed. Andrew P. Kelly and Kevin Carey (Cambridge, MA: Harvard Education Press, 2013), 9–43.

20. John R. Thelin and Richard W. Trollinger, *Philanthropy and American Higher Education* (New York:, Palgrave MacMillan, 2014), 67–93.

21. Ibid., 82.

22. National Center for Education Statistics, *Total Fall Enrollment in All Postsecondary Institutions Participating in Title IV Programs and Annual Percentage Change in Enrollment, by Degree-Granting Status and Control of Institution: 1995 Through 2012*, http://nces.ed.gov/programs/digest/d13/tables/dt13_303.20.asp?current=yes.

23. For a more robust discussion of quality assurance in higher education, see Kelly and James, *Untapped Potential*.

24. The full report can be accessed only through a subscription. See Council for Aid to Education, "Fundraising in Education: VSE Survey," http://cae.org/fundraising-in-educa-tion/vse-survey/. To access a free trial of the data miner tool, see Council for Aid to Education, "Data Miner Free Trial Information," http://cae.org/fundraising-in-education/data-miner/data-miner-free-trial-information/.

25. Kevin Carey, "Americans Think We Have the World's Best Colleges. We Don't," *New York Times*, June 28, 2014, http://www.nytimes.com/2014/06/29/upshot/americans-think-we-have-the-worlds-best-colleges-we-dont.html?abt=0002&abg=1.

26. Richard Arum and Josipa Roksa, *Academically Adrift: Limited Learning on College Campuses* (Chicago: University of Chicago Press, January 2011).

27. College Board, *Tuition and Fees and Room and Board over Time—Trends in Higher Education*, http://trends.collegeboard.org/college-pricing/figures-tables/tuition-fees-room-board-time.

28. Pew Research Center, *Is College Worth It? College Presidents, Public Assess Value, Quality, and Mission of Higher Education* (Washington, DC, May 15, 2011), http://www.pewso-cialtrends.org/2011/05/15/is-college-worth-it/.

29. Josh Sanburn, "Higher-Education Poll," *Time*, October 18, 2012, http://nation.time.com/2012/10/18/higher-education-poll/.

30. Elyse Ashburn, "Gates's Millions: Can Big Bucks Turn Students into Graduates?" *Chronicle of Higher Education*, August 8, 2010, http://chronicle.com/article/Can-Gates-Foundations/123824/.

31. Hilary Pennington and Greg Shaw, "Three Policy Priorities for Improving Success Beyond High School," *Spotlight on Poverty and Opportunity*, January 11, 2010, http://www.spotlightonpoverty.org/ExclusiveCommentary.aspx?id=353be617-6662-4d08-8d2f-2a9a2f8c2fab.

32. Jamie P. Merisotis, "The Changing Higher Education Agenda" (speech, National Energy Education Network meeting (CEWD), Indianapolis, IN, August 22, 2013).

33. Hall and Thomas, "Advocacy Philanthropy."

34. Marc Parry, Kelly Field, and Beckie Supiano, "The Gates Effect," *Chronicle of Higher Education*, July 14, 2013, http://chronicle.com/article/The-Gates-Effect/140323/.

35. For a comprehensive discussion of the completion agenda, see Andrew P. Kelly and Mark Schneider, eds., *Getting to Graduation: The Completion Agenda in Higher Education* (Baltimore: The Johns Hopkins University Press, 2012).

36. Hall and Thomas's list of fourteen was based on those foundations that ranked in the top twenty-five in giving to higher education at least seven out of the ten years from 2000 to 2009.

37. The Foundation Center, "Foundation States: Education," http://data.foundationcenter.org/#/fc1000/subject:education/all/top:foundations/list/2010.

38. Hall and Thomas, "Advocacy Philanthropy."

39. Lumina also made three large grants to a for-profit organization (HCM Strategists, a DC-based public policy consultancy) to administer a state-level initiative designed to boost higher education productivity, which is what accounts for the large relative size of that category in Lumina's budget.

40. Community College Research Center, "Community College FAQs," http://ccrc.tc.columbia.edu/Community-College-FAQs.html.

41. Examples of "advocacy and engagement" grants include: a $117,000 to the Alliance for Excellent Education to "employ its network of education stakeholders to make the case that the nation's federal student aid system is in urgent need of reform and to propose

viable reform options"; and $546,900 to the Texas Valley Communities Foundation to "lay advocacy groundwork for college readiness by creating structure that informs and engages community, builds strong base of diverse supporters and regrants funds to local grassroots organizations."

42. Michael Horn, "Gates Foundation Steps Up with Investments in Next-Generation Learning," *Forbes*, June 20, 2012, http://www.forbes.com/sites/michaelhorn/2012/06/20/gates-foundation-steps-up-with-investments-in-next-generation-learning/.

43. Doug Lederman, "How to Do More with Less," *Inside Higher Education*, November 24, 2009, http://www.insidehighered.com/news/2009/11/24/lumina.

44. Andrew P. Kelly, "Opening Up the University," *Philanthropy Magazine*, Spring 2012.

45. Ford Foundation, "Ford Foundation Appoints Hilary Pennington and Martin Abregu as Program Vice Presidents," September 9, 2013, http://www.fordfoundation.org/newsroom/news-from-ford/814.

46. Parry, Field, and Supiano, "The Gates Effect."

47. Robin Rogers, "The Price of Philanthropy," *Chronicle of Higher Education*, July 14, 2013, http://chronicle.com/article/The-Price-of-Philanthropy/140295/.

48. Michael McPherson, quoted in Doug Lederman, "Consensus or Groupthink?" *Inside Higher Education*, November 22, 2010, http://www.insidehighered.com/news/2010/11/22/foundations.

49. George Leef and Jenna Ashley Robinson, "Research That Isn't Luminous," The John William Pope Center for Higher Education Policy, February 6, 2013, http://www.pope-center.org/commentaries/article.html?id=2802.

50. Quoted in Parry, Field, and Supiano, "The Gates Effect."

51. Actor Matt Damon, now a poster boy for education reform skeptics, recently told a Reddit Q&A, "I've always believed that they have to invite teachers into the discussion to help design policy. We would never let business men design warheads, why would you cut out educators when you're designing education policy?" Quoted in Valerie Strauss, "Matt Damon: 'We Would Never Let Businessmen Design Warheads. Why Would You Cut Out Educators When You're Designing Education Policy?'" *Answer Sheet* (blog), *Washington Post*, February 8, 2014, http://www.washingtonpost.com/blogs/answer-sheet/wp/2014/02/08/matt-damon-we-would-never-let-businessmen-design-warheads-why-would-you-cut-out-educators-when-youre-designing-education-policy/.

52. Arthur Hauptman, "Where Do We Stand and How Can We Improve?" (presentation, Degrees of Difficulty: Can American Higher Education Regain Its Edge?, American Enterprise Institute, Washington, DC, February 11, 2011), http://www.aei.org/events/degrees-of-difficulty-can-american-higher-education-regain-its-edge/.

53. California Faculty Association, *The CSU Graduation and Achievement Gap Initiative: Doing Our Part to Educate 1 Million More Graduates by 2025* (Sacramento, CA, April 2010), http://www.calfac.org/sites/main/files/CFA_WPApr10_Grad_Initiative.pdf.

54. Susan Meisenhelder, "Higher Education at the Crossroads: The Graduation Rate Craze," *Huffington Post*, May 25, 2011, http://www.huffingtonpost.com/susan-meisenhelder/higher-education-crossroads-graduation-rate_b_829787.html.

55. George Leef, "Oh, but There *Is* a Great Debate Over That," *National Review Online*, Feburary 17, 2011, http://www.nationalreview.com/phi-beta-cons/259971/oh-there-iisi-debate-over-george-leef.

56. Diane Ravitch, "Now the Gates Foundation Is Destroying Higher Education," *Diane Ravitch's Blog*, July 17, 2013, http://dianeravitch.net/2013/07/17/now-the-gates-foundation-is-destroying-higher-education/.

57. Nicholas W. Hillman, David A. Tandberg, and Alisa H. Fryar, "Evaluating the Impacts of 'New' Performance Funding in Higher Education," *Educational Evaluation and Policy Analysis* (2015), 1–19.

58. David Tandberg, quoted in Doug Lederman, "Performance Funding Underperforms," *Inside Higher Education*, November 18, 2013, http://www.insidehighered.com/news/2013/11/18/studies-question-effectiveness-state-performance-based-funding.

59. William J. Goggin, quoted in Doug Lederman, "Completion-Focused Financial Aid," *Inside Higher Education*, August 7, 2012, http://www.insidehighered.com/news/2012/08/07/new-effort-gear-federal-financial-aid-programs-college-completion.

60. Sara Goldrick-Rab, "Reflections on Foundations, ALEC, and Higher Ed Reform in Wisconsin," *The Education Optimists*, June 24, 2012, http://eduoptimists.blogspot.com/2012/06/reflections-on-foundations-alec-and.html.

61. Hall and Thomas, "Advocacy Philanthropy."

62. Richard L. Hall and Alan V. Deardorff, "Lobbying as Legislative Subsidy," *American Political Science Review* 100, no. 1 (2006): 69–84.

63. Andrew P. Kelly and Frederick M. Hess, *Beyond Retrofitting: Innovation in Higher Education* (Washington, DC: The Hudson Institute, June 2013), http://www.hudson.org/content/researchattachments/attachment/1121/beyond_retrofitting-innovation_in_higher_ed_%28kelly-hess,_june_2013%29.pdf.

64. Ibid.

65. Paul Fain, "Establishment Opens Door for MOOCs," *Inside Higher Education*, November 14, 2012, http://www.insidehighered.com/news/2012/11/14/gates-foundation-and-ace-go-big-mooc-related-grants.

Chapter 5

1. Sam Dillon, "Teacher Ratings Get a New Look, Pushed by a Rich Watcher," *New York Times*, December 3, 2010, http://www.nytimes.com/2010/12/04/education/04teacher.html; Anya Kamenetz, "Updated: New Details on Bill Gates's $5 Billion Plan to Film, Measure Every Teacher," *Fast Company*, April 15, 2013, http://www.fastcompany.com/3007973/creative-conversations/updated-new-details-bill-gatess-5-billion-plan-film-measure-every-tea; Larry Abramson, "Watch Again: Helping Teachers Improve Via Video," *Weekend Edition Saturday*, NPR, December 26, 2010, http://www.npr.org/2010/12/26/132313779/watch-again-helping-teachers-improve-via-video.

2. Lyndsey Layton, "Gates Foundation Study: We've Figured Out What Makes a Good Teacher," *Washington Post*, January 8, 2013, http://www.washingtonpost.com/national/gates-study-weve-figured-out-what-makes-a-good-teacher/2013/01/08/05ca7d60-59b0-11e2-9fa9-5fbdc9530eb9_story.html.

3. Joy Resmovits, "Gates Foundation MET Report: Teacher Observation Less Reliable Than Test Scores," *Huffington Post*, January 8, 2013, http://www.huffingtonpost.com/2013/01/08/gates-foundation-met-report-teacher-_n_2433348.html.

4. Eleanor Chute, "Gates Foundation Airs Model to Evaluate Teachers," *Pittsburgh Post-Gazette*, January 9, 2013, http://www.post-gazette.com/news/education/2013/01/09/Gates-Foundation-airs-model-to-evaluate-teachers/stories/201301090265.

5. Stephen Sawchuk, "Combined Measures Better at Gauging Teacher Effectiveness, Study Finds," *Education Week*, January 8, 2013, http://www.edweek.org/ew/articles/2013/01/08/17teach_ep.h32.html.

6. Leslie Lenkowsky, "The 'Best Uses' of Philanthropy for Reform," in *With the Best of Intentions: How Philanthropy is Reshaping K–12 Education*, ed. Frederick M. Hess (Cambridge, MA: Harvard University Press, 2005).

7. Dana Goldstein, *The Teacher Wars: A History of America's Most Embattled Profession* (New York: Doubleday, 2014) and Carnegie Forum on Education and the Economy, *A Nation Prepared: The Report of the Task Force on Teaching as a Profession* (New York, 1986).

8. Sarah Reckhow, *Follow the Money: How Foundation Dollars Change Public Schools* (New York: Oxford University Press, 2013).

9. Andrew Rotherham, "Teaching Fishing or Giving Away Fish? Grantmaking for Research, Policy, and Advocacy," in Hess, *With the Best of Intentions*, 206.

10. Steven Cantrell, interview by Dana Goldstein, Dec. 11, 2014.

11. Bill & Melinda Gates Foundation, *2013 Annual Report*, http://www.gatesfoundation.org/Who-We-Are/Resources-and-Media/Annual-Reports/Annual-Report-2013.

12. US Department of the Treasury, Internal Revenue Service, Carnegie Foundation for the Advancement of Teaching Form 990 (Washington, DC, 2013).

13. Walton Family Foundation, *2013 Grant Report*, http://www.waltonfamilyfoundation.org/about/2013-grant-report.

14. US Department of the Treasury, Internal Revenue Service, Spencer Foundation Form 990 (Washington, DC, 2013).

15. For the history of value-added measurement, see Goldstein, *The Teacher Wars*, 204–211.

16. Robert Gordon, Thomas J. Kane, and Douglas O. Staiger, "Identifying Effective Teachers Using Performance on the Job," Hamilton Project paper (Washington, DC: The Brookings Institution, April 2006).

17. Thomas Kane, interview by Dana Goldstein, November 20, 2014.

18. Thomas Toch, "Small Is Still Beautiful," *Washington Monthly*, July/August 2010.

19. American Institutes for Research and SRI International, *Evaluation of the Bill & Melinda Gates Foundation's High School Grants Initiative: 2001–2005 Final Report*," August 2006, https://docs.gatesfoundation.org/Documents/year4evaluationairsri.pdf.

20. The New Teacher Project, *The Widget Effect: Our National Failure to Acknowledge and Act on Differences in Teacher Effectiveness*, June 8, 2009, http://tntp.org/publications/view/the-widget-effect-failure-to-act-on-differences-in-teacher-effectiveness.

21. All Gates Foundation grant numbers are drawn from the foundation's searchable grantee database, available online at http://www.gatesfoundation.org/How-We-Work/Quick-Links/Grants-Database.

22. Steven Cantrell et al., *National Board Certification and Teacher Effectiveness: Evidence from a Random Assignment Experiment*, June 11, 2008, http://cepr.harvard.edu/cepr-resources/files/news-events/ncte-national-board-certification--cantrell-fullerton-kane-staiger.pdf.

23. Ibid.

24. Thomas Kane, interview by Dana Goldstein, November 20, 2014.

25. For state responses to Race to the Top, see Goldstein, *The Teacher Wars*, 213–217.

26. Thomas Kane, interview by Dana Goldstein, November 20, 2014.

27. Jesse Rothstein, interview by Dana Goldstein, November 14, 2014.

28. Robert Pianta, interview by Dana Goldstein, November 18, 2014.

29. Douglas Harris, interview by Dana Goldstein, November 21, 2014.

30. MET findings are drawn from the following papers, all published online by the Bill & Melinda Gates Foundation and available at http://www.metproject.org/reports.php:

Learning About Teaching: Initial Findings from the Measures of Effective Teaching Project (2010); *Gathering Feedback for Teaching: Combining High-Quality Observations with Student Surveys and Achievement Gains* (2012); *Have We Identified Effective Teachers? Validating Measures of Effective Teaching Using Random Assignment* (2013); *The Reliability of Classroom Observations by School Personnel* (2013); *A Composite Estimator of Effective Teaching* (2013); *Feedback for Better Teaching: Nine Principles for Using Measures of Effective Teaching* (2013); and *Ensuring Fair and Reliable Measures of Effective Teaching: A Practitioner Brief* (2013). In addition, findings are published in *Designing Teacher Evaluation Systems: New Guidance from the Measures of Effective Teaching Project*, ed. Thomas Kane, Kerri Kerr, and Robert Pianta (San Francisco: Jossey-Bass, 2014).

31. Jay P. Greene, "Understanding the Gates Foundation's Measuring Effective Teachers Project," *Jay P. Greene's Blog*, January 9, 2013, http://jaypgreene.com/2013/01/09/understanding-the-gates-foundations-measuring-effective-teachers-project/.

32. Kane, Kerr, and Pianta, *Designing Teacher Evaluation Systems*.

33. Robert Pianta, interview by Dana Goldstein, November 18, 2014.

34. Steven Cantrell, interview by Dana Goldstein, December 11, 2014.

35. Ibid.

36. Thomas Kane and Douglas Staiger, "Making Decisions with Imprecise Performance Measures: The Relationship Between Annual Student Achievement Gains and a Teacher's Career Value-Added," in Kane, Kerr, and Pianta, *Designing Teacher Evaluation Systems*.

37. Matthew Ronfeldt, Susanna Loeb, and James Wyckoff, "How Teacher Turnover Harms Student Achievement," *American Educational Research Journal* 50, no. 1 (2013): 4–36.

38. Information on new Gates Foundation research grants from Dana Goldstein interviews with Cantrell and Kane, 2014.

39. Thomas Kane, interview by Dana Goldstein, November 20, 2014.

40. Robert Pianta, interview by Dana Goldstein, November 18, 2014.

41. NEPC funding detailed at http://nepc.colorado.edu/support.

42. Jesse Rothstein and William Mathis, *Review of Two Culminating Reports from the MET Project*, NEPC paper, January 31, 2013, http://nepc.colorado.edu/thinktank/review-MET-final-2013.

43. Douglas Harris, interview by Dana Goldstein, November 21, 2014.

44. Ibid.

45. Spencer Foundation, "2012 Grant List," http://www.spencer.org/resources/content/2/9/documents/gl_2012.pdf; I have received a Spencer Foundation grant.

46. Douglas Reed, interview by Dana Goldstein, November 17, 2014.

47. C. Kirabo Jackson, Rucker C. Johnson, and Claudia Persico, *The Effects of School Spending on Educational and Economic Outcomes: Evidence from School Finance Reforms*, NBER working paper, January 2015.

48. Carmen Fariña, "Trust" speech, available at http://schools.nyc.gov/Offices/mediarelations/NewsandSpeeches/2014-2015/Chancellor+Carmen+Fari%C3%B1a+Lays+Out+Vision+for+NYC+Schools.htm. For media reaction, see Jessica Glazer and Sarah Darville, "Advocates Pushing City on Struggling Schools Choose an Unlikely Champion," *Chalkbeat New York*, October 13, 2014, http://ny.chalkbeat.org/2014/10/13/advocates-pushing-city-on-struggling-schools-choose-an-unlikely-champion/#.VJskVMAA8. For research on trust, see Anthony Bryk and Barbara Schneider, *Trust in Schools: A Core Resource For Improvement* (New York: Russell Sage Foundation Publications, 2004).

49. Janelle Scott and Huriya Jabbar, "The Hub and the Spokes: Foundations, Intermediary Organizations, Incentivist Reforms, and the Politics of Research Evidence," *Educational Policy* 1, no. 25 (2014).

50. Kane, Kerr, and Pianta, *Designing Teacher Evaluation Systems*, 5.

51. Goldstein, *The Teacher Wars*, 92.

52. Ibid., 228–229, 242.

53. Huriya Jabbar et al., "How Policymakers Define 'Evidence': The Politics of Research Use in New Orleans," *Policy Futures in Education* 12, no. 8 (2014).

54. Scott and Jabbar, "The Hub and the Spokes."

55. Jabbar et al., "How Policymakers Define 'Evidence.'"

56. Jeffrey Henig, *Spin Cycle: How Research Is Used in Policy Debates: The Case of Charter Schools* (New York: Russell Sage Foundation Publications, 2008).

57. Steven Cantrell, interview by Dana Goldstein, December 11, 2014.

58. MDRC press release available at http://www.mdrc.org/news/press-release/ new-findings-show-new-york-city-s-small-high-schools-boost-college-enrollment.

59. Steven Cantrell, interview by Dana Goldstein, January 21, 2015.

Chapter 6

1. Fred Dardick, "Bill Gates' Reckless Meddling with US Education Through Common Core," *RedState*, June 18, 2014, http://www.redstate.com/diary/fdardick/2014/06/18/ bill-gates-reckless-meddling-u-s-education-common-core/.

2. Teacherken, "What Bill Gates Really Thinks of the Common Core Standards," *Daily Kos*, October 16, 2013, http://www.dailykos.com/story/2013/10/16/1247790/-What-Bill-Gates-really-thinks-of-Common-Core-State-Standards.

3. Peter Dreier, "Why Are Walmart Billionaires Bankrolling Phony School 'Reform' in LA?" *Moyers & Company*, March 2, 2013, http://billmoyers.com/2013/03/02/ why-are-walmart-billionaires-bankrolling-phony-school-reform-in-la/.

4. Diane Granat, "Saving the Rosenwald Schools: Preserving African American History," The Alicia Patterson Foundation, 2002, http://aliciapatterson.org/stories/ saving-rosenwald-schools-preserving-african-american-history.

5. Jerald E. Podair, "The Ocean Hill-Brownsville Crisis: New York's *Antigone*," *The Gotham Center*, October 6, 2001, http://www.gothamcenter.org/festival/2001/confpapers/podair. pdf.

6. Peter Appleborne, "Annenberg School Grants Raise Hopes, and Questions on Extent of Change," *New York Times*, April 30, 1995, http://www.nytimes.com/1995/04/30/us/ annenberg-school-grants-raise-hopes-and-questions-on-extent-of-change.html.

7. Frederick M. Hess, "Rethinking America's Schools," *Philanthropy*, March/April 2005, http://www.philanthropyroundtable.org/topic/excellence_in_philanthropy/ rethinking_americas_schools.

8. Gary Rosen, "The Broad Foundation Infiltrates the Worcester Public Schools," *Worcester Magazine*, March 31, 2011, http://worcestermag.com/2011/03/31/ the-broad-foundation-infiltrates-the-worcester-public-schools-118950514/7312.

9. Michele McNeil, "Rifts Deepen Over Direction of Ed. Policy in U.S.," *Education Week*, May 7, 2013, http://www.edweek.org/ew/articles/2013/05/08/30debate_ep.h32.html.

10. Olivia Pulsinelli, "Laura and John Arnold Foundation Launch Education Database," *Houston Business Journal*, June 27, 2012, http://www.bizjournals.com/houston/ news/2012/06/27/laura-and-john-arnold-foundation.html.

11. Sara Rimer, "Gates Grants Aim to Help Low-Income Students Finish College, *New York Times*, December 8, 2008, http://www.nytimes.com/2008/12/09/education/09gates. html?_r=0.

12. Keith Ervin, "$2 Million Goes to Seattle Schools," *Seattle Times*, October 14, 2000, http://community.seattletimes.nwsource.com/archive/?date=20001014&slug=4047697.

13. Jay P. Greene, "Buckets into the Sea: Why Philanthropy Isn't Changing Schools and How It Could," in *With the Best of Intentions: How Philanthropy Is Reshaping K–12 Education*, ed. Frederick M. Hess (Cambridge, MA: Harvard Education Press, 2005).

Chapter 7

1. Ellen Lagemann, *The Politics of Knowledge: The Carnegie Corporation, Philanthropy, and Public Policy* (Chicago: University of Chicago Press, 1989); Barry Karl and Stanley Katz, "The American Private Philanthropic Foundation and the Public Sphere, 1890–1930," *Minerva* 19, no. 2 (1981): 236–270.

2. Frank Walsh, "Perilous Philanthropy," *The Independent*, August 1915, 262.

3. Jeffrey Hart as quoted in Robert Arnove and Nadine Pinede, "Revisiting the 'Big Three' Foundations," *Critical Sociology* 33, (2007): 391.

4. Diane Ravitch, *Death and Life of the Great American School System* (New York: Basic Books, 2010), 200.

5. Rick Cohen, *Strategic Grantmaking: Foundations and the School Privatization Movement*, (Washington, DC: National Committee for Responsive Philanthropy, 2007).

6. For an example of the charge of privatization of public schools coming from the political left, see the cartoon by Mark Fiore called "ProfitShip! Cashing in on Public Schools," commissioned by *The Progressive* and published in December 2014 at https://www.youtube.com/watch?v=opcHQ_v6PuU.

7. Charles Lindblom, *Politics and Markets* (New York: Basic Books, 1980); Joel Klein, "The Case for the Private Sector in School Reform," *The Atlantic*, August 2012, http://www.theatlantic.com/national/archive/2012/08/the-case-for-the-private-sector-in-school-reform/261215/; Michael Sandel, *What Money Can't Buy: The Moral Limits of Markets* (New York: Farrar, Straus & Giroux, 2012). For personal attacks, see Lyndsey Layton, "Center for Union Facts Says Randi Weingarten Is Ruining Nation's Schools," September 24, 2014, http://www.washingtonpost.com/local/education/center-for-union-facts-says-randi-weingarten-is-ruining-nations-schools/2014/09/24/6443fed4-441e-11e4-9a15-137aa0153527_story.html. Also see Alliance for Quality Education, *The Real Campbell Brown: Right-Wing. Elitist. Wrong About Public Schools*, August 2014, http://realcampbellbrown.com/wp-content/uploads/2014/08/TheRealCampbellBrown.pdf.

8. I use the phrase *policy elites* interchangeably with *top policy makers, civic and business leader coalitions, policy entrepreneurs*, and *reformers*. By *policy elites*, I mean loose networks of corporate leaders, public officials (including top educational policy makers), foundation officials, and academics who circulate ideas consistent with their views of problems and solutions, champion particular reforms, use both public and private funds to run projects, and strongly influence decision making. Not unlike policy elites in business and civic affairs who are involved in growing a stronger economy, improving health care, protecting national security, strengthening foreign policy, and safeguarding the environment, policy entrepreneurs and reformers have ready access to media and are capable of framing problems and shaping an agenda of change. Or, as one member in good standing wrote: "In public policy, it matters less who has the best arguments

and more who gets heard—and by whom" (Ralph Reed, cited in Dana Milbank, *Homo Politicus: The Strange and Barbaric Tribes of the Beltway* [New York: Doubleday, 2008], 68).

Political party labels do not define these elites, although there are clearly Republican and Democratic members who wear their affiliation on their sleeves and, when administrations change, move in and out of office. I do not use the term to suggest conspiratorial groups secretly meeting and designing action plans. Nor do I bash elites. I suggest only that these overlapping networks of like-minded individuals share values and tastes and seek school improvements aligned with those values and tastes. As "influentials," they convene frequently in different forums, speak the same policy talk, and are connected closely to sources of public and private influence in governments, media, businesses, academia, and foundations. They help to create a climate of opinion that hovers around no more than a few hundred national policy leaders and smaller numbers at state and local levels. Familiar with the ways of the media, they extend and shape that climate of opinion by closely working with journalists who report what they say, write, think, and do. Few members of these loosely connected networks, however, have had direct or sustained experience with school principals or teachers, much less experience in teaching. Yet their recommended policies—their "common sense" decisions about what the nation, states, districts, and teachers should do—touch the daily lives of both educators and children. See John Kingdon, *Agendas, Alternatives, and Public Policies* (Boston: Little, Brown, 1984); James Fallows, *Breaking the News* (New York: Random House, 1996); William Safire, "Elite Establishment Egghead Eupatrids," *New York Times Magazine*, May 18, 1997, 16. For a survey of experts on who the "influentials" currently shaping school reform policy are, see Christopher Swanson and Janelle Barlage, *Influence: A Study of the Factors Shaping Educational Policy* (Washington, DC: Editorial Projects in Education Research Center, December 2006).

9. David Tyack and Larry Cuban, *Tinkering Toward Utopia* (Cambridge, MA: Harvard University Press, 1995), 117–119; Lawrence Leak and Lois Williams, "Private Management of Public Schools: The Baltimore Experience" (paper presented to American Educational Research Association, Chicago, 1997); Keith Richburg, "Setback for Philadelphia Schools Plan," *Washington Post*, June 29, 2008, http://www.washington-post.com/wp-dyn/content/article/2008/06/28/AR2008062801637.html.

10. National Center for Education Statistics (NCES), "The Condition of Education, 2014" (Washington, D.C.: Institutes of Education Sciences, http://nces.ed.gov/programs/coe/). Some examples strengthen this point: Parental choice through charter schools, magnets, and vouchers are common in large and middle-sized cities enrolling about 13 percent of US students. Even in first-ring suburbs that have become largely minority, such as Prince George's County (MD) outside of Washington, DC (where 67 percent of the population is middle- and working-class African American), eight out of 204 schools were charters in 2014. Council of the Great City Schools, "Urban School Statistics," http://www.cgcs.org/Page/75; for Prince Georges County statistics on charter schools, see *Wikipedia*, http://en.wikipedia.org/wiki/Prince_George%27s_County_Public_Schools; National Center for Education Statistics, *Digest of Education Statistics*, Table 216.20: Number and enrollment of public elementary and secondary schools, by school level, type, and charter and magnet status: Selected years, 1990–91 through 2011–12, http://nces.ed.gov/programs/digest/d13/tables/dt13_216.20.asp.

11. Note that historian of education Diane Ravitch recognizes that "corporate reformers" and billionaire donors work from a mix of motives. Some no doubt are motivated by idealism.

Some think they are leading a new civil rights movement, though I doubt that Dr. King would recognize these financial titans as his colleagues as they impose their will on one of our crucial public institutions. Some hate government. Some love the free market. Some think that the profit motive is more efficient and effective than any public-sector enterprise. All of them share a surprising certainty that they know how to "fix" the public schools and that the people who work in those schools are lazy, unmotivated, incompetent, and not to be trusted (Diane Ravitch, "Bridging Differences," *Education Week*, November 15, 2011, http://blogs.edweek.org/edweek/Bridging-Differences/2011/11/billionaires_for_education_ref.html).

12. For the 2012 referendum on allowing charter schools in the state of Washington, major contributors were the Gates, Walton, and Broad Foundations. See *Cash Contributions for Yes on 1240 Washington Coalition for Public Charter Schools*, Public Disclosure Commission, http://www.pdc.wa.gov/MvcQuerySystem/CommitteeData/contributions?param=WUVTIFdDIDUwNw====&year=2012&type=initiative.

   I also include centralizing educational authority in state takeovers of lowest performing schools such as Louisiana's Recovery School District in Orleans Parish and Tennessee's Achievement School District and creating charter schools in such districts. The Walton and Broad Foundations have supported these ventures. See http://achievementschooldistrict.org/blog/2013/01/13/foundations-advance-growth-of-excellent-schools/ and http://www.broadeducation.org/investments/current_investments/investments_all.html; Janelle Scott, "The Politics of Venture Philanthropy in Charter School Policy and Advocacy," *Educational Policy* 23, no. 1 (2009): 106–136; Joanne Barkan, "Plutocrats at Work: How Big Philanthropies Undermine Democracy," *Dissent*, 2013, http://www.dissentmagazine.org/article/plutocrats-at-work-how-big-philanthropy-undermines-democracy.

13. Lorraine M. McDonnell, "No Child Left Behind and the Federal Role in Education: Evolution or Revolution?" *Peabody Journal of Education* 80, no. 2 (2005): 19–38. The phrase *muscular philanthropy* comes from Frederick Hess, "Philanthropy Gets in the Ring: Edu-funders Get Serious about Education Policy," *Phi Delta Kappan* 93, no. 8 (2012): 17–21.

14. Sarah Reckhow and Jeffrey W. Snyder, "The Expanding Role of Philanthropy in Education Politics," *Educational Researcher* 43, no. 4 (2014): 186–195; Lyndsey Layton, "How Bill Gates Pulled Off the Swift Common Core Revolution," *Washington Post*, June 7, 2014; Patrick McGuinn, "Fight Club: Are Advocacy Organizations Changing the Politics of Education?" *Education Next* 12, no. 3 (2012), http://educationnext.org/fight-club/; Natalie Hopkinson, "Why Michelle Rhee's Education 'Brand' Failed in D.C.," *The Atlantic*, September 15, 2010, http://www.theatlantic.com/politics/archive/2010/09/why-michelle-rhees-education-brand-failed-in-dc/63014/; Joanne Barkan, "Got Dough? How Billionaires Rule Our Schools," *Dissent*, Winter 2011, http://www.dissentmagazine.org/article/got-dough-how-billionaires-rule-our-schools; Nicolas Confessore, "Policy-Making Billionaires," *New York Times*, November 26, 2011.

15. Public education, like health care reform and efforts to pass climate change legislation, is only one of many venues where foundations have funded advocacy groups. Note the heavy presence of donors making grants to organizations that pressed for the Affordable Care Act since 2009. See Rick Cohen, "The Role of Philanthropy and Advocacy in Healthcare Reform Implementation," *NPQ*, February 21, 2013, https://nonprofitquarterly.org/philanthropy/21836-the-role-of-philanthropy-and-advocacy-in-healthcare-reform-implementation.html.

16. Rob Reich, "What Are Foundations For?" *Boston Review*, March 1, 2013, http://www.bostonreview.net/forum/foundations-philanthropy-democracy.

17. Edward Skloot, "The Gated Community," *Alliance Magazine*, September 2011, http://www.hudson.org/content/researchattachments/attachment/1197/alliance_magazine_edward_skloot.pdf.

18. David Callahan, "Be Afraid: The Five Scariest Trends in Philanthropy," *Inside Philanthropy*, October 31, 2014, http://www.insidephilanthropy.com/home/2014/10/31/be-afraid-the-five-scariest-trends-in-philanthropy.html. Frederick Hess makes the persuasive point that major educational foundations enjoy an "absence of scrutiny," with media and academics joining in a "conspiracy of silence" when it comes to asking hard questions of donors. See Frederick M. Hess, ed., *With the Best of Intentions: How Philanthropy Is Reshaping K–12 Education* (Cambridge, MA: Harvard Education Press, 2005), 9–11.

19. Walking away from a grant—usually three years in length—was common among donors when early returns appeared unpromising. See Gary Lichtenstein report on what happened at Denver's Manual High School in the early 2000s when the high school was reorganized to become three small schools. "Lessons Learned at Manual," July 2004 (in author's possession) and Gary Lichtenstein, "What Went Wrong at Manual High: The Role of Intermediaries in the Quest for Smaller Schools," *Education Week*, May 16, 2006.

20. Mark Smylie and Stacy Wenzel, *The Chicago Annenberg Challenge: Successes, Failures, and Lessons for the Future*, Final Technical Report, (Chicago: Consortium of Chicago School Research, 2003). The Gates Foundation's desertion of its small high schools venture after a few years led a close observer of donors to remark: "In an age of hands-on living mega donors, the possibilities for big screw-ups are self-evident and we've seen some doozies so far—like, say, turning urban school districts upside down to create small high schools and then realizing that this idea wasn't as brilliant as MS-DOS." (David Callahan, "Be Afraid.")

    Gates's walking away from small high schools may also have been premature, since recent studies have shown that small high schools, many of which were directly funded by the foundation, have higher graduation rates than larger neighborhood schools. See Atila Abdulkadiroglu, Weiwei Hu, and Parag Pathak, "Small High Schools and Student Achievement: Lottery-Based Evidence from New York City" (working paper no. 19576, National Bureau of Economic Research, Cambridge, MA, October 19, 2013); Rebecca Unterman, *The Effects of New York City's Small High Schools of Choice on Postsecondary Enrollment*, MDRC Policy Brief, October 2014, http://www.mdrc.org/publication/headed-college.

21. I thank Jeffrey R. Henig for suggesting the "slipping gear" phrase.

22. As many researchers and observers have pointed out, a major shift in education policy has occurred over the past half-century. Beginning after the US Congress passed the Elementary and Secondary Education Act (1965) and the subsequent Coleman Report (1966), a focus on student outcomes accelerated sharply after the *Nation at Risk* report (1983), moving the focus of decision-makers on school performance from inputs (for example, per-pupil spending, facilities, lab equipment) to district, school, and student accountability for outputs (for example, student test scores, graduation rates, college attendance). See Robert Linn, "Assessments and Accountability," *Educational Researcher* 29, no. 2 (2000): 4–16; Jal Mehta, "How Paradigms Create Politics: The Transformation of American Educational Policy, 1980–2001," *American Educational Research Journal* 50, no. 2 (2013): 285–324.

As for hostility to unions, early-twentieth-century philanthropists such as Andrew Carnegie and John D. Rockefeller displayed even stronger animosity toward unions when they headed steel and mining corporations. See Barry Karl and Stanley Katz, "The American Private Philanthropic Foundation and the Public Sphere, 1890–1930," *Minerva* 19, no. 2 (1981): 253.

23. David Tyack and I have written extensively about the marked differences between policy talk (the rhetoric and hype of, say, new technologies for students), policy action (adopting particular policies such as buying and deploying technological innovations), and policy implementation (putting adopted policies into classroom practice, teachers use new hardware and software as policy makers intended). See Tyack and Cuban, *Tinkering Toward Utopia.*

24. For an example of a foundation pressing for particular changes by staffing a state department of education with officials it paid for, see James Odato, "Education Reform Backed by the Wealthy," *Albany Times Union*, November 25, 2013, http://www.timesunion.com/local/article/Education-reform-backed-by-the-wealthy-5006670.php.

25. Michael Janofsky, "Vergara Ruling Stands, Judge Rules in Final Review," *LA Report*, August 28, 2014, http://laschoolreport.com/just-in-vergara-ruling-stands-judge-rules-in-final-review/; Bill Raden and Gary Cohn, David Welch, "The Man Behind *Vergara v. California*," *Capital & Main*, February 20, 2014, http://capitalandmain.com/david-welch-the-man-behind-vergara-versus-california/.

26. The literature about policy implementation, especially those measures dubbed as "reforms," has become increasingly detailed and sophisticated over the past half-century. It is a research literature rich in examples of policies and their implementation that would be disheartening to either current or prospective policy makers. Some key studies over the decades are the following: Jeffrey Pressman and Aaron Wildavsky, *Implementation* (Berkeley: University of California Press, 1973); Paul Berman and Milbrey McLaughlin, *Federal Programs Supporting Educational Change*, Vol. VIII, *Implementing and Sustaining Innovations* (Santa Monica, CA: RAND, 1978); Meredith Honig (ed.), *New Directions in Education Policy Implementation* (Albany: State University of New York Press, 2006); Joseph McDonald et al., *American School Reform: What Fails and Why* (Chicago: University of Chicago Press, 2014).

Over decades, researchers have repeatedly documented how top-down policy formation and adoption seldom spurred practitioners to put policies into classroom practice that bore much resemblance to what policy makers intended. Research has also shown that as the policy traversed district and school offices into classrooms, teacher adaptations and adjustments occurred.

27. In 2011, 48 percent of US schools failed to meet Adequate Yearly Progress (AYP). Variation in states ranged from 89 percent in Florida to 11 percent in Wisconsin failing to make AYP. See Alexandra Usher, *AYP Results for 2010–2011* (Washington, DC: Center on Education Policy, December 2011), 2. Also see Sam Dillon, "Failure Rate of Schools Overstated, Study Says," *New York Times*, December 15, 2011, http://www.nytimes.com/2011/12/15/education/education-secretary-overstated-failing-schools-under-no-child-left-behind-study-says.html?_r=0.

28. Brian Stecher et al., "Consequences of Large-Scale High-Stakes Testing on School and Classroom Practice, in *Making Sense of Test-Based Accountability in Education*, ed. Laura Hamilton et al. (Santa Monica, CA: RAND, 2002), 79–100; James Spillane et al. "Organizational Routines as Coupling Mechanisms: Policy, School Administration, and the Technical Core," *American Educational Research Journal* 48, no. 3 (2011): 586–619.

29. Motoko Rich, "A Walmart Fortune, Spreading Charter Schools," *New York Times*, April 25, 2014; Philip Gleason et al., "Do KIPP Schools Boost Student Achievement?" *Education Finance and Policy* 9, no. 1 (2014): 36–58; Howard Bloom, "Charter Schools Get Boost," *Los Angeles Times*, January 17, 2008; Sam Dillon, "School Is Turned Around but Cost Gives Pause," *New York Times*, June 24, 2010. For within-district competition and borrowing from charter schools, see the Apollo 20 project in Houston, Texas, public schools, http://www.houstonisd.org/Page/78350; also see Marc Holley et al., "Competition with Charters Motivates Districts," *Education Next*, Fall 2013, http://educationnext.org/competition-with-charters-motivates-districts/.

30. CREDO, *Multiple Choice: Charter School Performance in 16 States* (Stanford, CA: Center for Research on Education Outcomes, 2009); Matthew DeCarlo, "The Evidence on Charter Schools and Test Scores," policy brief (Washington, DC: Albert Shanker Institute, 2011).

31. Katie Ash, "Computers in the Classroom, Then and Now," *Education Week*, April 22, 2009, http://blogs.edweek.org/edweek/DigitalEducation/2009/04/computers_in_the_classroom_the_1.html.

32. Jason Ravitz et al., "Cautionary Tales About Correlations Between Student Computer Use and Academic Achievement" (paper presented at annual meeting of the American Educational Research Association, New Orleans, LA, April 2002); Larry Cuban, *Inside the Black Box of Classroom Practice: Change Without Reform in American Education* (Cambridge, MA: Harvard Education Press, 2013), 43–45.

33. Mark Windschitle and Kurt Sahl, "Tracing Teachers' Use of Technology in a Laptop Computer School," *American Educational Research Journal* 39, no. 1 (2002): 165–205; Larry Cuban, *Oversold and Underused: Computers in the Classroom* (Cambridge, MA: Harvard University Press, 2001); Cuban, *Inside the Black Box*.

34. Larry Cuban, *Hugging the Middle: How Teachers Teach in an Era of Testing and Accountability* (New York: Teachers College Press, 2009); Cuban, *Inside the Black Box*, 155–171.

35. Anyone familiar with the level of hardware and software used in schools over the past thirty years has seen extraordinary changes in software programs and hardware miniaturization. The software that ninth-graders were using in 1985 was gone and forgotten five years later. Preparing students for jobs in a labor market prizing the use of information and rapid communication means constant changes in what software and hardware students will use in schools, a condition that districts can hardly afford to keep purchasing every few years. Thus, built-in obsolesence of machines and software makes it difficult to plan on current students being prepared for jobs. Current interest in teaching all students to learn to code recognizes the constant turnover in technological equipment and skills. See, for example, Nick Wingfield, "Fostering New Tech Talent in Schools," *New York Times*, September 30, 2012.

36. "Bill Gates School Crusade," *Bloomberg Businessweek*, July 15, 2010, http://www.businessweek.com/magazine/content/10_30/b4188058281758.htm#p2.

37. For press releases from Broad Superintendents Academy, see http://www.broadcenter.org/academy/newsroom/category/press-releases. For a highly critical view, see Sharon Higgins, a parent who has followed Broad graduates of the Academy and other programs: http://thebroadreport.blogspot.com/p/parent-guide.html. As of 2011, there were 165 graduates. The foundation released no figures for 2012 and 2013.

38. Angela Pascopella, "Superintendent Staying Power," *District Administration*, April 2011, http://www.districtadministration.com/article/superintendent-staying-power.

39. Further evidence of the struggle to go from policy to practice is the announcement that The Broad Foundation will no longer give a $1 million prize, begun in 2002, to urban districts that have improved student achievement and reduced the test score gap between minorities and whites. See Howard Blume, "Broad Foundation Suspends $1-million Prize for Urban School Districts," *Los Angeles Times*, February 8, 2015. For a recent study of the correlation between superintendents and student achievement, see Larry Cuban, "Superintendents and Test Scores," *Larry Cuban on School Reform and Classroom Practice*, October 14, 2014, https://larrycuban.wordpress.com/2014/10/08/superintendents-and-test-scores/.

40. Lyndsey Layton, "How Bill Gates Pulled Off the Common Core Revolution," *Washington Post*, June 7, 2014, http://www.washingtonpost.com/politics/how-bill-gates-pulled-off-the-swift-common-core-revolution/2014/06/07/a830e32e-ec34-11e3-9f5c-9075d5508f0a_story.html; Tim Murphy, "Tragedy of the Common Core," *Mother Jones*, September/October 2014, 31–43, 68.

41. That the Common Core standards are not a curriculum and local officials, including teachers, determine what is taught in lessons is stated directly as a "Fact" in the Common Core standards' website. See http://www.corestandards.org/about-the-standards/myths-vs-facts/.

42. Two national consortia will produce assessments for most of the states adopting Common Core standards. PARCC, or the Partnership for Assessment of Readiness for College and Career, has nine states and the District of Columbia signed up and Smarter Balanced Assessment Consortia has seventeen states committed to this test. Both tests will be used in the 2014–15 school year. The remaining states plan to use their own or other commercially prepared tests. See Catherine Gewertz and Andrew Ujifusa, "State Plans for Testing Fragmented," *Education Week*, May 21, 2014. In the wake of imminent testing, a backlash has developed. See, for example, Patrick O'Donnell, "Test Mania? Teachers Say 'High Stakes' of Testing Leads to More Tests, Less Teaching," *Cleveland Plain Dealer*, October 22, 2014; Lisa Wolff, "Too Early for High Stakes Testing on Common Core," *NJ Spotlight*, http://www.njspotlight.com/stories/14/06/15/op-ed-too-early-for-high-stakes-testing-based-on-common-core-state-standards/; Liz Bowie, "Local School Leaders Ask State To Delay High-Stakes Graduation Tests," *Baltimore Sun*, October 16, 2014, http://www.baltimoresun.com/news/maryland/education/blog/bs-md-graduation-requirements-20141016-story.html#page=1.

43. Alexandra Neason, "The 'Common' in Common Core Fractures as State Support Falters," *The Hechinger Report*, June 18, 2014, http://hechingerreport.org/content/common-common-core-fractures-state-support-falters_16420/; Motoko Rich, "States Given a Reprieve on Rating Teachers," *New York Times*, August 21, 2014.

44. Valerie Strauss, "Gates Foundation Backs Two-year Delay in Linking Common Core Test Scores to Teacher Evaluation, Student Promotion," *Answer Sheet* (blog), *Washington Post*, June 10, 2014, http://www.washingtonpost.com/blogs/answer-sheet/wp/2014/06/10/gates-foundation-backs-two-year-delay-in-linking-common-core-test-scores-to-teacher-evaluation-student-promotion/.

45. Valerie Strauss, "Common Core Supporters Back Moratorium on New Tests' High Stakes," *Washington Post*, June 6, 2013; Motoko Rich, "States Given a Reprieve on Rating Teachers," *New York Times*, August 21, 2014. The US Secretary of Education allowed states to ask for an additional year before using Common Core tests to evaluate teacher performance.

46. Louise Locock and Annette Boaz, "Research, Policy and Practice—Worlds Apart?" *Social Policy and Society* 3, no. 4 (2004): 375–384.

47. Rick Hess, "Thinking Policy: Four Tips for Educators," Rick Hess Straight Up, *Education Week*, August 8, 2012, http://blogs.edweek.org/edweek/rick_hess_straight_up/2012/08/thinking_policy_four_tips_for_educators.html.

48. David Labaree, *Someone Has to Fail* (Cambridge, MA: Harvard University Press, 2010), 158.

49. Richard Elmore and Milbrey McLaughlin, *Steady Work* (Santa Monica, CA: RAND Corporation, 1988), 5–14; Locock and Boaz, "Research, Policy and Practice."

50. The primacy of the teacher as the significant in-school factor in getting students to learn is embedded in the experiential wisdom of parents who seek out particular teachers, move to different districts, get in lotteries for charter schools, and seek out vouchers. Researchers have said as much over the decades. From the work of William Sanders in Tennessee to John Hattie's meta-analyses to the recent findings of the Measures of Effective Teaching Project, all—and others—reaffirm what students, parents, and principals have said for years. See William Sanders and Sandra Horn, "Research Findings from the Tennessee Value-Added Assessment System (TVAAS) Database: Implications for Educational Evaluation and Research," *Journal of Personnel Evaluation in Education* 12, no. 3 (1998): 247–256; John Hattie, *Visible Learning for Teachers: Maximizing Impact on Learning* (London: Routledge, 2011); Thomas Kane, *Learning About Teaching: Initial Findings from the Measures of Effective Teaching Project* (Seattle: Bill & Melinda Gates Foundation, 2013).

51. Cuban, *Oversold and Underused*, 168.

52. Labaree, *Someone Has To Fail*; Tyack and Cuban, *Tinkering Toward Utopia*.

53. David Tyack and Elisabeth Hansot, *Managers of Virtue* (New York: Basic Books, 1982); Labaree, *Someone Has To Fail*; Diane Ravitch, *Left Back: A Century of Failed School Reform* (New York: Simon & Schuster, 2000).

54. Such tissue-paper reforms are characterized far more by policy talk, media hype, and scattered adoption rather than being sustained over time to become part of schooling structures and classroom lessons. See Tyack and Cuban, *Tinkering Toward Utopia*, 40–42, 111.

55. Robert Merton, "The Unanticipated Consequences of Purposive Social Action," *American Sociological Review* 1, no. 6 (1936): 894–904; Albert Hirschman, *The Rhetoric of Reaction: Perversity, Futility, and Jeopardy* (Cambridge, MA: Harvard University Press, 1991).

56. Robert Arnove and Nadine Penede, "Revisiting the 'Big Three' Foundations," *Critical Sociology* 33 (2007): 389–425; Hirschman, *Rhetoric of Reaction*, 1991.

57. Donald Schön, *Beyond the Stable State: Public and Private Learning in a Changing Society* (New York: Norton, 1973); Cuban, *Hugging the Middle*.

58. Historians writing about northern white philanthropy in the South in the late nineteenth and early twentieth centuries have largely agreed on what donors have done in these decades. However, they are deeply divided over donors' motives and the consequences of donors' actions (both planned and unplanned) in making grants to get black schools built, helping black teachers, and supplying services that white school boards had failed to provide. See James Anderson, *The Education of Blacks in the South, 1860–1935* (Chapel Hill: University of North Carolina Press, 1988); Mary Hoffschwelle, *The Rosenwald Schools of the American South* (Gainesville: University Press of Florida, 2006); Eric Anderson and Alfred Moss, Jr., *Dangerous Donations: Northern Philanthropy and Southern Black Education, 1902–1930* (Columbia: University of Missouri Press, 1999).

Consider further that donors like John D. Rockefeller, Henry Ford, and Andrew Carnegie were openly accused of making grants that reinforced existing conditions during the Progressive reform movement a century ago. Historian Merle Curti researched the influence of turn-of-the century philanthropists and the criticisms they received from the liberals of the day: "[M]uckrakers, progressives and socialists contended that large-scale giving placed far too much power over public policy in the hands of a few men whose fortunes after all had been created only because of prevailing social and economic conditions. It was argued that philanthropy was intended to patch up the shortcomings in the existing order and thus to preserve a status quo that did not deserve preservation." Merle Curti, "American Philanthropy and the National Character," *American Quarterly* 10, no.4 (1958): 420–437.

59. The Harlem Children's Zone is an area of New York City where low-income families have access to an array of services for infant to adults in schools and other agencies. See http:// en.wikipedia.org/wiki/Harlem_Children%27s_Zone.

Chapter 8

1. Unless otherwise noted, all quotations from interviewees are from phone or email communication with the author. Former Broad Foundation staffer Dan Katzir and former *Education Week* editor Erik Robelen (who covered philanthropy before moving to the Education Writers Association) were also interviewed, although they have not been explicitly cited in the chapter.

2. Foundations have also had enormous success with funding research in key areas of interest, counting on research findings to drive changes. Tom Kane's MET study is an example of a study that had a big impact, according to Weiss. "Project Reports," *Measures of Effective Teaching*, http://metproject.org/reports.php. TNTP's Widget Effect report is another example: The New Teacher Project, *The Widget Effect: Our National Failure to Acknowledge and Act On Differences in Teacher Effectiveness*, http://tntp.org/assets/documents/TheWidgetEffect_2nd_ed.pdf. Studies like this show the "power of doing research that's practical, directly on the system, that you can apply to the system itself," Weiss notes. Properly disseminated, studies like these "both had impact on policy and took to scale much faster than it would otherwise have gotten to scale."

3. Fear of taking a side is also sometimes an issue within reform-minded grantmakers, according to Rhee. She describes both foundation staff and donors themselves—cutthroat capitalists in at least some cases—expressing fear of offending various stakeholders. "I don't get it. They'll talk the good talk half the time, pound their chests in certain circles, but when it comes down to it they're much meeker, much more kowtowing to special interests."

4. Lyndsey Layton, "How Bill Gates Pulled Off the Swift Common Core Revolution," *Washington Post*, June 7, 2014, http://www.washingtonpost.com/politics/ how-bill-gates-pulled-off-the-swift-common-core-revolution/2014/06/07/a830e32e-ec34-11e3-9f5c-9075d5508f0a_story.html.

5. Walton alum Jim Blew agrees that Common Core advocacy was rushed and unwise. "They felt some weird pressure to move too quickly and too comprehensively and without a strong understanding of how standards interact with the other parts of the reform formula," he says. "The blow-back was inevitable and predictable, and it has derailed progress on the other parts of the [reform] formula."

6. See Thomas B. Fordham Institute, "Can Philanthropy Fix Our Schools?" http://edex. s3-us-west-2.amazonaws.com/publication/pdfs/annenberg_6.pdf.

7. Tom Vander Ark, "Strategic Philanthropy is Making Foundations Less Responsive," *Getting Smart*, June 7, 2012, http://gettingsmart.com/2012/06/strategic-philanthropy-is-making-foundations-less-responsive/.

8. The focus on data and short-term accomplishments meeting benchmarks was also a complaint among those charged with implementing ED in '08, who were locked into biweekly reporting periods and only able to access funding depending on their short-term success at hitting certain marks.

9. While Walton is typically characterized as the most highly focused and aggressive of the new funders, some grantees like 50CAN's Porter-Magee credit it for flexibility and patience. "I don't think Walton gets enough credit for the balance they strike in holding grantees for results . . . but not presuming to tell grantees how to do their work."

10. Steven Teles and Mark Schmitt, "The Elusive Craft of Evaluating Advocacy," *Stanford Social Innovation Review*, Summer 2011, http://www.ssireview.org/articles/entry/the_elusive_craft_of_evaluating_advocacy/.

11. According to Schwartz, the best example to illustrate the danger of short-term thinking and preestablished goals is the 1990s' Pew- and MacArthur-funded New Standards initiative, which clearly failed at its original goal of developing new assessments for a quarter of the nation's schools but succeeded at a much larger and longer-lasting goal. The standards documents it developed "influenced the way many states went about developing their own standards," according to Schwartz. And its subject-area leaders, Phil Daro and Sally Hampton, have played a big role in the standards movement since, including the current Common Core effort.

12. Chester E. Finn Jr., "The State of Education Reform," *Defining Ideas* (Hoover Institution), http://www.hoover.org/research/state-education-reform.

13. One alternative might be a hybrid approach that includes some strategic thinking along with a values- or vision-based focus that uses community capacities. That's what Ford tried, according to Jeannie Oakes. Instead of relying entirely on building community infrastructure and letting ideas percolate from the ground up, the foundation picked one idea—"more and better learning time." Granted, it was a clear, noncontroversial idea with no strong ideological attachments and no particular formula or fixed idea of how it could be accomplished. But the simple act of focusing on one thing seems to have been constructive. "It was a very strategic goal, but we used a more field-building, capacity-building structure to try and achieve it," says Oakes. "There were multiple versions of what might count. We tried hard to avoid saying we have a model." Juxtaposing a strategic focus with a community-oriented implementation strategy, Ford kept close to its deeply held belief that those who are most affected by a problem should play a prominent role in helping to understand and shape the solutions while also making sure not to spread its funding so broadly or randomly that there was little chance it would result in any concrete improvements.

Conclusion

1. Jay P. Greene, "Buckets Into the Sea: Why Philanthropy Isn't Changing Schools, and How It Could," in *With the Best of Intentions: How Philanthropy Is Reshaping K–12 Education*, ed. Frederick M. Hess (Cambridge, MA: Harvard Education Press, 2005), 49–76.

2. Jeffrey R. Henig, *Spin Cycle: How Research Is Used in Policy Debates: The Case of Charter Schools* (New York: Russell Sage Foundation/Century Foundation, 2008); Frederick M. Hess, ed., *When Research Matters: How Scholarship Influences Education Policy* (Cambridge, MA: Harvard Education Press, 2008); Christopher Lubienski, Janelle Scott,

and Elizabeth DeBray, "The Politics of Research Production, Promotion, and Utilization in Educational Policy," *Educational Policy* 28 (2014): 131–144.

3. Paul J. DiMaggio and Walter W. Powell, "The Iron Cage Revisited: Institutional Isomorphism and Collective Rationality in Organizational Fields," *American Sociological Review* 48, no. 2 (1983): 147–160.

4. Alice M. Rivlin, *Reviving the American Dream: The Economy, the States, and the Federal Government* (Washington, DC: Brookings Institution, 1992); Paul E. Peterson, *The Price of Federalism* (Washington, DC: Brookings Institution, 1995).

5. Morton Grodzins, *The American System* (New York: Transaction Publishers, 1966).

6. Frederick M. Hess, *Spinning Wheels: The Politics of Urban School Reform* (Washington, DC: Brookings Institution, 1998).

Acknowledgments

For the past few years, we have spent more than a little time discussing with one another a topic that has loomed large in today's education policy debates: the role of education philanthropy. For all its visibility and import, it's received less examination and less scholarly exploration than we would have expected. During the course of 2013 and 2014, we hosted several convenings of scholars, funders, and policy analysts at Columbia University in New York and at the American Enterprise Institute in Washington, DC. In February 2015, informed by these discussions, we hosted a research conference at AEI to explore the subject in greater depth. The volume you hold in your hands is the fruit of those efforts.

The chapters that you have just read each seek to explore an important component of the new philanthropy in education. How much do new and old philanthropies give to education advocacy and research? What do foundation officials think they've learned in the past several years? How much backlash is there against philanthropic influence in education?

We are indebted to all of those who have been involved in this project and pushed our thinking on these ideas, but we especially thank the following people for providing outstanding and concentrated feedback during our February conference: Joanne Barkan of *Dissent* magazine, Jim Blew of Students First, Stacey Childress of NewSchools Venture Fund, and Howard Fuller of Marquette University. We also owe our appreciation to the William T. Grant Foundation and the Spencer Foundation for generously provided financial support for this project, and we are deeply grateful for their involvement and encouragement throughout the process. We also greatly appreciate the Ford Foundation's support, which helped to fund earlier conversations that shaped this effort.

We thank AEI and Teachers College at Columbia University for the support and the resources that helped make this project possible. We'd also like to thank the terrific staff at AEI, especially Jenn Hatfield for her work managing and overseeing this project and coordinating the conference; Meg Cahill and Sarah DuPre for their efforts in promoting the scholarly contributions; and Max Eden, Elizabeth English, and Rooney Columbus for their vital assistance. Finally, we express our gratitude to the Harvard Education Press team, particularly our editor, Caroline Chauncey, who offered skillful and timely guidance throughout the course of this project.

About the Editors

Frederick M. Hess is director of education policy studies at the American Enterprise Institute (AEI). An educator, political scientist, and author, he studies K–12 and higher education issues. His books include *The Cage-Busting Teacher, Cage-Busting Leadership, Breakthrough Leadership in the Digital Age, The Same Thing Over and Over, Education Unbound, Common Sense School Reform, Revolution at the Margins,* and *Spinning Wheels.* He is also the author of the popular *Education Week* blog, *Rick Hess Straight Up,* and is a regular contributor to *The Hill* and to *National Review Online.* Hess's work has appeared in scholarly and popular outlets such as *Teachers College Record, Harvard Education Review, Social Science Quarterly, Urban Affairs Review, American Politics Quarterly, Chronicle of Higher Education, Phi Delta Kappan, Educational Leadership, U.S. News & World Report, USA Today, Washington Post, New York Times, Wall Street Journal, The Atlantic,* and *National Affairs.* He has edited widely cited volumes on the Common Core, the role of for-profits in education, education philanthropy, school costs and productivity, the impact of education research, and No Child Left Behind. Hess serves as executive editor of *Education Next,* as lead faculty member for the Rice Education Entrepreneurship Program, and on the review board for the Broad Prize for Public Charter Schools. He also serves on the boards of directors of the National Association of Charter School Authorizers and 4.0 SCHOOLS. A former high school social studies teacher, he teaches or has taught at the University of Virginia, the University of Pennsylvania, Georgetown University, Rice University, and Harvard University. He holds an MA and PhD in government, as well as an MEd in teaching and curriculum from Harvard University.

Jeffrey R. Henig is a professor of political science and education at Teachers College, Columbia University, where he also serves as chair of the Department of Education Policy and Social Analysis. He is the author, coauthor, or coeditor of ten books, the most recent being *The End of Exceptionalism in American Education: The Changing Politics of School Reform* (Harvard Education Press, 2013). His book *Spin Cycle: How Research Gets Used in Policy Debates: The Case of Charter Schools* (Russell Sage Foundation, 2008) won the American Educational Research Association's Outstanding Book Award in 2010. In addition, his coauthored books *The Color of School Reform: Race, Politics and the Challenge of Urban Education* (Princeton University Press, 1999) and *Building Civic Capacity: The Politics of Reforming Urban Schools* (University Press of Kansas, 2001) were each named the best book written on urban politics by the Urban Politics Section of the American Political Science Association. Henig's scholarly work on urban politics, racial politics, privatization, and school reform has appeared in journals including the *American Journal of Education, Educational Evaluation and Policy Analysis, Journal of Urban Affairs, Policy Sciences, Political Science Quarterly, Social Science Quarterly,* and *Urban Affairs Review.* His more popular writing has appeared in outlets such as *Education Week, Chronicle of Higher Education, Boston Globe, Los Angeles Times, Washington Post,* and *New York Times.*

About the Contributors

Larry Cuban is professor emeritus of education at Stanford University. His major research interests focus on the history of curriculum and instruction, educational leadership, school reform, and the uses of technology in classrooms. His recent books include *Inside the Black Box: Change Without Reform in Classrooms* (Harvard Education Press, 2013), *As Good as It Gets: What School Reform Brought to Austin* (Harvard University Press, 2010), *Against the Odds: Insights from One District's Small School Reform* (Harvard Educational Publishing Group, 2010), and *Hugging the Middle: How Teachers Teach in an Era of Testing and Accountability* (Teachers College Press, 2008). Before becoming a professor, Cuban taught high school social studies for fourteen years, directed a teacher education program that prepared returning Peace Corps volunteers to teach in inner-city schools, and served for seven years as a district superintendent.

Dana Goldstein is a journalist who reports on education and other social issues. She is the author of *The Teacher Wars: A History of America's Most Embattled Profession* (Doubleday, 2014). She is also a staff writer at The Marshall Project and has contributed to *Slate*, *The Atlantic*, and other national magazines. She was previously a Schwartz Fellow at the New America Foundation and a Puffin Fellow at the Nation Institute. Goldstein is also a former associate editor at the *Daily Beast* and in 2010 won the Spencer Fellowship in education journalism at Columbia University.

Jay P. Greene is department head and holds the 21st Century Chair in Education Reform at the University of Arkansas. He is the author of *Education Myth: What Special Interest Groups Want You to Believe About Our Schools and Why It Isn't So* (Rowman & Littlefield, 2005), *Why America Needs School Choice* (Encounter, 2001), and dozens of articles in scholarly and popular publications. His scholarly work has appeared in journals such as *Education Finance and Policy*, *Educational Researcher*, *Economics of Education Review*, and *Sociology of Education*, while his popular work has appeared in outlets such as the *New York Times*, *Wall Street Journal*, *Washington Post*, and *Education Next*.

Jenn Hatfield is a research assistant in education policy studies at the American Enterprise Institute. Her research focuses on school choice, teacher quality, and state and federal politics in K–12 education.

Kevin J. James is a research fellow with the Center on Higher Education Reform at the American Enterprise Institute, where he researches and writes about higher education financing, quality assurance in colleges and universities, and traditionally underrepresented populations' access to higher education. Before joining AEI, James worked on a variety of issues as a legislative aide to Representative Tom Petri (R-WI), a senior member of the House Education and Workforce Committee. James worked on labor, health care, energy, the environment, issues dealing with the Department of the Interior, and education. In particular, he focused on higher education reform initiatives and led the development of an extensive student loan reform bill.

Andrew P. Kelly is the director of the Center on Higher Education Reform and a resident scholar in education policy studies at the American Enterprise Institute. His research focuses on higher education policy, innovation, financial aid reform, and the politics of education policy. Previously, he was a research assistant at AEI, where his work focused on the preparation of school leaders, collective bargaining in public schools, and the politics of education. His research has appeared in the *American Journal of Education*, *Teachers College Record*, *Educational Policy*, *Policy Studies Journal*, and *Education Next* as well as popular outlets such as *Education Week*, *Inside Higher Ed*, *Forbes*, *The Atlantic*, *National Affairs*, the *Weekly Standard*, and *Huffington Post*. He is coeditor of *Stretching the Higher Education Dollar: How Innovation Can Improve Access, Equity, and Affordability* (Harvard Education Press, 2013), *Getting to Graduation: The Completion Agenda in Higher Education* (Johns Hopkins University Press, 2012), *Carrots, Sticks, and the Bully Pulpit: Lessons from a Half-Century of Federal Efforts to Improve America's Schools* (Harvard Education Press, 2011), and *Reinventing Higher Education: The Promise of Innovation* (Harvard Education Press, 2011). In 2011, Kelly was named one of sixteen Next Generation Leaders in education policy by the *Policy Notebook* blog on *Education Week*.

Michael Q. McShane is a research fellow in education policy studies at the American Enterprise Institute. He is coeditor, with Frederick M. Hess, of *Common Core Meets Education Reform* (Teachers College Press, 2013). He is also coauthor of *President Obama and Education Reform: The Personal and the Political* (Palgrave MacMillan, 2012). His analyses have been published widely in technical journals and reports, including *Education Finance and Policy*. He has contributed to more popular publications such as *Education Next*, *Huffington Post*, *National Review*, *Chronicle of Higher Education*, and the *St. Louis Post–Dispatch*. He began his career as an inner-city high school teacher in Montgomery, Alabama.

Sarah Reckhow is an assistant professor in the department of political science at Michigan State University. Her book *Follow the Money: How Foundation Dollars Change Public School Politics* (Oxford University Press, 2012) examines the role of major foundations, such as the Bill & Melinda Gates Foundation, in urban school reform. Her work has appeared in *Educational Researcher*, *Urban Affairs Review*, *Policy Studies Journal*, and *Planning Theory*.

Alexander Russo is a freelance writer, blogger, and author whose work has been published in *Slate*, the *Washington Monthly*, *The Atlantic*, *Washington Post*, *Huffington Post*, and *USA Today*. His blog, *This Week in Education*, is one of the nation's longest-running education policy blogs. He won a 2009 Spencer Education Journalism Fellowship at Columbia University. His book *Stray Dogs, Saints, and Saviors: Fighting for the Soul of America's Toughest High School* (Jossey-Bass, 2011) chronicled a group of teachers seeking to rescue a struggling Los Angeles high school. Before he began writing, Russo served as an education adviser to two US senators and to the chancellor of New York City Public Schools. He was also (briefly) a high school English teacher and education researcher. You can find him at @alexanderrusso.

Jeffrey W. Snyder is a postdoctoral research fellow in education, philanthropy, and advocacy at the University of Michigan and Michigan State University. His research focuses on education politics, policy, and governance. His recent coauthored research, published in *Educational Researcher*, finds evidence of increased foundation giving to national-level K–12 policy advocacy and nontraditional education groups (such as Teach For America). Snyder's other recent work can be found in *Educational Policy* and the *American Journal of Education* and is forthcoming in *Journal of Public Administration Research and Theory*.

Megan Tompkins-Stange is an assistant professor at the Ford School of Public Policy at the University of Michigan. Her research interests focus on the role of private philanthropic foundations in public education policy in the United States. She is the author of a book on how foundations advance K–12 education reform, forthcoming from Harvard Education Press.

Index